# ARTUR IMMANUEL LOEWENTAL
# 1879-1964

A brief introduction to his life and work, together with a select list of his sculpted works

## John T. Turner

Published by
THE SOCIETY FOR LINCOLNSHIRE HISTORY AND ARCHAEOLOGY
2014

ARTUR IMMANUEL LOEWENTAL

First published by the Society for Lincolnshire History and Archaeology 2014
© Society for Lincolnshire History and Archaeology

ISBN 978 0 903582 50 6

British Library Cataloguing in Publication Data
A CIP catalogue record for this book is available from the British Library

This book was produced with the aid of a grant from the Spalding Gentlemen's Society

Production Editor: Ken Redmore
Designed by Ros Beevers

Printed in the United Kingdom by Ruddocks, Lincoln

*Front cover:*
*Artur Loewental sculpts Professor Albert Einstein, Berlin, 1930*
*© collectionsCEGES/SOMA – Brussels, Image No.126746*
*Medals by Artur Loewental of Mark Twain, 1898, 90mm 1:2, LOE001, Rudyard Kipling, 1935, 140mm 1:3, LOE191,*
*Sir Winston Churchill, general issue death medal, 1965, 50mm actual size, LOE267*

*Back cover:*
*A bronze self-portrait medal of the sculptor Artur Immanuel Loewental to commemorate his 70th birthday, Lincoln, 1949*
*140mm (actual size) (LOE230)*
*From the Fennell private collection*

# CONTENTS

# PREFACE

THE PURPOSE and primary aim of this brief biography of the sculptor and medallist Artur Immanuel Loewental is to establish, for the first time, a record of his life in England. Although articles have been published in German over the years detailing his early life in Austria and Germany and listing many of the works that he produced while living in those countries, most, if not all, have been based on a single short article by Suhle published in 1927. Accordingly, the early part of his life has only been given in outline here. Some of the more important published references in German and French have, however, been noted in the sources. The present work thus concentrates in detail on the latter part of his life – some thirty years or so – which he spent living in England, having moved from Berlin with the rise of the Nazi party in the early nineteen-thirties.

The idea of researching the life and work of Artur Loewental was initiated in the early nineteen-eighties by Anthony Gunstone, who was at that time Director of Lincolnshire Museums. Unfortunately his ill health meant that this ambition was soon to be thwarted and his original plans had to be modified merely to produce an information sheet on the sculptor. But even this watered down aim was cut short by his worsening illness. Instead he laid down plans for the Usher Gallery (now part of The Collection, Lincoln) to keep an illustrated catalogue of its collection of Artur's works, while he himself would augment the gallery's Loewental collection by the purchase of further examples. He was able to put this latter idea into operation and during his short period in office was able to add four important examples before his untimely death in March 1984, at the early age of forty-seven, brought a halt to his plans. Subsequently the gallery's large collection of Artur's works was consigned to a strong room within the Usher Gallery building where it has resided ever since, while Gunstone's own research notes are now contained in a slim file kept at The Collection, Lincoln.

My first introduction to the work of the sculptor Artur Loewental was through the gift of a modern reproduction of a portrait medal produced by him depicting the well-known Lincoln solicitor Alderman Francis Hill, the original having been sculpted by Artur in Lincoln in 1948. The workmanship was of such high quality that I decided to delve deeper into the life of this sculptor. Almost at once I discovered that a second bronze medal, obviously from the same mould, had been produced, c1958, probably to coincide with Francis Hill's knighthood. An enquiry to the Spalding Gentlemen's Society brought news of a magnificent collection of Chinese china and glassware that had been purchased from Artur in 1948. The Society was also able to show me a medal of one of their former presidents, Ashley K. Maples, dated 1948, which had been sculpted by Artur, having been commissioned and paid for by members of the Society. Inevitably I was to be drawn to the large collection of Artur's works stored in the strong room of the Usher Gallery building, Lincoln, which was to flame my enthusiasm for further research into the life and work of this highly skilled sculptor who, due to circumstances beyond his control, almost vanished without trace from the recorded scene once he fled Nazi Germany for England in 1934. An even greater discovery was the extensive collection of his works that still survives in the possession of the Bauer family at Wellingore, near Lincoln. This collection had been left to Gizella Bauer by the terms of Artur's will. Its true extent is still unclear as much continues to remain in storage and unavailable for research at this time.

I have included in this volume all the examples of his work that I have so far traced and that survive outside Germany and Austria, many of which he sculpted while living in England. It is indeed unfortunate that Artur does not appear to have kept a record of his output so that, as will become apparent in the following account, there are still many gaps left in our knowledge of his life and work. Many major museum collections still remain un-catalogued, while there must be many private estates that unknowingly harbour examples of his work. Hopefully, this present account may act as a catalyst to others to search their records and collections.

It is perhaps pertinent at this stage to clarify Artur's family name and his nationality, both of which seem to cause some confusion. Artur was born in Vienna, at that time in Austria-Hungary, and thus held Austrian papers; however, after the First World War and under the terms of the Treaty of Versailles, 1919, both he and his wife, Rosa, chose Czechoslovakian nationality. When they later obtained British nationality in 1941 their Czechoslovakian nationality was not relinquished due to their age. As far as the family name is concerned it may be spelt Löwenthal, Löwental, Loewenthal or Loewental. Artur himself used all of the variations during his life but I have restricted myself to the variation Loewental throughout the present work.

# ACKNOWLEDGEMENTS

My THANKS are due to the many individuals who have helped me during my ten years of research. Many remain anonymous, but a few deserve special mention. Very early in my research I was fortunate enough to meet Sally McNichol, Artur's grand-niece, and over many years we have engaged in a protracted correspondence, each encouraging the other in our respective research into the history of the Loewental family. Sally was also able to provide much valuable documentary information about Artur.

The extensive collection of Artur's work held by The Collection, Lincoln, was made available to me for recording through the kindness and help of Andrea Martin, the former Collections Access Officer, as the items are, unfortunately, all now in storage. Gerard Bauer kindly photographed part of the large collection owned by the Bauer family, which had been left to his mother under the terms of Artur's will. Dr Volker Heuchert, Collections Manager of the Heberden Coin Room at the Ashmolean Museum, Oxford, undertook the photographing of the entire collection of Artur's work in their collection. Dr Ira Rezak, New York, USA, provided photographs of his extensive collection. I also need to thank Sir Desmond Fennell and Lady Susan Fennell for their hospitality and for allowing me to record their collection at their home in Winslow.

I would also thank the curators and staff of the following museums and institutions for their help: The American Numismatic Society, New York, USA; The Ashmolean Museum, The Heberden Coin Room, Oxford; The Association for Jewish Refugees in Great Britain, Stanmore; Blenheim Palace, Woodstock; Beethoven-Haus Vertriebs-GmbH, Bonn, Germany; Bibliothéque Nationale de France, Département des Monnaies, Médailles et Antiques, Paris, France; The British Art Medal Society, London; The British Museum, Department of Coins and Medals, London; The British Numismatic Society, London; Chartwell, Westerham; The Collection, Lincoln; The Devonshire Collection, Chatsworth, Bakewell; Eretz Israel Museum, The Kadman Numismatic Pavilion, Tel-Aviv, Israel; The Fitzwilliam Museum, Department of Coins and Medals, Cambridge; The Hebrew University of Jerusalem, The Jewish National and University Library, Department of Manuscripts and Archives, Jerusalem, Israel (The Albert Einstein Archives); The Honourable Society of the Inner Temple, Inner Temple Library, London; The Imperial War Museum, Department of Art, London; The Jewish Museum, New York, USA; The Jewish Museum, Camden Town; The Jewish Museum, The Sternberg Centre, Finchley; Kunsthistorisches Museum mit MVK und ÖTM Münzkabinett, Numismatic Department, Vienna, Austria; Lincoln Cathedral Works Department, Lincoln; Lincoln Central Library, Lincoln; The Lincoln Red Cattle Society, Grange-de-Lings; Lincolnshire Archives Office, Lincoln; Lincolnshire Illustrations Index, Lincoln; The London Jewish Museum of Art, Ben Uri Gallery, St John's Wood; The Mark Twain House and Museum, Hartford, USA; The Middle Temple Library, London; The National Archives, Kew; Provincial Sterckshof Museum, Deurne, Belgium; The National Art Gallery, South Kensington; The National Maritime Museum, Greenwich; The Royal Academy of Arts, London; The Society for Lincolnshire History and Archaeology, Lincoln; The Spalding Gentlemen's Society, Spalding; Staatliche Museen Preußischer Kulturbesitz, Berlin, Germany; Upton House, Banbury; The Victoria and Albert Museum, Department of Sculpture, Metalwork, Ceramics and Glass, South Kensington; Waddesdon Manor, Waddesdon; The Wellcome Institute for the History of Medicine, London.

The staff at the following companies have provided invaluable help: Alexander Autographs, Inc, Cos Cob, USA; Andrew & Company LLP, Lincoln; Bonhams, Retford; CEGES/SOMA, Photo Department, Brussels, Belgium; Simon Chorley Art & Antiques, Prinknash Abbey Park; Daniel Fearon, London; The Home Office, Records Management Services, London; Israelitische Kultusgemeinde Wien, Vienna, Austria; Thos Mawer & Son Limited, Lincoln; N. M. Rothschild & Sons Limited, London; Whitechapel Bell Foundry, London.

Help has also been solicited from and freely given by the following individuals: David Ashton-Hill, Eran Bauer, C. P. Carter, Bridget Cracroft-Eley, Stephanie Gilbert, Lady Anne Glenconnor, Keith Gretton, Dr Edward Jackson, Pamela Lee, Leah Lucas (Artur's grand-niece living in Canada), Flora Murray, Philip Race, Mona Skehel, J. W. Michael Smith (Kipling Society), Paul Smith, Tessa Tennant, and Thora Wagstaffe.

Credits for the illustrations supplied and used are acknowledged to:

Alexander Autographs, Inc: LOE146.

The Ashmolean Museum: LOE029, 050, 056, 060, 068, 085, 116, 124, 126, 142, 151, 158, 159, 163, 165, 166, 167, 182, 187, 194, 195, 221, 232, 248.

Gerard Bauer: LOE019, 020, 028, 112, 115, 120, 132, 135, 138, 141, 148, 150, 152, 169, 171, 172, 178, 215, 247, 259, 260, 261.

The British Museum: LOE018, 040, 069, 118, 133, 160, 198.

Collections CEGES/SOMA: Fig.9.

The Kadman Numismatic Pavilion: LOE054.

Pamela Lee: LOE079.

Leah Lucas: LOE246.

The Lincolnshire Illustrations Index: Fig.28.

Dr Ira Rezak: LOE011, 014, 027, 081, 082, 121, 136, 143, 147, 149, 235.

Sally McNichol: Figs.1, 4, 23, 31.

Paul Smith: Fig.14.

Upton House (National Trust): LOE196, 203, 207.

All other illustrations were taken by the author and thanks are due to the following for allowing me to record their collections: Andrew & Co. LLP; Gerard Bauer (trial plaster casts); The Collection, Lincoln; Sir Desmond Fennell; Stephanie Gilbert; Dr Edward Jackson; Pamela Lee; Sally McNichol; and Spalding Gentlemen's Society.

Finally my thanks are due to Ros Beevers for her sterling work in preparing the publication for the printers; Philip Attwood for kindly providing a foreword, and Ken Redmore for his tireless work in seeing the publication through the many changes that have been made, and for providing an index. Last but certainly not least my eternal thanks to my beloved wife, Anna, who has shared my passion for all things Lincolnshire for over fifty years.

# FOREWORD

A RECURRING feature of the history of art medals in Britain is the contribution made by artists coming from other countries: Steven van Herwijck from the Netherlands in the sixteenth century; the various members of the Roettier family in the seventeenth, also from the Low Countries; the Dassiers from Switzerland in the eighteenth; the Italian Benedetto Pistrucci in the early years of the nineteenth century and the French man Alphonse Legros in its final decades. Without artists such as these British medallic art would have been much the poorer and would lack much of its interest and diversity.

For most of the twentieth century Britain is generally considered to have been, if not exactly a medallic desert, at least very sparingly watered. Given this unpromising situation, it is particularly fortunate that artists continued to arrive from abroad, bringing with them that appreciation of medal-making that was such a feature of continental European artistic practice. The threat that in the 1930s spread throughout central Europe from Nazi Germany was the catalyst for this development, which saw the arrival in this country of Fritz (soon Fred) Kormis from Germany, Paul Vincze from Hungary, the Croatian Oscar Nemon, and the Austrian / Czechoslovakian Artur Loewental, the subject of this book. Desperate personal stories were to have a very positive effect on British medal production.

As John Turner relates, Loewental arrived in England in 1934. Settling first in the London artists' quarter of St John's Wood, he moved to Lincoln in 1941 and this was to remain his home until his death in 1964. Like Kormis and Vincze, and unlike most British-born sculptors of the time, he understood the possibilities offered by medals and continued to make them his speciality. In this way an unlikely link was created between turn-of-the-century Vienna – the Vienna of the Secession and the famed sculptor and medallist Joseph Tautenhayn – and post-war Lincoln. Equally noteworthy, the man whose medals had celebrated so many German military figures of the First World War now turned his hand to the commemoration of the allied victory and Winston Churchill. Given their personal histories, it is in no way surprising that Kormis, Vincze and Nemon also produced portraits of Churchill, the man who most clearly personified the fight against the oppression from which they had fled.

Until now none of these artists has been the subject of a scholarly study. Art histories have a tendency to be written along nationalist lines, and it is often the case that artists who fail to fit neatly within the traditions of one country are ignored, despite the fact that their achievements may have a greater significance because of those very travels. In the case of Loewental, this omission is now rectified by the present volume.

Artur Loewental was an accomplished sculptor and engraver and an energetic collector, but it is the medals that he made over more than half a century that are his most enduring legacy: documents of both the vicissitudes and friendships of an eventful life and a traumatic period in world history.

*Philip Attwood*
*Keeper of Coins and Medals*
*British Museum*

# INTRODUCTION

THE RESEARCHING of the life and works of Professor Artur Immanuel Loewental has been fraught with difficulties. The disruptions and destructions caused by two world wars together with the itinerant lifestyle that his work and interests demanded of him have meant that much that might be expected to survive under more normal circumstances has been lost forever. He seems not to have kept a record of his travels or of the commissions that he undertook. A further problem is that, although many of his works still survive in both museums and private collections, in many instances their existence has either still to be recorded or they remain unrecognised due to the fact that he omitted, in many cases, to sign his work.

Artur was a highly skilled sculptor concentrating almost exclusively on true-to-life portraits, which he produced as bronze medals or plaques. He refused to be swayed by the artistic influences of the times in which he lived, and it is rare to find any sign of the Art Nouveau or Art Deco movements included on his medals, as was the practice of many of his contemporaries. The insistence on his part for photographic accuracy in his portraiture has had the drawback of him being listed in the past as a 'minor Jewish sculptor', whereas his output must have been quite large and certainly included many of the prominent personages of Central Europe in the first half of the twentieth century. His initial commissions were from members of the Jewish community who supported his work, but later subjects included many great names both living and dead.

His sculptures range from private family portraits, always intended to circulate solely within the family circle and thereby often being unique or nearly so, to major commissions such as the busts of Beethoven commissioned for the Moscow Philharmonic Association in 1912 and the busts of Professor Albert Einstein commissioned by the German State in 1930.

It is to be regretted that some avenues of investigation that would have enhanced this record of Artur's life and work have proved to be unavailable at this time; nevertheless, it was thought important that a record should be made available so that those who take an interest in his work or may own examples of it will be able to better assess their collections. A further regret is that the Home Office found it necessary at some time in the past to fillet the five files that were compiled by them when Artur was in the process of applying for British nationality to just one: much further detail might have been forthcoming if these files had survived intact.

As will be evident in the main body of this work, it is staggering the large amount of his personal effects and works that he was able to bring with him when he left Germany in 1934, much of which he retained until finally starting to unload large portions of it in 1948 in order to ease his financial situation. A member of the Krupp family, many of whom he had sculpted in 1918, is said to have assured him that the situation in Germany would stabilise in about six months' time, after which he would be able to return to Berlin, and they may also have been instrumental in easing Artur's exit from the country. Certainly, in 1948 he was able to sell a very valuable collection of Chinese glassware and other items that he had brought with him to the Spalding Gentlemen's Society for £5,000, a very large sum at that time.

The sale of his own works appears to have been slow, since the same bronze medals and other items repeatedly appear in his exhibitions in England. He constantly worried over the final resting place of the many examples of his own work and on one occasion stated that he would have liked them to have gone to the Spalding Gentlemen's Society. In the event many of his portraits were either purchased by or given to the Usher Galley, Lincoln, which had acted as a store for many of his works over the years. Further major gifts were made to the Ashmolean Museum, Oxford, although the bulk of his remaining works were still in his possession when he died and thus by the terms of his will passed to Mrs Gizella Bauer, the lady who looked after him for the last five years of his life.

It is difficult to envisage the many skills and wide knowledge that Artur possessed. As with so many other individuals, the ravages of two world wars had serious consequences for his life. His early fight to establish himself as a sculptor, against his father's wishes, was finally coming to fruition when the First World War broke out and lost him his possessions and home in Cairo. After an enforced programme of medal production to commemorate German events and personages of the war, peace in 1918 must have given him hope of a more settled existence. Unfortunately, with the rise of the Nazi party in 1933, his new life was to be short lived. Again he was to lose his home and many of his possessions as he moved to England. Even with a few settled years in England the outbreak of the Second World War deprived him of his livelihood, only to be saved by obtaining British nationality, which enabled him to work for the war effort throughout the hostilities. Peace in 1945 was again to see a renewed spur for his sculpting, but advancing years and the death of his beloved wife, Rosa, forced him to move from his home in Lincoln to spend the last five years of his life in lodgings in Wellingore, a village close to Lincoln, where his unsteady hands and failing eyesight must have saddened the final years of one so talented and renowned.

His work is illustrated in this review to a large extent by examples from local museums, augmented by other individual pieces that have been traced, both in national collections and in private ownership in Britain and abroad. The large collections of his work that survive in Germany and Austria have been omitted as these have already been covered by catalogues published in Germany. The large holding of The Collection, Lincoln, consists of many examples of his output including plaster of Paris casts for his medals, the subsequent bronze medals themselves, and intaglios carved in hard gemstones and rock crystal. Perhaps the only type of work produced by Artur that is not represented in The Collection are his original models in wax; five of these are, however, preserved in the collection of the Ashmolean Museum in Oxford.

His working methods may be glimpsed from his correspondence with Ashley Maples, president of the Spalding Gentlemen's Society, during his preparations for producing a bronze medal of him. His first model would be executed using beeswax, in which he would be able to carve out the intricate detail required. This wax sculpture would in most cases be melted down afterwards for reuse, although a few of his wax portraits do survive. From this wax model a plaster of Paris cast would be made, many of which still survive. It is very unlikely that Artur would make any of his own bronze castings, and it is thought that he used a bell founder in London at some time and possibly one of the local brass founders in Lincoln. At the end of the process Artur himself would burnish the rough casting, add the patina, and finish off the medal to his own satisfaction and the customer's requirements.

His skill and patience in working hard gemstones and rock crystal – materials that are intractable and brittle – has not been covered here, but an example of his work in rock crystal may be seen in the Panther Vase in the collection of The Collection, Lincoln. Although this piece is damaged, it nevertheless gives an indication of the time and effort involved in its production. Still greater skill and patience would have been required to produce what was perhaps Artur Loewental's greatest sculpture, the 'Cup of Dionysos', an illustration of which was published in *The Illustrated London News* 15 June 1935. However, the location of this sculpture, if it still survives, is not known.

# 1. THE EARLY YEARS, IN EUROPE AND THE NEAR EAST

ALTHOUGH Artur Immanuel Loewental and his four siblings were all born in Vienna, Austria-Hungary, their Jewish parents both came from Moravia, a province of Bohemia. Their father, Samuel, was born in Kojetin, central Moravia, on 30 August 1837 and, in common with many other Moravian Jews, migrated to Vienna in the mid nineteenth century following the Jewish Emancipation and their re-admission into Austria in 1848. In Vienna he attended grammar school and technical college where his abilities and hard work enabled him to acquire a qualification in mechanical engineering as well as a first class certificate in English. He returned to Moravia in order to marry Antonia Eisler, born in Braunseifen (now Ryžoviště), eastern Moravia, on 23 May 1850. The marriage took place in Austerlitz (now Slavkov u Brna) on 25 May 1874, after which Samuel took his new bride back to Vienna to set up home. Their first born was Clara Ottilie, on 30 April 1875, followed by Camilla Angelika, on 21 September 1876. Artur Immanuel was their third child, born on 28 August 1879, followed by Paula Auguste, in August 1882, and finally Oskar Alexander, on 21 October 1885. It is curious to note that, unusual among

Jews, each of Samuel's daughters remained unmarried. Artur's own marriage was childless. Thus it is from Oskar, Artur's brother, that the present branch of the family is descended.

The Jewish migrants who had moved to Vienna during the second half of the nineteenth century worked hard to establish an accepted and respected community and it is within this community that Samuel was to earn an important position as a machine and railway construction engineer (*Maschinen-und Eisenbahnbauingenieurs*) on the NordWestBahn railway. Having reached a high degree of respectability together with a good standard of living as a result of his hard work, he made sure that his children were given the best possible education in order to maintain their position in society and thereby in their turn to make a suitable contribution to the Jewish community and, if possible, even cement the family's standing within the Jewish community. It would therefore come as a great shock and disappointment to him when Artur, at a very early age, displayed a fervent interest in the arts. Artur himself was later to claim that he had in

*Fig.1. A pencil sketch by the sculptor depicting his father, Samuel Loewental, n.d. (The McNichol private collection).*

*Fig.2. LOE107. A bronze portrait plaque of Antonia Loewental, the sculptor's mother, Berlin, 1924. 130 x 170mm. 1:2. (The Jackson private collection).*

fact mastered the ancient art of engraving hardstone by the age of twelve, being inspired by the reopening of the Kunsthistorisches Museum in Vienna with its collection of sculptures and ancient cameos. His early trials to copy these pieces would, it has been claimed, later lead him to engrave in the style of Dürer and create medals in the style of Holbein.

The details of Artur's early schooling are unclear, but the friction that was generated between him and his father over his love of the arts, rather than taking up a reputable profession, finally came to a head when he was aged sixteen and a half. As a direct consequence he left the family home and travelled around Europe, accompanied by a friend, earning a living by wood carving as well as working for stonemasons and goldsmiths, while at the same time improving his sculpting skills whenever an opportunity presented itself. His early experiences in sculpting had been in wood and soft rock, such as soapstone, but now he was able to add to his skills by turning his hand to the engraving of hardstones, cornelian and rock crystal.

By the age of nineteen in 1898 he was back in Vienna where he began producing portrait medals and plaques of prominent members of the Jewish community, while at the same time attending grammar school. He quickly acquired an international recognition of his skills by surreptitiously sculpting the American writer and humorist Mark Twain, who happened to be staying in Vienna at the time. He subsequently produced several cast bronze medals from his portrait of Twain and this fact was reported in *The New York Times* of 13 November 1898:

> *At an art dealer's in the Graben are now to be seen medallions with a life-like portrait of Mark Twain, and they are very much liked. They by no means betray the fact that he sat without intending it. Unsuspicious of what awaited him, he went to the Deutsches Volkstheater one night, where he greatly enjoyed the performance. Meanwhile, however, a young artist in the next box was drawing away, all through the four acts, in fact, taking the unconscious author's portrait. Then the young fellow at home modelled the head so beautifully that the Austrian Art Industrial Museum bought one of his medallions. The artist is still attending the grammar school, and is named Arthur Loewenthal. He did not conceive the idea of catching the illustrious American at*

> *the theatre until after the latter had kindly but decidedly refused to sit for him, declaring that he had already sat for his portrait so often he could not bear any more sittings.*

An example of this medal is still in the collection of the museum in Vienna, while a further example has recently been acquired by the Mark Twain House and Museum, Hartford, USA. It clearly depicts the realistic technique he was to adopt for the rest of his life and which became his hallmark, described later as 'realistic naturalism'. Among the prominent people he sculpted at this time are numbered Moriz Kanitz, 1898, and Wilhelm Trinks, a famous Viennese numismatist, 1899. The wax model and lithographic stone matrix of this latter sculpture were brought to England by Artur in 1934 and the wax model was exhibited by him in Lincoln in 1941, although the present whereabouts of neither is known. He also sculpted a small medal in soapstone of August Ritter von Loehr, the first president of the first camera club in Austria, 1899, which is now in the collection of The Collection, Lincoln. Artur's desire to reacquire this in later years would suggest that it may have been a test piece to gain him entry into the Academie.

Artur entered the Academie der Bildenden Künste, Vienna, in 1900. While there he is said to have studied under Edmund Hellmer, the famous sculptor, and Joseph Tautenhayn, the famous medallist; his training thereby

*Fig.3. LOE001. A bronze portrait medal of Mark Twain, Vienna, 1898. 90mm. (The McNichol private collection).*

including both sculpting and gem-cutting. During his time at the Academie he continued with his sculpting activities and among his subjects were:

| | | | |
|---|---|---|---|
| Eduard Gaertner | singer of light opera | 1900 | |
| Rudolph Alter von Waldhof | chief of Austrian judiciary | 1900 | The Collection, Lincoln |
| Salo Cohen | director of the Jewish community, Vienna | 1901 | |
| The musician Gärtner | | 1901 | |
| Mrs Lewis of Vienna | | 1902 | |
| Dr Adolph Hoffmann | | 1902 | |
| Professor V. W. Russ | member of Austrian parliament | 1902 | private collection, USA |

During this period of his life Artur also sculpted small statuettes. While examples are rare they occasionally appear in salerooms in Germany and Belgium, although no details of this aspect of Artur's artistic skills have been included in the present work. The statuettes do display his undoubted skill in depicting the human form, and a particularly fine example depicts the goddess Hebe offering wine as a posing female nude, with grapes and vine leaves in her hair, holding a small jug in one hand and a small bowl in the other. Several examples of this are known to survive, cast in bronze, one of which is gold plated. In describing one of Artur's portraits at this time, of the musician Gärtner, in 1901, Suhle, 1927, states that every detail of the head, every little wrinkle of the face, is modelled down to the finest detail, though still maintaining the overall expression of the person depicted. Although Suhle heaped praise upon this portrait, he was to be happier with Artur's later portraits, which he said had less detail and were concerned more with the personality of the sitter.

Artur graduated from the Academie in 1903, being awarded the *Spezialschul-preis* together with the sum of four hundred Kronen. Possibly due to his work engraving hard stones Artur suffered from a severe lung ailment and was forced to move to Egypt and other Mediterranean countries about this time, living for a time in Cairo. He continued, however, to study the engraving techniques of ancient civilisations, building up his knowledge and skill while at the same time taking part in archaeological excavations and studying languages. In later years he claimed to be fluent in seven languages, including Arabic, as well as being a Greek scholar. During the years following his graduation he established his reputation as a sculptor and medallist and among the portraits produced were included:

| | | | |
|---|---|---|---|
| Baroness Newlinski | | 1903 | |
| Wilhelm Lichtenstern | an advocate | 1904 | |
| Dr Franz Hartmann | German theosopher and author who founded the German Theosophical Society | 1904 | British Museum |
| Dr H. Stiassing | a lawyer from Prague | 1904 | private collection, England |
| Princess Adelgunde of Bavaria | She and her husband Francis V had been exiled to Vienna after Italian Unification and Artur produced a very small stuck plaque in bronze of the princess in celebration of Christmas. | 1905 | |
| Alexander Girardi | singer of light opera | 1905 | |
| Evelyn Baring* | First Earl of Cromer, who was Consul General and virtual ruler of Egypt between 1883 and 1907. | 1906 | The Collection, Lincoln |
| Dr Alfred Hoffman | | 1906 | |

*Suhle is full of praise for this particular portrait as it depicts Baring facing the viewer. He states that it is extremely hard for a medallist to achieve a portrait from this angle and therefore rarely succeeds; indeed he states that Artur, in spite of further attempts, could not recreate a similar work of art.*

*Fig.4. Rosa Katharina Josepha, the sculptor's wife, n.d. (The McNichol private collection).*

A firm of engravers and die sinkers was established in Vienna at some period, which has been attributed to Artur, and that was able to produce many examples of his later medals.

In 1910 Artur married the attractive Rosa Katharina Josepha Sagorc (née Maric). Rosa was born in Castelnuova, in the Tyrol province of Austria-Hungary, on 18 May 1881. After the fall of the Austro-Hungarian Empire Castelnuova was incorporated into Italy in 1918, and Rosa thereafter always insisted that she was Italian and would speak Italian whenever possible. Her family originated from Dalmatia and thus she was of Slavic stock. The marriage took place on 4 January 1910 at the Temple of the Israelitische Kultusgemeinde, in Vienna. Artur's address at the time was given as Josefinengasse 6, while Rosa's was Tiefer Graben 13, both located in Vienna. Probably in celebration of his marriage Artur sculpted a portrait of Rosa, dated 1910 (private collection in England and the Ashmolean Museum). One of Artur's small statuettes depicting a posing female nude, holding a small jug, as noted earlier, and a bronze plaque of a dancing lady, both dated 1910, may also depict Rosa (the latter plaque is now in the author's collection). Artur and other contemporary members of his family always referred to Rosa as Ida, although the reason for this is now lost. Interestingly he was, on her death, to place a flower vase on her grave that still survives and is inscribed 'Ida'.

Also in 1910 Artur sculpted the famous Austrian architect Adolf Loos. Loos rejected the then current Art Nouveau style of architecture and the use of ornamentation and was to become one of the pioneers of the modern functional style in Europe. Artur produced a lifesize bust of Loos in bronze, which for many years resided in the Loos Haus in Vienna. It is believed to have been removed by the Nazis during World War Two and its present whereabouts is unknown. Fortunately, a plaster cast of the bust is preserved in the Kunsthistorisches Museum in Vienna.

Throughout this early period of his life Artur built up a large collection of *objets d'art*, which were later to become an impressive and very valuable asset, and much of which he was able to bring with him to England in 1934. The precise details of Artur's movements during this period have proved to be elusive as he seems to have been constantly on the move. In 1909 he is recorded as living at Rosenbursenstr 8, Vienna, while his marriage certificate records his address as Josefinengasse 6. By 1911 he had moved again, to Klimschgasse 2. A year later *Die Fackel* announced that he had recently moved to Berlin.

Two important commissions may be noted for 1912: the first to sculpt Professor Fritz Kreisler, the Austrian-born

*Fig.5. LOE028. A bronze portrait medal of Rosa Katharina Josepha, the sculptor's wife, Vienna, 1910. 186mm. 1:2. (The Bauer private collection).*

violinist, and his wife Harriet Woerz, and the second a prestigious commission from Sergei Koussevvitzky, the Russian conductor, composer and double bassist with the Moscow Philharmonic Association, for a portrait of the German composer Ludwig van Beethoven (1770-1827) who had spent the major part of his life in Vienna. For this commission Artur was to produce several sculptures of Beethoven including a cast bronze mask and several busts. Artur is said to have achieved an expression of Beethoven's innermost feelings in the final sculptures by quietly listening to his C Minor Symphony while working. The Collection in Lincoln has an example of his life-size bust of Beethoven cast in bronze and emphasised

by a black patina, while the Beethoven Haus in Bonn, Germany, has two similar life-size busts carved in marble.

The move to Berlin in 1912 proved to be very unfortunate for Artur and Rosa as both had registered Austrian citizenship. With the declaration by Germany of war on Russia on 1 August 1914, followed by Britain's declaration of war on Germany on 4 August 1914, they found themselves trapped, and compelled to remain in Germany until hostilities came to an end in 1918. This is said to have meant the loss of their home and possessions in Cairo, while their lives for the duration of the war were to be dictated by the German State.

*Fig.6. LOE033. A bronze life-size bust of Ludwig van Beethoven, Berlin, 1912. (The Collection, Lincoln).*

# 2. WORKING IN BERLIN DURING WORLD WAR 1

ARTUR'S enforced stay in Berlin for the duration of the war had dramatic consequences for his lifestyle, which previously had been characterised by being that of an itinerant. He was later to record that he was engaged by the German State upon research, although what this involved he did not divulge. As was characteristic of the German State, it wished to record the various battles and personalities of the war, whether they were successful or not. To achieve this several sculptors were engaged to produce commemorative medals over the period of the war. Artur was engaged by Hugo Grünthal, the owner of the minters Robert Ball Nachfolger, to contribute to this project and as a result he produced many medals including a fine series in silver.

Artur's production of commemorative medals was further promoted by the formation of the *Freunde der deutschen Schaumünze* (Friends of the German Medal) formed in 1915 by Dr Julius Menadier, the Director of the Kaiser Friedrich Museum in Berlin. Although initially intended as a social gathering of those with similar interests, it soon encouraged the production of medals in aid of the war effort, and many of the examples produced by Artur are included in their contemporary catalogue.

A few of the best well-known examples of his commemoratives produced at this time that reflect the German custom of recording both their successes and failures may be noted, although the latter usually are in praise of the commanders in the field. The victory of the German army over the Russians at Tannenberg, 26-30 August 1914, is said to have been the most complete victory of World War 1, and Artur produced numerous versions of this medal both in honour of von Hindenburg and to commemorate the victory itself. They were struck in bronze, silver and gold, with castings also in bronze.

The victory over the French at St Quentin, 29-30 August 1914, was recorded on a medal to honour von Bülow, and the advance on Paris in September 1914, although halted within 13 miles of the city, and not a victory in itself, was recorded on a medal issued to honour von Kluck. A plaster of Paris cast of Artur's design for the obverse of this medal is in the collection of The Collection, Lincoln. The defeat of the German fleet in the Battle of the Falklands

on 8 December 1914 was recorded on a medal issued to honour von Spee, who died in the battle. The initiation of the submarine blockade of Britain on 18 February 1915 is commemorated to honour von Tirpitz. A more definitive loss was the destruction of the German submarine U29 on 18 March 1915, with the loss of its commander Otto Weddigen who, however, was subsequently honoured on a medal depicting him as a Viking warrior standing aboard a sinking boat. A medal to honour von Mackensen was produced to commemorate his success in the Galician offensive of April 1915. For other examples of Artur's work in this series see Zetzmann, 2002, and Steguweit, 1998.

At about this time Artur received a private commission from the Österreichischen Aero-Club for an award medal. The reverse of this medal depicts a female winged guardian with her right arm stretched out above the city of Vienna, and it is interesting to note that Artur, when living in England, was to use a similar figure on a medal to commemorate the end of the Second World War. As well as his engagement on this series of 'official' medals Artur was able to continue to produce many other portraits during the war of prominent people in Central Europe: members of the royal households of Germany and Prussia, and individuals drawn from academia and industry.

This period seems to have proved to be his most productive. How many of his subjects he actually met in the flesh is not known; some must have been modelled from photographs. An indication of this may be gleaned from a series of photographs found among his effects following his death that depict the 'Red Baron', although it is fairly certain that he never actually produced a medal of him as other sculptors had done. There also appears to have been some co-operation with other sculptors on some of his war medals.

It is also interesting to speculate upon his use of the title 'professor', which he occasionally used during the latter part of his life. Artur's brother Oskar believed it to have been an honorary title bestowed on him at about this time in order that the Kaiser and ladies of the court might have a title by which to address him when they came into contact with him during sculpting sessions. Certainly, most later academic references to him omit the title.

Among those sculpted at this time may be noted:

| | | | |
|---|---|---|---|
| Dr Karl Domanig | Director of the Vienna Münzkabinett To commemorate his death in 1913 | 1914 | British Museum |
| Professor von Schmoller | scientist and political economist | 1914 | |
| Rudolph Herzog | German author and poet | 1914 | |
| Professor Wilhelm von Bode | General Director of all the royal Prussian museums | 1914 | Ashmolean Museum, Oxford |
| Kaiser Wilhelm II | German Kaiser and King of Prussia | 1915 and 1916 | |
| Count Arthur von Posadowsky-Wiehner | Minister of State | 1915 | |
| Alexander Girardi | famous singer of light opera | 1915 | |
| Professor Adolph Wagner | economist and financier, professor of political science at Berlin University | 1915 | |
| Prince Guido Henckel von Donnersmarck | major Silesian industrialist and landowner and a member of the Prussian upper chamber | 1915 and 1916 | the wax model for the obverse of this medal is in the collection of the Ashmolean Museum |
| Gustav Krupp von Bohlen und Halbach* | German industrialist | 1916 | |
| Margarethe Krupp | The wife of Friedrich Alfred Krupp, who became involved in the planning and building of the Margarethenhöhe housing estate and other company benefit schemes. Buildings depicted on reverse of medal. | 1916 | The Collection, Lincoln |
| Baron Moritz von Bissing and his wife Baroness Alice von Bissing | Governor General of occupied Belgium 1914-1917 | 1916 | |
| Otto Wolff | Cologne steel industrialist | 1916 | Ashmolean Museum |
| Alexandra Viktoria von Schleswig-Holstein-Sonderburg-Glücksburg | Princess August Wilhelm of Prussia | 1916 | |
| the Duke of Donnersmarck | | 1916 | |
| Count Andreas Maltzan | | 1916 | |
| Countess Mengerson | German head of the Red Cross in Belgium | 1916 | The Collection, Lincoln |
| Professor Fritz Rausenberger | professor, Militärtechnische Akademie, Charlottenburg | n.d | |
| Professor Emmo Friedrich Richard Ulrich von Wilamowitz-Moellendorff | Greek historian and Rector, University of Berlin | 1916 | |
| Countess von Maltzan | | 1917 | |
| Baron Hans Eberhard von Bodenhausen-Degener | | 1917 | |
| Dr Johannes Hass | leader of the Centrum Party, Bavarian Catholics | undated but possibly of this period | |

* Artur also sculpted Gustav's two sons Alfried and Claus at about this time and this close involvement with the family may account for their help in 1934 when he decided to leave Berlin.

This continual output of medals demanded of him during the war years must have put a severe strain on Artur, so it would have come with some relief when the end of the war allowed him a return to normal life. Arthur Suhle (Suhle, 1927) states that many of Artur's sculptures at this time were produced quickly, some in a single night, although he considered the results to have been generally most successful and praiseworthy. He also records that a number of the subjects were sculpted from photographs and that good intentions often had to suffer.

# 3. POST-WAR LIFE AND WORK

WITH the declaration of peace in 1918 Artur and his wife returned to Vienna for a short while. Under the terms of the 1919 Treaty of Versailles, which dismantled the old Austro-Hungarian Empire, they both opted for Czechoslovakian nationality to replace their current Austrian citizenship, a recourse that was to stand them in good stead when the Second World War broke out. This decision may have been prompted by Artur's memory of what had happened to them in 1914. His itinerant ways also seem to have taken over again as he embarked on further travels around Europe and the Near East. One of the most important acquisitions towards his collection at this time was a two-handled canthorus or *vasa murrina*, a first century Roman drinking vessel carved from fluorspar, a material said to give wine a particular pleasant flavour. Artur records that the vessel was excavated somewhere near the Turco-Syrian border by an army officer who had been digging for water. He purchased this artefact in 1919, and his article describing the discovery remains the only provenance for the find and the constant reference used in subsequent articles written on the *vasa murrina*.

There can be little doubt of the deep affection Artur had for his wife, Rosa, and it is likely that in recognition of this he produced a medal entitled 'Rosa Lavorosa'. When he actually sculpted this portrait is not known but he was to reproduce copies of it over many years to follow. It depicts a portrait of Rosa and is thought to be allegorical. She is shown wearing a peasant's head-scarf, perhaps a hint of her Slavic ancestry, while the legend might be a reference to the two finest marbles used by sculptors – rosa and lavorosa – both of which are mined close to where Rosa was born. At about the same time he sculpted a self-portrait, which is also undated. Were the two portraits produced to celebrate fifteen years of marriage? The Collection, Lincoln, has an example in bronze of both, as well as a plaster of Paris cast of the 'Rosa Lavorosa' medal.

Artur believed that his skills and future would be better developed in Berlin, which led him to return with Rosa after their travels and set up home there. The commissions carried out at this time include: Otto Wolff, steel industrialist of Cologne, 1919; Princess Fulvia Orsini of Italy, 1920; Herr Sterne, 1920. How Artur and Rosa fared during the period of rapid inflation in 1923 is not known. Certainly no dated portraits of this period

*Fig.7. LOE113. A bronze portrait medal entitled 'Rosa Lavorosa', depicting the sculptor's wife, n.d. 130mm. 1:2. (The Fennell private collection).*

*Fig.8. LOE110. A bronze self-portrait medal of the sculptor, Artur Immanuel Loewental, n.d. 142mm. 1:2. (The Collection, Lincoln).*

have been traced outside Germany and Austria, while commissions were probably non-existent and may have led him to concentrate on members of his own family. In 1924 he sculpted his mother, Antonia, producing it in both medal and plaque form (examples of each type are in private collections in England) while the self-portrait and the 'Rosa Lavorosa' medals mentioned above may also date from this forced period of inactivity. Two life-size plaster female busts, now in the collection of The Collection, Lincoln, are thought to depict two of Artur's sisters: Paula Auguste and Clara Ottilie. Both are undated but may perhaps originate from this period.

Once the period of hyyper-inflation was over, Artur's output steadily increased and many famous names were added to his list of subjects. Examples include:

| | | | |
|---|---|---|---|
| Paul von Beneckendorff und Hindenburg | President of the Weimar Republic | 1925 | |
| Professor Fritz Kreisler* | | 1926 | The Collection, Lincoln |
| Adolph Donath | Czechoslovak poet and connoisseur | 1926 | The Collection, Lincoln, and Ashmolean Museum, Oxford |
| Professor Wilhelm Bode | Director General of German museums | 1926 | |
| Theodor Däubler | Italian artist and poet | 1927, 1929 | The Collection, Lincoln |
| Dr Friedrich Wilhelm Karl Thimme | historian and political publicist | 1927 | |
| Dr Alfred Kerr | poet, journalist and drama critic | 1927 | private collection, England |
| Dr Otto Merckens | to mark his appointment as Chairman, NSU-Werke, Neckarsulm | 1927 | Ashmolean Museum, Oxford |
| Gustav Böss | Burgermaster of Berlin | 1927 | (known from a contemporary photograph in the author's collection) |
| Charles Ahl | Finnish goldsmith | 1928 | Ashmolean Museum, Oxford |
| Robert Weismann | last democratic Secretary of State of Germany | 1928 | |
| Herr Matter | Clerk to the Burgermaster of Berlin | 1928 | |
| Johannes Hass | leader of trade unionism in Germany | 1928 | |
| Paul Loebe | President of the Reichstag | 1928 and 1930 | |
| Alfred Flechtheim | art dealer of international repute | 1928 | |
| Professor Ulrich von Wilamowitz-Moellendorff | Greek historian and Rector, University of Berlin | 1928 | British Museum |
| Captain Geyger | a noted connoisseur | 1928 | |
| Max Jacob Friedlaender | Director General of German museums, successor to Bode | 1928 | private collection, England. 1929 plaster cast in The Collection, Lincoln |
| Dr Höpker-Aschoff | last democratic Minister of Finance of Prussia | 1929 | private collection, England, and Ashmolean Museum, Oxford |
| Baron Ehrenfried Günther von Hünefeld | German aviation pioneer and initiator of first E-W trans-Atlantic flight. Probably sculpted to commemorate his death | 1929 | private collection, USA |
| Professor Jacob Gould Shurman | American Ambassador to Germany | 1929 | |

*On 18 December 1926 The Watertown Daily Times reported the presentation of Artur's medal to Kreisler during a concert in Berlin in recognition of his benefactions to starving Austrian children, the presentation having been made by Dr Felix Frank, the Austrian Minister to Germany, on behalf of the Austrian Aid Society.

In 1930 Artur received what is perhaps his most important commission, this time from the German State, to produce a bust of the now world-famous theoretical physicist Professor Albert Einstein. In 1929 Einstein, having not only celebrated his fiftieth birthday but also having his *Unified Theory* published, had come to be held in high esteem by the German State, so it was perhaps to celebrate these two events that Artur was commissioned to produce a portrait. Einstein sat for Artur in Berlin, with the sculpting process of the wax model being captured on camera and published by the *New York Times*, on 13 April 1930. A typical sculpting session with Einstein was to be recounted years later by Artur in an interview for the *Lincolnshire Echo* of 9 January 1950:

> *There, clad in baggy flannel trousers, wearing a grey woollen jersey, his hair dishevelled, Einstein sat relaxed in an arm chair, deep in thought, oblivious to everything and everyone in the room. Opposite in another chair with paper and pencil sat expert mathematician, Professor Walther Mayer of Vienna. Einstein was, so to speak, in a coma, he was just leaning back. His cheeks were hollow. His temples were caved in. His eyes sank deep. His whole frame shrank like a dying man. It was as though life had stopped and everything was being drawn inside him. Einstein, the inventor, was grasping out of nothing, a new fundamental idea. It was as if I could see the air around him begin to scintillate, fulminate, like something supernatural. Then his eyes became alight again. His cheeks rounded. His forehead bulged. It was as if some extraordinary force would have lifted the whole man. The whole being of Einstein began to radiate. He rose, hand upraised, excitely pouring out words, figures, mathematical equations and formulae. Opposite, Professor Mayer, the mathematics expert, the workman who hammered together the ideas which teemed out of Einstein's brain, began to write furiously. He would look at Einstein, taking in every word he ejaculated, translating them into mathematical formulae. He worked with the rapidity of which only a skilled mathematician is capable. Sheet after sheet of paper dropped from his hand until the floor was littered with them. There was nothing of a pose about the scene. It was the most natural happening. Einstein was aware of nobody. Had the Emperor of China been in the room it would have been all the same to him.*

Artur brought an example of the cast of the bronze bust produced from this effigy with him to England in 1934, where it is now in the collection of The Collection, Lincoln.

Einstein must have been pleased with the subsequent portrait as, in a letter to Max Liebermann, the famous German-Jewish portrait painter, dated 30 March 1930, he is full of praise for Artur's skills as a sculptor.

It is interesting to note that Einstein mentions two reliefs and one bust in his letter, which neatly ties up with types traced outside Germany, although other examples must exist. This commission is said to have led to a close friendship between Artur and Einstein, although Artur notes that at first Einstein regarded him as one who just 'had to be tolerated', but that 'later on he began to take a personal interest in me'. Artur also recalled that they became friends, visiting each other's homes for meals.

It is clear that Artur was always deeply involved in his art, living an isolated academic existence, oblivious to events in the outside world around him and in particular to the developing plight of the Jews in Austria and Germany.

*Fig.9. Artur Loewental sculpts Professor Albert Einstein, Berlin, 1930. (© collections CEGES/SOMA – Brussels, Image No.126746).*

Einstein on the other hand, although engrossed with his physical theories and feted at this time by the German State for his discoveries, was always the intuitive realist: he saw what lay ahead for the Jews in Europe. As a consequence Einstein wrote to the director of the Metropolitan Museum in New York on 24 March 1930, recommending that he should encourage Artur to move to America. He emphasised at length Artur's artistic productivity as a sculptor and deplored the growing impoverishment of European artists. According to Einstein there was no future for an artist like Artur in Europe, and he hinted that the director should write to encourage Artur to go over to America. Einstein wrote a further letter dated 16 October 1930, which was addressed to Boyce Thompson, a renowned lapidary in New York, pointing out Artur's skills in crafting gems, and again trying to pave a path for Artur to go to America. Artur, for his part, does not seem to have shown any interest or desire to go to America, but he did write to Einstein from Lugano, Switzerland, in October or November 1930, urging Einstein to help his friend Carlo Klein, whose application for residency in Switzerland had been refused. Only a fragment of this letter survives in the Einstein Archive, Israel, and written on the only surviving page is a draft reply, believed to be in the writing of Einstein's wife, which supports the view of the close friendship between Artur and Einstein.

Despite the turbulent times for Jews in Germany at this time Artur was able to continue carrying out commissions for portraits and among those sculpted were:

*Fig.10. LOE145. A bronze life-size bust of Professor Albert Einstein, Berlin, 1930. (The Collection, Lincoln).*

| | | | |
|---|---|---|---|
| Dr Friedrich Eichberg | inventor of electrical machinery | 1930 | private collection, USA |
| Professor Fritz Kreisler | Austrian violinist and composer | | |
| Dr Wilfrid Greif | Director of J. G. Farben, New York | n.d. | private collection, USA |
| Dr Otto Braun | last democratic Prime Minister of Prussia | 1930 | private collections, England and USA, and Ashmolean Museum, Oxford |
| Paul Loebe | President of the Reichstag | 1930 | private collection, England |
| Theodor Däubler | | 1931 | bronze medal and original wax model on slate in Ashmolean Museum, Oxford |
| Professor Max von Planck | President of the Academy of Science, and expounder of Quantum Theory | 1931 | British Museum |
| Johann Wolfgang von Goethe | to mark his centenary | 1932 | |
| Professor Robert Schmidt | Director, Schloss Museum, Berlin | 1932 | Ashmolean Museum, Oxford |

| | | | |
|---|---|---|---|
| Alex Veeck | | 1932 | plaster cast in The Collection, Lincoln |
| Jean Babelon | Director, Bibliotique Nationale, Paris | 1933 and 1937 | |
| Mrs Anna Winkler, of Berlin | | n.d. but may date from this time | private collection, England. |

Throughout his life Artur carved portraits and subjects in hard gemstones and other hard minerals such as rock crystal. As most are unsigned and unrecorded his large output of intaglios is for the most part untraceable, except for a few instances where there is a definite provenance. Three of his larger works in rock crystal may be mentioned: two from descriptions in publications and one known survival. Even as late as 1932 Artur was being feted in the German press for his outstanding engraving skills in rock crystal, in particular his major and possibly finest work known as the 'Dionysos Cup', which was copied in general form from the cup in agate called 'des Ptolémées', held by the Cabinet des Médailles de France, Paris. Artur recalled that he did not have the necessary equipment to cut the natural rock crystal from which it was to be carved in his workshop in Berlin and had to travel to Idar Oberstein, a major centre for stone cutting, in Rheinland-Pfalz, in southwest Germany.

When completed, the two-handled and partially gilded cup depicted a scene of the god Dionysos teaching humans how to make wine. In an article in *Der Kunstwanderer*, 1932, Robert Schmidt describes in detail the methods that Artur had used to carve the cup from a solid block of rock crystal. The article is accompanied by illustrations of both sides of the finished cup. It was presented to the city of Berlin in 1932 and the article names Director Alfred Frankfurter as the 'owner'. Its present whereabouts is unknown and it may perhaps have been a victim of Nazi looting during the Second World War. Artur contributed a long and detailed article on the engraving techniques used on large rock crystal vessels and their origins in *La Gazette des Beaux-Arts*, January 1934, while the *Illustrated London News*, 15 June 1935, elevates Artur to the modern counterpart of Benvenuto Cellini:

> *Professor Artur Loewental, whose recent exhibition at the Beaux Arts Gallery was opened by the Austrian Minister Baron*

> *Franckenstein, is a master of klein-plastik, comprising the arts of the medallist, carver, and engraver in hard stones. His work, it has been said, has not been surpassed since the days of Benvenuto Cellini. In a foreword to the exhibition catalogue, Sir George Hill, Director of the British Museum, said of his engravings in rock crystal that 'he need not fear comparison with the most famous masters of the Renaissance'; adding that he is 'not one of those who think that in order to attain "self-expression" it is essential to avoid fidelity of representation. Portraiture, accordingly, is one of his greatest points.'*

Two further examples of his work in rock crystal that Artur brought with him to England in 1934 may be noted. The first is a circular bowl depicting 'Prometheus bringing the fire' which was commissioned by Ivar Kreuger of Sweden. Unfortunately Kreuger died before its completion. Artur exhibited this bowl in London in 1935, and in 1980 it was included in the Bauer sale. Its present whereabouts is unknown. The second, although damaged, does survive and is now in the collection of The Collection, Lincoln. It too was exhibited in London in 1935 and is known as the 'Panther Cup' in reference to the two handles that are carved as panthers.

The early years of the 1930s became ever more difficult for Jews in Germany and Austria. The increasing anti-Semitism associated with the rise of Hitler and the Nazi party applied more and more pressure on Jews to leave those countries. Further pressures included a series of laws preventing Jews from working in the professions. Einstein, feted for his achievements by the German State in 1930 and originally a pacifist, soon became opposed to the Nazi regime and could foresee a future Germany where Jews would be excluded from every form of employment.

The Reichstag elections of 5 March 1933 brought the Nazi party into power, and confirmation of Einstein's fears came through the Enabling Act of 23 March. Einstein himself wisely chose not to return to Germany from a visit to America. Instead, having landed in Antwerp on 28 March, he set up a temporary home in Belgium, before moving to England and lecturing there, and finally leaving Europe for ever in the following October. Was Artur's reluctance to leave a case of naivety or indifference? Certainly he appears to have always been totally engrossed in his work, to all appearances living in an isolated academic world and taking little, if any, interest in politics or local events. So the sudden absence of his friend Einstein from the scene and the increasing plight of ordinary Jews may have been the final prompts needed to convince him that it might be expedient to leave Berlin himself. Hitler's policy towards the Jews at this time was to encourage them to leave Germany, but with the crippling condition that they should only be allowed to take a small suitcase of their personal possessions with them – forfeiting their homes, wealth and possessions for a chance to escape tyranny. It was under these changed circumstances that Artur finally decided to leave Berlin for England. The precise circumstances of his departure are not known, but it is remarkable that, compared to other Jews leaving Germany at this time, he was allowed to leave and to take with him a considerable quantity of very valuable possessions, even returning in subsequent years up to 1939 to collect further possessions and even visit his mother in Vienna, although he did lose his home and its contents. The question remains as to how Artur managed to leave with so much of value, although both he and Rosa would be travelling on Czechoslovak passports. A possible answer may be his acquaintance with the Krupp family, several of whom he had sculpted in 1916. It is even recounted by his descendants that one of the members of the Krupp family assured him before he left for England that the present in Germany would be over in six months, after which he would be able to return. It is also believed that he left many of his possessions in safe keeping in Berlin – perhaps with a member of the Krupp family. This 'return' was never to happen and Artur and his wife Rosa would spend the rest of their lives in England.

Anti-Semitism in Germany came to a head in 1933, the first year of the Third Reich and the year in which Adolf Hitler became Chancellor of Germany. The *Gesetz zur Wiederherstellung des Berufsbeamtentums* (Law for the Restoration of the Professional Civil Service) was passed on 7 April 1933. It was the first of a series of anti-Semitic laws intended to outlaw Jews from prominent positions enacted after Hitler's rise to power, although its full force was not to be felt until after the death of von Hindenburg on 2 August 1934. It may have been the loss of an important ally that finally signalled to Artur that it was time to leave. Certainly, his exit was to come soon afterwards, on 20 November. Einstein's sudden exodus, together with the increasing restrictions being imposed upon himself as a Jew, would have made him question his own future and finally reach the decision to leave for England.

In 1934, the year in which Artur and Rosa came to England, Jews were not only excluded from the German stock exchanges, but by 15 September 1935 the Nuremberg Laws had deprived Jews of German citizenship and outlawed marriage and extramarital relationships with Aryans. This was to be followed in 1938 by the legal decree banning Jews from the professions and business, although by this time Artur and Rosa were firmly established in England.

# 4. THE MOVE FROM BERLIN TO ENGLAND IN 1934

ARTUR and Rosa arrived in England on 20 November 1934, and by 18 December are recorded as guests at the Kingsley Hotel, Hart Street, London. Despite his arrival so late in 1934 Artur was almost immediately able to produce portrait commissions for several prominent British people including: Sir Robert Abdy, 5th Bt., a connoisseur, art dealer and collector with premises in Paris and to whom Artur had sold an amethyst vase in the past, 1934 (private collection, England); Baron Georg von und zu Franckenstein, Austrian Ambassador at the Court of St James, 1934 and 1935 (The Collection, Lincoln); Lady Betty Hambro, 1934. Although it is said that, whilst he spent many hours on the larger medal version, it was probably unsolicited and never accepted. However, it always took pride of place in his home after he moved to Lincoln and was in his effects when he died. It is now in a private collection in England; Lord Christopher Glenconnor (Christopher Grey Tennant, 2nd Baron Glenconnor), and his two sons James and Colin, c.1934. The Collection, Lincoln, has a plaster cast of the former, while examples of the latter two are in the Ashmolean Museum and a private collection in England.

Artur already had an important contact in England in Sir George Francis Hill, the Director and Principal Librarian at the British Museum, whose association with him will have been due to his specialisation in numismatics and enthusiasm for medals, and the subsequent dealings with European museums. In fact Hill had already praised

Artur's medallic work as early as 1919, while *circa* 1920 the British Museum published a set of picture postcards depicting German medals issued during the First World War. This set included several examples of works by Artur, among which were: XL4, Grand Admiral von Tirpitz; XL7, General-Oberst von Hindenburg; XL9, General-Oberst von Kluck; and XL10, 'To Paris – 1914', the reverse of which is by Artur. There is no doubt that this set was promoted by Hill, who again praised Artur's skills in his *Catalogue of commemorative medals in the collection of the British Museum*, published in 1934. Hill was to prove to be a very supportive friend to Artur, particularly in 1940, during the Second World War, when he helped him obtain British nationality. His initial help was forthcoming by promoting a major exhibition of Artur's works that was held within months of his arrival in England. The items chosen for display were intended to show visitors the quality and skill of Artur's sculpting, hopefully encouraging new commissions in order to establish his reputation in England and provide him with an income. The exhibition was held at the Beaux Arts Gallery, Bruton Place, Bruton Street, London, and ran from 28 May to 8 June 1935. It was opened by His Excellency Baron Georg von und zu Franckenstein, the Austrian Minister at the Court of St James. Franckenstein was well known as an ardent supporter of the arts and for his sponsorship of artistic endeavour. There is little doubt that he added his considerable weight behind Artur in his bid to establish himself in England. The catalogue for the

*Fig.11.LOE187. A bronze portrait medal of Sir George Francis Hill, London, 1935. 140mm. 1:2. (The Ashmolean Museum, Oxford).*

## CATALOGUE

*(The prices can be had on application)*

————

1. Professor Albert Einstein (*bronze head*)
2. Dr. Braun, former Minister-President (*bronze bust*)
3. Beethoven (*bronze bust*)
4. Beethoven (*bronze mask*)
5. Cup with two handles in the form of Panthers (*carved in rock crystal*)
6. Round Bowl with engraved relief of " Prometheus " (*carved in rock crystal*)
7. " Dragon " seal (*carved in rock crystal*)
8. Professor A. Einstein (*silver-mounted medallion in rock crystal*)
9. Two-handled Amphora (*carved in sardonyx*)

### BRONZE RELIEFS

10. Geheimrath von Planck, President of the Academy of Sciences
11. Wilamowitz von Mœllendorf, former Rector of Berlin University
12. Dr. Braun, former Minister-President of Prussia
13. Dr. Hoepker-Aschoff, former Finance Minister of Prussia
14. Jacob Shurman, former American Ambassador in Berlin
15. Dr. Wilfried Greif, Director of J. G. Farben, New York
16. Professor Fritz Kreisler, violinist
17. Dr. Franz Hartmann, theosophist
18. Freiherr von Hünefeldt, aviator
19. Madame von Bissing
20. Countess Mengersen
21. Fulvia Orsini
22. Frau von Krupp
23. Gustav Krupp von Bohlen Halbach
24, 25, 26. The Children of Gustav Krupp von Bohlen Halbach
27. Lord Christopher Glenconner
28, 29. Lord Glenconner's Children
30. Mrs. Betty Hambro
31. Geheimrath Max Friedlander, Director of the Kaiser-Friedrich Museum, Berlin
32. An Old Man
33. Wilhelm von Bode, Chief Director of the German Museums
34. Theodor Daübler, poet
35. Otto Wolf, of Cologne

36. General Litzmann, the victor of Kovno
37. General von Kluck (*silver medal*)
38. General Field Marshal von Hindenburg, as the victor of Tannenburg (*silver medal*)
39. Reichspräsident von Hindenburg (*silver medal*)
40. Professor von Schmoller
41. Alexander Girardi, actor
42, 43. The Artist's Wife—" Ida "
44. Fuerst Henkel Donnersmark
45. Lord Cromer, Viceroy of Egypt
46. Adolph Donath
47. Jean Babelon, Director of the Musée des Antiques et Médailles, Paris
48. Sir Robert Abdy
49. Rudolf Herzog, poet
50. Rudolf Herzog (*reverse of the medal*)
51. Freiherr von Franckenstein, the Austrian Minister (*plaster cast*)
52. Freiherr von Franckenstein (*small medallion, plaster*)
53. Johannes Hass
54. " La Semeuse " (*silver medal*)

————

55. Mrs. Betty Hambro (*relief carved in ivory*)
56, 57. Lord Glenconner's Children (*reliefs carved in ivory*)

| MEDALLIONS ENGRAVED IN ROCK CRYSTAL | INTAGLIOS ENGRAVED IN CARNELIAN |
|---|---|
| 58. The Austrian Minister | 70. Professor Robert Schmidt |
| 59. Wilhelm von Bode | 71. The Artist's Wife |
| 60. Geheimrath Max Planck | 72. The Artist's Wife |
| 61. Otto Braun | 73. Ancient Greek Horse |
| 62. Paul Loebe | 74. Amazon Riding |
| 63. Allegory of War | 75. A Young Lady |
| 64. Allegory of World Commerce | 76. Harriet Kreisler |
| 65. Sir Robert Abdy | 77. Fritz Kreisler |
| 66. Adolph Donath | 78. Alexander Pichler |
| 67. Otto Wolf | 79. Head of an Athlete |
| 68. The Artist's Wife | 80. Otto Wolf (*cameo carved in agate*) |
| 69. Gustav Böss | 81. Portrait of a Child (*engraved topaz*) |

82. Cigarette Box in gold repoussé with engraved carnelian
83. Goethe (*bronze medallion obverse*)
84. Goethe (*bronze medallion reverse*)
85. Charles Ahl, goldsmith

*The copyright is strictly reserved*

exhibition includes a glowing foreword written by Hill. Of his engraving skills he says:

> In the work of Artur Loewental one sees the Viennese qualities at their best: a combination of delicacy with virility, a complete mastery of technique guided by an unerring scholarship and inspired by an intensive study of the methods of his forerunners.

While of his portraiture:

> A glance at this exhibition reveals him as not one of those who think that in order to attain 'self-expression' it is essential to avoid fidelity of representation. Portraiture, accordingly, is one of his strongest points.

The pages from the exhibition catalogue reproduced here give some idea of the range of Artur's work and of the many personages that he sculpted. Some 85 items were exhibited, most of which he had brought with him from Berlin. Although a price list was available with the catalogue, there is little evidence that any major sales took place, and many of the same items were to appear in his subsequent exhibitions. A photograph of Artur's 'Panther Cup' appears on the cover of the catalogue. The exhibition was certainly given much publicity and *The Times*, 8 June 1935, records the visit of the Princesses Marie Louise and Helena Victoria of Schleswig-Holstein, the granddaughters of Queen Victoria, to view the exhibition, no doubt at the suggestion of Franckenstein.

Shortly after the closure of this exhibition Artur and Rosa travelled to Switzerland, leaving on 27 August and landing back in Dover on 4 October. In London they rented a partially furnished house, 35 Elm Tree Road, St John's Wood, with a rent of £16 per month, and where Artur set up his studio in a glass fronted room on the top floor of the property.

No doubt in recognition of the enormous help he had received on his arrival in England Artur produced several portrait medals of Hill dated 1935 (The Collection, Lincoln, the Victoria and Albert Museum and Ashmolean Museum, Oxford), 1936 (the Ashmolean Museum and a private collection in England), and 1938 (the Ashmolean Museum and a plaster cast in The Collection, Lincoln).

For others sculpted at this time see the following table:

| | | | |
|---|---|---|---|
| Rufus Daniel Isaacs, 1st Marquis of Reading, politician, judge and ambassador | | 1935 and 1936* | The Collection, Lincoln, and British Museum |
| Lady Bearsted | | 1936 and 1938 | Upton House, Banbury |
| Mary Gascoigne-Cecil, Marchioness of Hartington, who became Duchess of Devonshire in 1938 | | 1936 | private collection, England |
| Paul Channon | son of Lady Honor Channon | 1937 | plaster cast in The Collection, Lincoln |
| Anton Maric | | 1938 | |
| Lord Bearsted | | 1939 | Upton House, Banbury |

*The 1936 example seems to have been popular and many are known in the UK and USA.

For most of Artur's commissions precise details and dates are unknown, so the portraits he sculpted of Rudyard Kipling are of particular interest. Rudyard Kipling, the celebrated English short story writer and novelist, celebrated his seventieth birthday on 30 December 1935, and to commemorate this achievement Artur sculpted a small portrait medal (140mm in diameter) with the legend 'Rudyard Kipling' and the date '1935'.

It is unknown whether this was a commission or rather a commercial venture similar to his Mark Twain medal of 1898. A rare survival, in a private collection in England, is a series of progressive trial plaster casts taken as he developed the portrait. At least three examples of the finished bronze casting survive, one in the collection of the American Numismatic Society and two in private collections. Sadly Kipling died within a few days of his birthday, on 18 January 1936, and to commemorate his life Artur used the same portrait to produce a much larger medal (239mm in

*Fig.12. LOE191. A bronze portrait medal of Rudyard Kipling, London, 1935. 140mm. 1:2. (The Bauer private collection).*

*Fig.13. LOE198. A bronze portrait medal of Rudyard Kipling, London, 1936. 239mm. 1:2. (The British Museum, London).*

diameter) with a revised legend 'Rudyard Kipling 1865-1936' and the date '1936'. On 10 February 1936 *The Times* reported the presentation of an example in bronze of this larger medal to the British Museum by a Captain John Ball. The closeness of this presentation to Kipling's death must indicate either that Artur had anticipated his death and prepared the medal in advance, or had added the date later.

On 20 October 1937 Yarrow Shipbuilders Limited, Glasgow, began the construction of a Javelin class destroyer for the Royal Navy to be named HMS Kipling. This was the first time that a Royal Navy vessel had been named after Kipling and quite naturally the Kipling Society took an active interest in its construction. It was felt by the Society that a 'plaque of Kipling in Bas-relief' might be presented to the vessel. *The Kipling Journal* of December 1938 announced that the Lords Commissioners of the Admiralty had accepted the offer made by the Society, and invited subscriptions from members towards the cost of the plaque. In April 1939 *The Kipling Journal* reported that 'a plaque of Kipling's head and shoulders has been ordered for presentation to HMS Kipling which will be commissioned in December next'. To fulfil this commission Artur supplied the Society with two castings in bronze of his earlier, larger, 1936 medal. One of these is preserved in the Society library at Bateman's, Burwash, while the other was presented on board HMS Kipling at a ceremony on 6 April 1940, being unveiled by the founder of the Society, Mr J. H. C. Brooking. It is sad to relate that on 11 May 1942, while returning to Alexandria with three other destroyers, HMS Kipling was sunk by an anti-ship group of German JU88 bombers in the eastern Mediterranean north of Sidi Barrani, Egypt. Of the ship's 250-strong company 221 survived. The wreck was never salvaged so one of Artur's medals now rests at the bottom of the Mediterranean Sea.

In 1997 the Kipling Society authorised the copying of their example of the Kipling medal for presentation to the Sir J. J. Institute of Applied Art in Bombay (now Mumbai), an institute that has close historical associations with the Kiplings. The sculptor Janet Leech was commissioned to undertake this task and, having cleaned the medal, she made a mould in 'stone-plaster' from which a number of replicas in various materials were produced. In 1998 one of these replicas was delivered to the Sir J. J. Institute of Applied Art in Bombay, while a second example now forms part of the HMS Kipling exhibit in the Kipling Room at The Grange, Rottingdean. Other replicas were intended for presentation to outstanding members of the Society, while members were also offered the chance to purchase examples at a price of around £40.

Artur continued to exhibit his work, with displays at the Royal Academy in 1936, 1937 and 1939. A further

## Exhibition of the Work of Artur Loewental at the Fine Arts Society, London, May 1939

### List of Exhibits

1. Round intaglio (rock crystal) – His Excellency Dr Bode
2. Round intaglio (rock crystal) – 'Allegory of the World Trade'
3. Oval intaglio (rock crystal) – President Loebe
4. Round intaglio (rock crystal) – Professor Max v Planck
5. Round intaglio (rock crystal) – 'The Fury of War on Horseback'
6. Oval intaglio (rock crystal) – Adolph Donath
7. Oval intaglio (cornelian) – Portrait of a young Italian
8. Oval intaglio (cornelian) – Greek Horse
9. Oval intaglio (sard) – Sir George Franckenstein
10. Oval intaglio (cornelian) – 'Head of Hercules'
11. Large round intaglio (rock crystal) – The Duchess of Devonshire
12. Oval intaglio (sard) – Professor Dr Robert Schmidt
13. Oval intaglio (cornelian) – Amazon on Horseback
14. Round intaglio (rock crystal) – Sir Robert Abdy
15. Cameo in agate – Otto Wolff of Cologne
16. Small intaglio (cornelian) – 'My wife'
17. Oval intaglio (cornelian) – Mrs Harriet Kreisler
18. Small intaglio (cornelian) – Head of a Girl
19. Round intaglio (rock crystal) – Dr Gustav Boss
20. Round intaglio (rock crystal) – Dr Braun
21. Oval intaglio (cornelian) – 'Ida'
22. Large oval intaglio (rock crystal) – 'Bacchant'
23. Oval intaglio (cornelian) – Fritz Kreisler

24. Large round intaglio (rock crystal) – Sir George Franckenstein
25. Oval intaglio (rock crystal) – Roman head
26. Oval intaglio (amethyst) – 'The Poet and Muse'
27. Oval intaglio (rock crystal) – Portrait head 'Italiana'
28. Medal (rock crystal) (mounted in leather case) – The late Lord Reading
29 and 30. Medals (ivory) – The children of Lord Glenconnor
31. Intaglio on stand (topaz) – Portrait of Countess Maltzan
32. Oval intaglio (sard) – Sir George Franckenstein
33. Oval intaglio (cornelian) – Anton Maric
34. Large round intaglio (rock crystal) – Lady Bearsted
35. Small intaglio (cornelian) – 'After the Bath'
36. Oval intaglio (cornelian) – Head
37. Round intaglio (rock crystal) – 'Baby'
38. Oval intaglio (rock crystal) – Portrait of a thoroughbred horse
39. Round intaglio (rock crystal) – Lady Honor Channon
40. Oval intaglio (amethyst) – Paul Channon
41. Round intaglio (rock crystal) – The late Duchess of Rutland
42. Oval intaglio (rock crystal) – Mrs Wolff
43. Mounted medal (rock crystal) – Mr Anthony de Rothschild's daughter Anne
44. Silver mounted medal – Portrait of Professor Einstein
45. Bowl (rock crystal) engraved 'Prometheus bringing the Fire' (made for the late Ivor Kreuger of Sweden)
46 Amphora in Greek style (sardonyx)
47. Mounted gilded silver (rock crystal) – Lady Bearsted
48. Medal (ivory) – Mr Anthony de Rothschild's daughter Anne
49. Bronze medal – The Duchess of Devonshire
50. Bronze medal – Fritz Kreisler
51. Bronze medal – The late Lord Reading
52. Bronze medal – Sir George Franckenstein
53. Bronze medal – Dr Hopker-Aschoff

important though smaller exhibition, also promoted by Hill, was held in May 1939 at the Fine Arts Society, London. This exhibition concentrated almost exclusively on his engraved intaglios and carvings in hard minerals, the vast majority of which have not been traced. The catalogue for this exhibition lacks illustrations but a photographic negative from the same period, now in a private collection in Canada, depicts some trial casts from his intaglios and gives some impression of the fineness of his work in this field. The foreword to the catalogue was again written by Hill. Fifty-three items were exhibited, 48 of which give a glimpse into the side of Artur's artistic skills as an engraver not covered in this present work, but a list of the exhibits is given above.

In Germany the Nazi party issued their final laws against the Jewish population, and Hitler's ambitions for his Third Reich were about to throw Europe into chaos. On 1 September 1939 German troops invaded Poland and as a consequence Great Britain, honouring its treaty with Poland, declared war on Germany two days later. It was under these changed circumstances that the decision by Artur and Rosa to opt for Czechoslovakian nationality seems to have paid off. Together with the influential contacts he had made since moving to England this was no doubt the reason why they were not interned at the beginning of hostilities, a fate which was to befall his only relative living in England, his nephew Tony Lucas (aka Anton Ignaz Loewental) who had arrived in England 13 September 1938 and lodged with Artur and Rosa in London. Although he was initially able to find work by designing for the textile industry, the prospect of war in late 1939 meant that his work dried up. The subsequent financial straits he found himself in, exacerbated by Artur's dwindling commissions and income, eventually caused friction between Tony and Rosa, and he moved out. With the outbreak of war, however, Tony was interned for a while on the Isle of Man. As a consequence of the restrictions and austerities caused by the war Artur also found himself unable to carry out his work, and commissions ceased. This situation was compounded by the fact that he was unable to use his glass-roofed workshop on the top of the house in Elm Tree Road due to the risks from German bombing raids. His financial position soon became desperate and he was compelled to live off his savings. In a report by the Metropolitan Police Special Branch, 18 October 1940, his assets and liabilities were summarised:

> Mr Loewental pays £16 per month inclusive for his partly furnished house. He has there a number of artistic works and materials of his own; a number of old masters, together with some Egyptological antiquities. He also stated that he had left the more valuable of his art possessions in the care of a friend in Beckenham, Kent, where they are stored in a bomb proof shelter. He was not able to compute the value of these, but valued a precious stone in his possession at approximately £2,000. He produced Post Office Savings Bank books which show that he and his wife have deposited the total sum of £1,553. He also has £500 in a deposit account at the Union Bank of Scotland.

Artur approached several manufacturers with a view to doing war work, knowing that his knowledge of working with hard gem stones, and in particular with diamonds, was an asset that was greatly needed for the war effort in Britain. In fact many Jews from Europe were being encouraged to come to England to use their expertise and, if possible, to bring diamonds with them. Kelvin, Bottomley & Baird, manufacturers of aeronautical instruments, and the GEC Research Laboratory, Wembley, both offered him a position working on diamond dies. Even the Ministry of Supply, Diamond Dies Control, wrote to Artur commissioning him to set up a laboratory in a studio near his home where he could conduct experiments in drilling rough diamonds to the finest possible diameters, the rough diamonds being supplied by the Ministry. Diamond dies are used to draw the extremely fine wires used, for instance, in aeronautical instruments. There was one major problem, however, in that he could not be employed in war work unless he became a British subject. In order to remedy this situation he completed the appropriate paperwork and submitted his application for naturalisation in January 1940. It was unfortunate that at this particular time the Home Office was reluctant to process applications, which greatly delayed progress. In a letter to Oswald Peake MP, 12 July 1940, Sir George Hill wrote:

> I can vouch for him in every way. But I should not press his case were it not that, if naturalised, he would be of the greatest use to this country. As an engraver in crystal and hard stones he has a European reputation; I personally consider him the finest living technician in that craft. The point is that, as he informs me, he has a personal assurance from Major MacAlpine of Kelvin, Bottomley and Baird, Basingstoke, manufacturers of Aeronautical Instruments, that if he can obtain naturalisation, they will give him employment; and they consider that his unique skill will be of great value to them in the production of scientific instruments. There would also be an opening for him in the G.E.C. Research Laboratory, Wembley (Dr Peterson and Mr Leeds) where he could be employed to solve the problems of the diamond dies. Mr A. J. Philpot of the British Scientific Research Association and Sir Frank Smith of the Ministry of Supply, are also, I understand, acquainted with Mr Loewental's special qualifications. I beg leave most earnestly to recommend this case to you for special consideration, such as, from what Sir John Anderson has said, it being accorded to exceptionally qualified persons.

Four well known figures agreed to sponsor Artur, all of whom he had sculpted since his arrival in England: Sir George Francis Hill, Sir Robert Abdy, Lord Christopher Glenconnor, and Lord Bearsted. In the event, Glenconnnor unfortunately could not be contacted as he was on a war mission in Turkey, but the other three communicated their support, although their reference forms are tinged with some reserve.

Reference form by Lord Bearsted, 2 October 1940:

> I have known Mr Loewenthal since his arrival in England some five years ago. I was originally introduced to him by Sir George Franckenstein, then Austrian Minister, who called my attention to his great qualities as an artist & sculptor. I have since given him several commissions. He is primarily an artist, & has little interest outside his work. In his own way he is, & has been for many years, an outstanding figure. His work is in most European museums & I am sure he would prove a loyal British subject.

Reference form by Sir George Hill, 3 October 1940:

*I was familiar with Mr Artur Loewental's work as an artist before I made his personal acquaintance when he came and settled in London. Since then I have seen a great deal of him, more especially in connexion with his professional work, and we have associated on very friendly terms. He has frequently consulted me with regard to his personal circumstances. I am confident that he can be trusted to be a loyal British subject. I may add that if he can obtain naturalisation it will make it easier for him to obtain employment in which his exceptional ability as an engraver of hard stones – his reputation in this art is international – could be used for work of the highest national importance.*

Reference form by Sir Robert Abdy, Bt, 6 October 1940:

*Acquaintance made in Paris about 1934 through a business acquaintance. After acquiring a bowl carved in amethyst purporting of early Byzantine period (£2000) no further meeting for 2 years or more occurred. When he reappeared in Paris at my (antiques business) shop he showed me numerous carvings in hard stone, photographs of same & medals & related he was without money. His possessions of Chinese carvings and money hidden were in his home at Berlin. I am still unaware of his nationality – religion and politics. (His wife is an Italian). Admiring the rare and talented skills(?) displayed in the carvings & being prepared to imagine he is a Jew on account of the declared impossibility of regaining his Chinese stones, etc., I did numerous actions to assist the gaining of his livelihood. Firstly with money then arranging exhibitions of his work & influencing others to give him work. When living in London he regained his Chinese vases etc. Personally I remain prepared to continue giving recommendations, give work & believe Mr Loewental to be in financial need; nor do I imagine him to have friends to assist him.*

Despite these recommendations the naturalisation formalities dragged on for nearly a year. Hill made repeated pleas on Artur's behalf, while a special report by the Metropolitan Police Special Branch, 18 October, finding nothing to prevent the application being granted, failed to hurry things along. In a memo dated 6 December it was concluded that Artur's case might be considered to have satisfied the necessary conditions, namely, the residence conditions, he was of good character, would be in a position to support himself, had an adequate knowledge of English, and had no political associations. It is interesting to note that while this same memo approved of Artur's application on the basis that it would be in the 'national interest', it still reflects doubts concerning Rosa's position, as she herself could make no such claim. However, having finally submitted his details for his certificate of naturalisation to the Under-Secretary of State at the Home Office, together with a fee of £9 on 21 December, Artur was sworn on 25 January 1941, upon which his Aliens Registration Card was transferred to the Dead Section on 26 February. Notice of his naturalisation was announced in the *London Gazette*, 18 March, after which Artur wrote a letter on his wife's behalf, signed by her, requesting that in light of her husband's successful application she, too, be granted naturalisation. Finally, a letter from the Chief Constable of Lincoln City Police, 18 October 1941, confirmed that Rosa had been granted British Nationality and her Aliens Registration Card had been transferred to the Dead Section.

Despite the constraints of the war and the undoubted pressures being suffered by the delays, Artur was still able to supply fifteen bronze medals shortly before his move to Lincoln for exhibition at the Royal Academy of Arts, London, in 1940. One of Artur's main benefactors when he came to England in 1934 was Baron Georg von und zu Franckenstein who received a knighthood in 1938 to become Sir George Franckenstein. In the collection of The Collection, Lincoln, there is a plaster cast of a portrait medal dated 1941 that Artur might perhaps have produced in commemoration of this honour, although no subsequent bronze casting has been traced.

# 5. THE MOVE TO LINCOLN IN 1941

ONCE British nationality had been granted things began to move swiftly. Artur and Rosa moved up to Lincoln, from where he was able to register his certificate with the Under Secretary of State, on 20 February 1941. The provisional address that he gave was the Industrial Cutting Tools Limited, Diamond Works, Lincoln. One of the major engineering companies in Lincoln, Clayton & Shuttleworth Limited, had been founded in 1842 and subsequently constructed office buildings and workshops at a site on Waterside South, Lincoln. A forge on the north side of the River Witham, known as Abbey Works, and large construction bays and offices on Waterside South, known as the Titanic Works, were added later.

By the 1920s the firm's fortunes had declined. In 1928 the company Clayton Dewandre Company Limited was formed and took over the Titanic Works. This was followed in 1929 by the sale of the Abbey Works to Thomas Smith of Coventry, to be renamed Smith Clayton Forge. In February 1930 a liquidator was appointed and in December 1936 Clayton & Shuttleworth Limited was wound up and the original buildings on Waterside South abandoned.

The United Carborundum and Electrite Works (UC&EW) was registered as a private limited company on 21 January 1933, with 100 £1 shares, the company address being Blenheim Works, Blenheim Road, Lincoln. H. A. Allman of 3 Albert Crescent, Lincoln, was listed as Engineer and Company Director, and Thomas Joseph Ball, stated as of the same address, was described as a Subscriber to the company. On 26 October 1936 Industrial Cutting Tool Alloys (ICTA) became a limited company, and by 25 June 1937 had a capital of 1,000 £1 shares; Allman and Ball held equal shares in ICTA with four other shareholders having a lesser number. On 24 February 1940 the share capital of UC&EW had increased to £15,000, possibly due to government contracts.

Both of these companies moved into the former buildings vacated by Clayton & Shuttleworth at Waterside South *circa* 1941. ICTA moved into a large brick building with UC&EW in a similar building next door. Products made by the two companies during the war included the manufacture of cast-iron dies, lathe tools, coalface cutters, and diamond setting. At the rear of the site farthest from the river was a small two-storey brick building, which became known as the Diamond

*Fig.14. The building within Industrial Cutting Tools Limited, Diamond Works, Waterside South, Lincoln, where Artur Loewental worked during the Second World War. (© Paul Smith, 2007).*

# CATALOGUE

## MEDALS AND PORTRAIT PLAQUES.

### In Bronze unless otherwise stated.

1. HARALD. Portrait of a Child. 1927.
2. PROFESSOR V. W. RUSS, Member of the Austrian Parliament. 1902.
3. WILHELM BODE, Director-General of German Museums. 1926. *See also Nos.* 66, 67, 103.
4. MRS. LEWIS OF VIENNA. 1902.
5. DR. KARL DOMANIG, Director Vienna Art Museum. 1914.
6. DR. FRIEDRICH EICHBERG. Famous as an inventor of electric machinery. 1930.
7. MEDAL SYMBOLISING WORLD TRADE. *c.* 1930. *See also No.* 101.
8. KREISLER AND HIS WIFE. 1912. (Silver). *See also No.* 48.
9. ANDREAS, COUNT MALTZAN. 1916.
10. SIR ROBERT ABDY, BT. 1933. *See also Nos.* 30, 106.
11. COUNT POSADOWSKY, Minister of State. 1915.
12. HARALD, Portrait of a child. 1918.
13. BARONESS NEWLINSKI. 1903.
14. PORTRAIT OF AN OLD GENTLEMAN. 1901.
15. MARIA CANDIDA. *c.* 1913.
16. TITY. Portrait of a child. 1903.
17. NUDE STUDY FROM LIFE. 1901.
18. HERR MATTER, Clerk to the Burgermaster of Berlin. 1928.
19. SIR GEORGE FRANCKENSTEIN, Austrian Ambassador to the Court of St. James.
    (*a*) First model in wax.
    (*b*) Modified cast in bronze, 1935.
    (*c*) Further modification in plaster, 1941, representing the Artist's final conception. *See also No.* 114.
20. WEISMANN, the last democratic Secretary of State of Germany, 1928.
22. RUDYARD KIPLING, 1936.
23. DR. FRANZ HARTMANN, Leader of Theosophists, 1904.
24. RUDOLF ALTER, Chief of the Austrian Judiciary. *c.* 1900.

## MEDALS AND PORTRAIT PLAQUES.

25. DR. HAAS. Leader of the Centrum Party, Bavarian Catholics. *c.* 1918.
26. OTTO WOLFF, Steel Industrialist of Cologne. 1919. *See also No.* 116.
27. THE ARTIST'S WIFE. *c.* 1906. *See also Nos.* 72(*a*), 118.
28. JEAN BABELON, Director of the Bibliotique Nationale at Paris. 1933.
29. HERBERT, Portrait of a child. 1927.
30. SIR ROBERT ABDY, BT., 1933. *See also Nos.* 10, 106.
31. DR. WILFRID GREIF, of New York. *c.* 1930.
32. ANTON MARIC of Dalmatia. 1938.
33. CLAUS, son of Krupp von Bohlen. 1916.
34. LORD CROMER, High Commissioner for Egypt. 1906.
35. "VIEL GLUCK"—GOOD FORTUNE. *c.* 1914.
36. COUNTESS MENGERSEN, German head of the Red Cross in Belgium. 1916.
37. MAX FRIEDLAENDER, Director-General of German museums, successor to Bode. 1929. *See also No.* 49.
38. FLECHTHEIM, art dealer of international repute. 1928.
39. HERR STERNE, 1920.
40. PROFESSOR JACOB SHURMAN, American Ambassador to Germany. 1929.
41. PRINCESS FULVIA ORSINI OF ITALY. 1920.
42. THEODOR D'AUBLER, Italian Artist and Poet. 1929. *See also No.* 79.
42A. AUGUST RITTER VON LOEHR, President of the first Camera Club in Austria. 1899. In stone.
43. SON OF LADY HONOR CHANNON. Plaster cast, together with small steel die with specimen strike from same.
44. (*a*) LORD CHRISTOPHER GLENCONNER. Plaster.
    (*b*) His son JAMIE.
    (*c*) His son COLIN.
    *See also Nos.* 87, 87 (*a*).
45. DR. HOPKER-ASCHOFF, the last democratic Minister of Finance of Prussia. !929.
46. DR. OTTO MERCKENS. 1927.
47. GUSTAV BOSS, Burgermaster of Berlin. 1928. *See also Nos.* 65, 108.
48. KREISLER. Obverse and Reverse. 1930. *See also No.* 8.
49. MAX FRIEDLAENDER. *See also No.* 37.

## MEDALS AND PORTRAIT PLAQUES.

50. OTTO BRAUN, last democratic Prime Minister of Prussia. 1928. *See also Nos.* 95, 98, 113.
51. Stone die and bronze cast, reverse of medal of DUKE OF DONNERSMARCK. 1916.
52. LORD READING. 1936. *See also No.* 69.
53. GOETHE. 1932.
53A. Reverse of medal of GOETHE.
54. JOHANNES HASS, Leader of Trade Unionism in Germany. 1928.
55. DR. ALFRED KERR, Poet, journalist and dramatic critic. 1927.
56. ALEXANDER GIRARDI, famous singer in light opera. 1915.
57. SIR GEORGE HILL, K.C.B., Director of the British Museum. Obverse in plaster ; reverse in bronze. 1938.
58. GENERAL VON KLUCK, medal in silver, and plaster cast of reverse from original model—an allegory on the march to Paris. 1914.
59. GUSTAV KRUPP VON BOHLEN UND HALBACH. The munitions magnate of Germany. 1916.
60. CHARLES AHL, Finnish goldsmith. 1927.
61. BARONESS VON BISSING. 1916.
62. ALEX VEECK. 1932. Plaster.
63. MAX VON PLANCK, President of the Academy of Science ; he expounded the quantum theory. 1931. *See also No.* 105.
64. PAUL LOBE, President of the Reichstag. 1928. *See also Nos.* 80, 104.
65. GUSTAV BOSS. *See also Nos.* 47, 108.
66. WILHELM BODE, obverse and reverse. 1926. *See also Nos.* 3, 67, 103.
67. WILHELM BODE, Director-General of German Museums. 1926. *See also Nos.* 3, 66, 103.
68. COUNTESS VON MALTZAN. 1917.
69. LORD READING. 1936. *See also No.* 52.
70. GUNTHER VON HUNEFELD. 1929.
70A. Ditto.
    Von Hunefeld was famous for an early transatlantic flight.
71. CAPTAIN GEYGER, a noted connoisseur. 1928.
72. SELF-PORTRAIT OF THE ARTIST. *c.* 1925.
72A. THE ARTIST'S WIFE. 1914. *See also Nos.* 27, 118.

## MEDALS AND PORTRAIT PLAQUES.

73. ALFRED, SON OF KRUPP VON BOHLEN.
74. GENERAL LITZMAN. 1915. *See also No.* 94.
75. ADOLPH DONATH, Czechoslovak poet and connoisseur. Obverse and reverse. 1926. *See also No.* 107.
76. RUDOLF HERZOG. German author and poet. 1914.
77. FIELD MARSHAL VON HAESELER. 1915.
78. FRAU MARGARETHE KRUPP. Obverse.
78A. Ditto, reverse. 1916.
79. THEODOR D'AUBLER. 1931. *See also No.* 42.
80. PAUL LOBE. 1928. *See also Nos.* 64, 104.
81. FIELD MARSHAL VON HINDENBURG as President of the Reich. 1925. Silver.
82. Reverse of the first Hindenburg medal commemorating the Battle of Tannenberg. 1914. Silver.
83. ADMIRAL VON TIRPITZ. 1915. Obverse and reverse.
84. THE KAISER WILHELM II and EMPEROR FRANZ JOSEPH. 1914. Silver.
84A. Reverse of larger model of No. 84.
85. WILHELM TRINKS, famous Viennese numismatist. 1899. Wax model on slate.
86. DUCHESS OF DEVONSHIRE. 1936. *See also No.* 109.
87. SON OF LORD GLENCONNOR.
87A. ANOTHER SON OF LORD GLENCONNOR.
    Both above are in ivory. *See also No.* 44b and c.
88. PROFESSOR VON SCHMOLLER, scientist and political economist. 1914.
89. ROBERT SCHMIDT, Director of the Schloss Museum, Berlin, 1932.
91. Tribute to woman in agriculture. 1915.
92. ULRICH VON WILAMOWITZ, Greek historian and Rector of the University of Berlin. 1928.
93. HANS EBERHARD, BARON VON BODENHAUSEN—DEGENER. 1917.
94. GENERAL LITZMANN, obverse and reverse. *See also No.* 74.
95. OTTO BRAUN. *See also Nos.* 50, 98, 113.
96. DR. HOPKER-ASCHOFF. 1929.

### PORTRAIT BUSTS.

97. PROFESSOR ALBERT EINSTEIN. Bronze. *See also No.* 100.
98. OTTO BRAUN. Bronze. *See also Nos* 50, 95, 113.
99. LORD BEARSTEAD. Plaster.

### INTAGLIOS IN ROCK CRYSTAL.

100. PROFESSOR ALBERT EINSTEIN. *See also No.* 97.
101. SYMBOLICAL REPRESENTATION OF WORLD TRADE. *See also* No. 7.
102. CLASSICAL STUDY.
103. WILHELM BODE. *See also Nos.* 3, 66, 67.
104. PAUL LOBE. *See also Nos.* 64, 80.
105. MAX PLANCK. *See also No.* 63.
106. SIR ROBERT ABDY. *See also Nos.* 10, 30.
107. ADOLPH DONATH. *See also No.* 75.
108. GUSTAV BOSS. *See also Nos.* 47, 65.
109. DUCHESS OF DEVONSHIRE. *See also No.* 86.
110. DUCHESS OF RUTLAND.
111. LADY BEARSTEAD.
112. LADY BEARSTEAD'S FAVOURITE HORSE.
113. OTTO BRAUN. *See also Nos.* 50, 95, 98.
114. SIR GEORGE FRANCKENSTEIN. *See also No.* 19.
115. " WAR FURY." *See also No. 58 reverse.*
116. OTTO WOLFF. *See also No.* 26.
117. WIFE OF OTTO WOLFF.
118. THE ARTIST'S WIFE. *See also Nos.* 27, 72 (*a*).

### INTAGLIO IN TOPAZ.

119. COUNTESS MALTZAN.

### INTAGLIO IN AMETHYST.

120. THE MUSE AND THE ARTIST.

### INTAGLIOS IN CARNELIAN.

121. KREISLER.
122. KREISLER'S WIFE.
123. THE ARTIST'S WIFE (2).
124. SIR GEORGE FRANCKENSTEIN.

### INTAGLIOS IN CARNELIAN.

125. PROFESSOR ROBERT SMITH.
126. ANTON MARIC.
127. SENOR CHIAPPA.
128. HEAD OF HERCULES.
129. HEAD OF A YOUNG GIRL.
130. " BATHING."
131. A GREEK HORSE.
132. AMAZON ON HORSEBACK.

### CAMEO IN AGATE-ONYX.

133. OTTO WOLFF. *See also Nos.* 26, 116.

### 134. SMALL AMPHORA CARVED IN SARDONYX.

### CARVINGS IN ROCK CRYSTAL.

135. THE PROMETHEUS BOWL. Made for Ivor Kreuger who died before its completion.
136. Series illustrating artist's method of hollowing a cup from rock crystal.
    (*a*) A virgin block.
    (*b*) 1st core removed after grinding.
    (*c*) 2nd ditto.
    (*d*) 3rd ditto.
137. A cup hollowed and partly shaped.
138. A bowl partly shaped.

### CARVING IN PRIME AMETHYST.

139. Unfinished double handled cup with artist's design for completion.

### CARVING IN CARNELIAN AGATE.

140. Roughly shaped calix before hollowing process.

.   .   .   .   .

141. PORTRAIT OF THE ARTIST BY BEGAS. 1913.

*Fig.15. Artur Loewental's first home in Lincoln, 81 West Parade, pictured in 2003.*

Works and in which wire drawing dies with a diamond centre were produced during the war. Artur, who is said to have kept himself to himself and was referred to as 'The Prof', worked on the first floor while a small team of machinists worked on the ground floor. The rough diamonds would be mounted on a steel mandrel and the required minute holes 'pecked' with a 'pecking machine' employing hardened steel needles and fine diamond paste – this process was capable of producing holes as small as 0.01mm (0.0004in). This two-storey building was still standing in 2007 (Fig.14) although most of the remainder of the site had been cleared.

Artur and Rosa moved into a house at 81 West Parade, Lincoln. Being engaged on war work would restrict Artur's sculpting but this did not prevent him, in 1941, from staging the most extensive exhibition of his works ever to be held in England. With the help of Francis John Cooper, the director of Lincoln Museums, Library and Art Gallery, who was to become a life-long friend, over one hundred and fifty examples of his work were displayed. Besides being the driving force behind the exhibition, Cooper also wrote the foreword to the exhibition catalogue.

*Fig.16. The sculptor Artur Loewental at his home in West Parade, Lincoln, 1955. (The Collection, Lincoln).*

Surprisingly, many of the examples already exhibited at the exhibitions in London in 1935 and 1939 were included, many of which had been brought with him from Berlin and depicted German and Austrian persons and events. To display such subjects at this period of the war was remarkable, even in a provincial city, and must say much for the esteem in which Artur's work was held, even in England. Cooper was quick to point out in the foreword to the exhibition catalogue that Artur was a true Anglophile and that his feelings 'are now firmly towards his new homeland'. The exhibition was held at the Usher Art Gallery, Lincoln, closed during hostilities except for occasional loan exhibitions. It included most aspects of his art as well as examples of techniques he used when working with hard minerals. One mysterious entry in the catalogue is a portrait of Artur said to be by Begas, dated 1913. If this refers to Reinhold Begas, the renowned German sculptor, he died in 1911, so there is some confusion here. However, this portrait has not been traced.

Artur wrote to his nephew with detailed descriptions of the exhibition on 2 December 1941, adding as a rider his concern about the fate of his collections should something happen to both himself and Rosa due to the hostilities. He stated that all of his collections of jade, china, hardstone, many valuable books, silver medals, coins etc were being stored in the Usher Art Gallery by Francis Cooper, and that in the case of anything happening to himself and Rosa his nephew was entitled to claim everything.

1942 proved to be a bad year for Artur. His mother, Antonia, who had managed to survive the rigours of living in Vienna during the war, died on 10 June. No longer protected by having to care for their elderly mother, two of Artur's sisters who had lived with her were transported to the concentration camp at Theresienstadt, Czechoslovakia, on 15 July, where they subsequently perished: Camilla Angelika on 12 March 1943, followed

*Fig.17. LOE246. A bronze portrait medal of Francis Cooper, Lincoln, 1950. 133mm. 1:2. (The Lucas private collection).*

by Clara Ottilie on 18 April 1944. Other Jews from Europe had come and settled in the Lincoln area but Artur 'made it clear that he wanted absolutely nothing to do with them, he shunned them' was how one member of the local Jewish community later expressed it in private correspondence.

At the 1943 AGM of the Lincolnshire Artists' Society his friend Francis Cooper was appointed Hon Secretary, and it was no doubt at his suggestion that Artur became a member of the Society, of which he remained an active member until Rosa's death in 1958. Artur was soon back on form and carrying out commissions, although it is not clear how many he actually received payment for or were produced as tokens of his thanks for the help he received. Three examples dated 1944 have been traced, viz: Sir George Franckenstein (a plaster cast in The Collection, Lincoln); Lady Ann Bontial (a plaster cast in The Collection, Lincoln); and Francis John Cooper (a bronze casting of this medal was sold in the USA in 2007). Artur exhibited at the Lincolnshire Artists' Society's annual exhibition in 1944 at the Usher Art Gallery, Lincoln, for the first time and his exhibits comprised:

| | |
|---|---|
| Winston Churchill, obverse | Plaster medal |
| Winston Churchill, reverse | Plaster medal |
| Sir George Franckenstein | Plaster medal |
| Rosa Loewental | Plaster medal |
| 'Portrait of a young girl' | Plaster medal |

| | |
|---|---|
| Winston Churchill intaglio | Rock crystal |
| 'Three intaglios' | Cornelian |

In 1944 the signs of an end to hostilities in Europe and the anticipated victory brought him his most prestigious commission of his time in England. Artur produced a proposed commemorative victory medal depicting a portrait of Winston Churchill on the obverse and a suitable text on the reverse quoting one of Churchill's

*Fig.18. LOE220. The general issue victory medal depicting Winston Churchill, struck in bronze, Lincoln, 1945. 63mm. 1:1.*

*Fig.19. LOE216. A bronze medal inscribed 'FOR THOSE WHO FOUGHT FOR LIBERTY 1939-1945', Lincoln, 1945. 202mm. 1:2. (The Fennell private collection).*

famous wartime speeches. Engstrom (1972) states that it was emitted by Harry Burrows, jewellers, of Manchester. Although the portrait was produced from photographs it was later to be praised as one of the finest of Churchill ever produced. The medal anticipated the end of the war in Europe, which in fact was to last into the next year, and large plaster casts and subsequent bronze castings were produced that bear the dates 1944 and 1945. With the surrender of the German General Staff, on 8 May 1945, Artur's final designs were reduced to 63mm diameter and John Pinches (Medallists) Limited, London, struck the issue in bronze. J. Eric Engstrom quotes the number minted as *one thousand* although in his history of the company John Harvey Pinches is more cautious at *'several hundred'*. The distribution of the medals was handled by B. A. Seaby, coin dealers, London, the cost being two guineas. Some of the known examples appear to have been lightly silver plated. By a fortunate chance the obverse and reverse steel working dies used to strike this medal came onto the market in 1977 at a Sotheby auction and were purchased for £130. They are now in the collection of The Collection, Lincoln.

A large bronze medal sculpted by Artur in 1945 entitled 'TO THOSE WHO FOUGHT' has been found in a private collection in England. It depicts a semi-nude winged Victory with outstretched arm holding an olive branch above a flaming altar inscribed 'FOR LIBERTY' and with the dates '1939-1945' in the exergue. The medal closely resembles the reverse of the award medal that Artur produced for the Österreichischen Aero-Club *circa* 1914. Why this medal was produced is unknown though it may have been an alternative reverse for the Victory medal, or perhaps to be presented to those who fought, as happened at the end of the First World War.

1946 saw Artur produce yet another bronze medal of Sir George Franckenstein, which, although exhibited in Lincoln in 1947 and 1955 and also in Antwerp in 1959, has not been traced. However, the wax model on slate for this medal is preserved at the Ashmolean Museum, Oxford, while a ticket attached to the back has the date 1936, which would suggest that the same model was used for all of his portraits of Franckenstein.

In this year Artur also sculpted Neal Green, a trawler owner, gentleman farmer, inventor and JP, who lived at Holbeck Manor, near Horncastle, and whose first love appears to have been the arts. A portrait was produced of him dated 1946 and the plaster cast and bronze casting

both survive in private collections. Green felt great sympathy for Artur's situation and would invite him over for lunch at Holbeck about once a fortnight, although Rosa would usually decline. Green's daughter Pamela was at this time a schoolgirl with hopes of becoming a sculptor and Artur would offer comments on her work and explained the techniques of casting, which she later felt helped her to gain a place in the Slade School of Art.

At about this period the Lincolnshire Red Shorthorn Association had an office a short distance away from Artur's home, at 14 West Parade. This close proximity was probably the reason he managed to obtain a commission from them to produce a design for their award medal that would be presented to the owner of the winning Lincolnshire Red bull at the various agricultural shows. The final design depicts a Lincolnshire Red bull in the foreground and a view, from the south, of Lincoln Cathedral in the background. The name of the association was changed to The Lincoln Red Shorthorn Society soon after and the legend on the exergue was revised to suit. The reverse was left plain for the name of the recipient to be engraved, a service that was undertaken by James Usher, jewellers, Lincoln. The medals were struck by John Pinches (Medallists), London.

At the Lincolnshire Artists' Society's annual exhibition in 1946 Artur's display comprised:

| | |
|---|---|
| Sir George Franckenstein | Plaster medal. |
| Neal Green | Plaster medal. |
| 'Rosa Lavorosa' | Plaster medal. |

*Fig.20. LOE244. The award medal created for the Lincoln Red Shorthorn Society, Lincoln, circa 1951 (the legend had previously read 'Lincolnshire Red Shorthorn Association'). 63mm. 1:1. (The Gilbert private collection).*

| | |
|---|---|
| Lincolnshire Red Shorthorn Association. | Bronze medal. |
| 'Hadassa' | Plaster medal. |
| 'Nude study' | Plaster medal. |

In 1947 Artur and Rosa moved into a larger house that Artur had purchased at 89 West Parade. He established a workshop at the bottom of the garden and converted the cellar of the house into a workplace for his lathes and other pieces of equipment. Sadly in the same year his brother Oskar, who had remained in Austria throughout the war and was put to hard forced labour under the Nazis, died on 7 March.

At the 1947 annual exhibition held by the Lincolnshire Artists' Society he was able to display some of his finished medals:

| | |
|---|---|
| Sir George Franckenstein | Bronze medal |
| Neal Green | Bronze medal |
| The artist's wife | Bronze medal |
| 'Vjera', a Swedish girl | Plaster medal |

He also exhibited a frame of one silver and nine bronze medals at the Royal Academy of Arts, London.

As has already been noted, Artur carried out few commissions during the war years, so it was to be in the late 1940s that his dwindling earned income seems to have caused real problems. Private personal portraits executed in bronze had been popular on the Continent in his early years and had provided him with a plentiful supply of work, whereas in England portraits of this kind were generally restricted to well-known personalities, and, in any case, photography was now well established for family portraits. Thus commissions were few and far between and usually came only from friends who felt sorry for his changed circumstances.

One significant commission, however, occurred in 1948 when the members of the Spalding Gentlemen's Society, Spalding, decided to honour their President and former Honorary Secretary, Ashley Kilshaw Maples, for his 'long association with the Society, first as Secretary and then as President during a membership extending over 56 years' by commissioning a portrait in bronze. Maples was a solicitor and served as Clerk to the Spalding Board of Guardians, the Spalding Rural District Council, and to the South Holland Magistrates.

It was during the annual excursion of the Spalding Gentlemen's Society to Lincoln on 10 July 1948, that Artur met Maples and preparations for the portrait

Fig.21. LOE224. A bronze portrait medal of Neal Green, Lincoln, 1946. 176mm. 1:2. (The Lee private collection).

must have begun soon after that date as on 25 July Artur wrote to Maples:

*I have much pleasure to inform you that I have in the meantime done all the preliminary work needed for the execution of the portrait medallion of yourself i.e. that I have modelled in modelling wax a sketch based partly on the photos partly on memory. Having done this I would now like to come to Spalding for a sitting... I can assure you that the sitting will be quite painless as you may sit quite comfortable in your easy chair at your home whilst I will sit in a corner studying your features. No preparations of any kind are needed and as I am working in modelling wax and not in wet clay your room will remain quite unsoiled ... .*

A letter from Artur to Mr G. W. Bailey, the Secretary of the Society, dated 25 September, after explaining why he had missed meeting Maples and Bailey due to a mix-up of train times when they came to Lincoln to see him, goes on to say:

*I learnt from my wife that you have seen one plaster cast but not the second mould I have prepared in my workroom. I would have loved to show you both in the proper light. ... I also would have liked to give you both some explanation about the final execution in bronze.*

*Fig.22. Artur Loewental's second home in Lincoln, 89 West Parade, pictured in 2003.*

An example of the finished portrait was exhibited at the Lincolnshire Artists' Society annual exhibition at the Usher Art Gallery, Lincoln, in 1949, while the completed commission comprised a bronze medal (195mm diameter) mounted on a mahogany panel, with a small bronze plaque mounted below that reads 'HON. SECRETARY. 24. APRIL. 1899 / PRESIDENT. 25. SEPT. 1930'. The finished portrait was presented to Maples at a special ceremony on 25 March 1949, being unveiled by Dr S. Herbert Perry, a senior member of the Society. Unfortunately Artur was unable to attend the ceremony due to ill health. Sadly Maples, already in poor health, was to die within a year, on 14 February 1950, but not before helping to give the Society he was so passionate about a valuable collection that will always be associated with his name.

What must be one of the most important and valuable possessions that Artur had been able to bring with him from Berlin was a magnificent collection of Chinese glass, ceramics, hardstone vessels and carvings, and Meissen porcelain. The collection had been built up over the years and would now be sold to put his finances onto a more stable footing. It had long been held by the Usher Art Gallery, Lincoln, with some of the larger items forming a small display in two cabinets, while the smaller items were kept in storage. Artur offered the collection to the

Gallery, which, being unable to pay cash, offered him an annuity instead. This he declined due to his advanced years and the fact that he had to make provision for his wife. An offer from the Ashmolean Museum, Oxford, was declined for the same reason. One definite offer was said to have come from a friend in America but, although he would probably have raised more money from such a sale, he declined it owing to his wish that the collection, if possible, should stay in England.

It is probable that, during one of the sculpting sessions with Maples, Artur raised the possibility of the Spalding Gentlemen's Society purchasing this collection. Certainly Maples seems to have jumped at the opportunity and wrote to the Society's Honorary Secretary, Mr C. F. Turner, on 31 October 1948:

*I am arranging to purchase a very fine collection of precious stones and carved crystal &c &c for the S.G. Society. As the price is about £5000 before I go further I should like your advice.*

Artur insisted that no one except the Society's chief officials should know of the proposed sale, so subsequently, at a meeting of the Society on 24 November, Maples put forward a resolution that the collection should be purchased for £5000 and the necessary steps taken. To back up his proposal he generously announced that he would personally contribute £3000 towards the purchase as 'a gift by me to the S.G. Society'. Approval was given and the purchase completed, the collection being delivered to the Society in the early summer of 1949. In order to display the collection, suitable cases were constructed in reused oak, gifted by Maples, from an old post mill at Weston Hills, the work being carried out by a member of the Society. A private viewing of the displayed collection was held on 2 December for members and friends. Unfortunately Maples was too ill to attend, and Artur, who was to have addressed the assembled company, was unable to come citing a breakdown on the railway. The collection is now on display within the strong room of the Society's museum. The catalogue produced at the time is reproduced overleaf to provide some idea of its scope and value.

On 18 December Artur wrote to Maples offering a further collection and also suggesting that his collection of his own works etc might find a home with the Society:

*On occasion of one of your last visits you asked me if I could provide you with a collection of precious stones. I am now in*

# Lœwental Collection

## Section I. CHINESE GLASS, ETC.

1 VASE with long neck, turquoise colour glass, K'ang-Hsi.
2 DEEP BOWL, translucent sapphire blue, Ch'ien-Lung.
3 VASE with long neck, turquoise blue glass, K'ang-Hsi.
4 DEEP BOWL, white jade colour glass, Ch'ien-Lung.
5 BOTTLE with long neck, sapphire blue, Ch'ien-Lung.
6 DEEP BOWL, purple red glass, Ming.
7 BOTTLE with long neck, sapphire blue, Ch'ien-Lung.
8 VASE with long neck, jade white glass, K'ang-Hsi.
9 VASE with short neck, deep amethyst glass, Ch'ien-Lung.
10 SCENT BOTTLE, cylindrical shape, brown opaque glass with multi-coloured spots.
11 SHALLOW DISH, round shape, amethyst glass, Ming.
12 SCENT BOTTLE, same as 10.
13 VASE, bellied shape ruby glass, Ch'ien-Lung.
14 SNUFF BOTTLE, rosy quartz coloured glass, Ch'ien-Lung.
15 VASE, double layer glass, ruby and creamish white with floral decoration carved from ruby layer, Ch'ien-Lung.
16 BOWL, sapphire blue glass, carved floral design, on coral coloured foot, also carved, K'ang-Hsi.
17 VASE with handle, sapphire blue glass with yellow ribs, Egyptian.
18 VASE, bellied shape, deep sapphire blue, Ch'ien-Lung.
19 DEEP BOWL, sapphire blue glass, Ch'ien-Lung.
20 BOTTLE with long neck, pale blue glass, K'ang-Hsi.
21 SNUFF BOTTLE, white glass, decorated in relief with floral decoration in coloured glass, Ch'ien-Lung.
22 BOTTLE with long neck, deep purple red glass, Ming (see note to 26).
23 SNUFF BOTTLE, double layer glass, ruby on white, carved floral decoration, Ch'ien-Lung.
24 DEEP ROUND DISH, clear amethyst glass, Ming.
25 SNUFF BOTTLE, clear glass painted on inside.
26 VASE with long neck, deep purple aubergine colour glass. Ming. (NOTE.—The material in this piece has been treated like a block of stone, because it is cut out of a solid block of glass and hollowed out in the same way as a stone vase, see also 22).

## Section II. CERAMICS, ETC.

1 DEEP BOWL, aubergine glaze, decorated with flowers in enamel, Ming.
2 BOWL, aubergine glaze, decorated with flowers in enamelled colours, Ming.
3 VASE, baluster shape, decorated with flowers in Mohammedan blue colour on white ground, K'ang-Hsi.
4 IMPERIAL HAT STAND, turquoise colour, K'ang-Hsi.
5 VASE, same as 3.
6 STAND of carved teak framing two square plates, decorated with flower designs in enamel colours, K'ang-Hsi.

7 BOTTLE, bellied shape "Tea" green glaze, K'ang-Hsi.
8 BOX with cover, Sang de Boeuf, K'ang-Hsi.
9 VASE, coral red colour, K'ang-Hsi.
10 BOTTLE, flat shape, soft green glaze, Ming.
11 BOX, ivory colour porcelain, inside turquoise, decorated with landscapes and figures.
12 VASE, baluster shape, "Mirror Black" glaze, K'ang-Hsi.
13 SHALLOW DISH, outside decorated with flowers, Ch'ien-Lung.
14 SNUFF BOTTLE, double layer glass, white and blue, with figures carved from blue layer, Ch'ien-Lung.
15 VASE, baluster shape Celadon with figure of dragon in relief, Ming, North China.
16 SNUFF BOTTLE, glazed stoneware, decorated.
17 DEEP BOWL, porcelain, decorated with geometrical ornament in relief, green enamel, medallions with flowers, Ming.
18 VASE, slender shape, Celadon, decorated with two mulberry leaves bearing a silkworm on each, green grey glaze, Sung.
19 BOTTLE, slender shape, "Peach Bloom" glaze, Ming.
20 DISH of large size, decorated with Peony tree and blooms in enamel colours, K'ang-Hsi (once in Dresden Museum).
21 SCENT BOTTLE in the shape of a peach, K'ang-Hsi.
22 VASE, baluster shape with long neck, apple green glaze, finely crackled K'ang-Hsi, made especially for Persia.

## Section III. HARDSTONE VESSELS AND CARVINGS

1 DEEP BOWL, carved from very thin translucent cornelian, with flower-like spot on one side, Indian.
2 DISH, round shape Indian mossagate, probably Roman.
3 BONBONNIERE, carved topaz, French Empire.
4 TEA POT with handle and cover, finely carved red marble, with traces of gilding, Japanese 18th century.
5 STAND of teak with finely carved open-work plate of green jade, Ch'ien-Lung.
6 SCENT BOTTLE, small size, carved from turquoise matrix, Tao-Kuang (1821).
7 DEEP BOWL, grey jade from Yunnan. On the outside carved stylised lotus leaves. The interior is treated in a peculiar way, giving the impression that it has been beaten like a silver vessel. It is of extreme thinness, late Ming or early K'ang-Hsi.
8 SEAL, handle representing a horse, so called Han jade material, Ming.
9 LOBED BOWL on 3 footstumps, emerald green avanturine jade, Ch'ien-Lung.
10 BRUSH VESSEL, miniature size, from turquoise, decorated with a rat and leaves, Ch'ien-Lung.
11 VASE of green translucent stone like nephrite.
12 SNUFF BOTTLE of red jasper, plain.
13 STANDING FIGURE of a Lohan carved from ivory coloured stone, Ming.
14 FLAT VASE with cover, delicate amethyst engraved with stylised ornaments, Ch'ien-Lung.
15 BOTTLE, translucent mossagate, Ch'ien-Lung.

16 VASE (KU), monolithic, of archaic form resembling bronze vases of the Chou period, green jade (Nephrite), height 14 inches. This vase was formerly in possession of a Russian Grand Duke, and was brought in 1916 to central Europe, being later brought to England where it was exhibited in the great Chinese Exhibition of 1935 at the Royal Academy. It is one of the jade replicas which were executed by the order of the emperor. Ch'ien-Lung.
17 KORO in miniature with ring handles and cover, on top the figure of a crouching Kinling, white jade with emerald green patches, Ch'ien-Lung.
18 INCENSE BURNER, white jade elaborately decorated, with hanging rings and open-work cover, Ch'ien-Lung.
19 SNUFF BOTTLE, clear rock crystal, plain, Ch'ien-Lung.
20 KYLIN, carved in rock crystal, Ming style.
21 WINE SCOOP for sacramental use, greyish jade, Ming.
22 WINE POT for sacramental use, rock crystal with handle, spout, and open-work cover, carved with scrolls outside, Ming.
23 WINE SCOOP for sacramental use, with handle, green nephrite.
24 BONBONNIERE, carved rock crystal, French Empire.
25 DEEP CUP, carved from striated Egyptian yellow quartzite, Roman period (exhibited at Ashmolean Museum).
26 BRUSH VESSEL in shape of a peach, milky white jade, top rose coloured, Ch'ien-Lung, probably made in court studios for use in the court.
27 OVAL LOBED DISH carved from translucent cornelian agate, the colour being honey yellow with red veins. It came from an old family descended from the Medici. Most probably it belonged once to the treasures of Lorenzo-il-Magnifico, and is probably identical with a vessel mentioned in the inventory as "Schodella antica die yellow agata," Florentine Renaissance.
28 POWDER BOX with cover, amethystine spar.
29 BOWL, oval shape, in yellow calcedony.
30 CALYX, amethystine spar, purple veins on amber ground, excavated in the Crimea, probably antique Roman.
31 DEEP BOWL, Indian cornelian, vivid red outside, inside milk white with red veins, probably late Roman.
32 BOTTLE, brown translucent agate with figures painted on the inside, K'ang-Hsi.
33 FLAT BOTTLE with cover carved from grey chicken bone jade which has been exposed to fire, perhaps in a burial ceremony. It is decorated with a carving representing a mountain slope with stairway or ladder, and the figures of two sages. A pilgrim bottle of the Sung period.
34 SNUFF BOTTLE carved from striated agate.
35 DEEP BOWL, round shape, open-work carving, mutton fat jade, on carved teak stand, Ch'ien-Lung.
36 BOWL, double-handled mutton fat jade, ceremonial object, decorated with "grain" pattern, K'ang-Hsi.
37 ROCK CRYSTAL, representing a mountain peak with engraved trees suggesting a mountain top in mist after a poem by Li-tai-pe from the Imperial Palace, Peking. It stood originally in a carved gold socket showing the two dragons with the pearl, and was evidently considered by the Chinese as a masterpiece as shown by its costly mounting, Ch'ien-Lung.

38 TWO PEACHES with leaves, Han jade material, a New Year's gift meaning "Good Luck," Ming.
39 VASE of lapis lazuli, carved with dragon decoration, Ming.
40 BOTTLE, flat shape, striated agate onyx.
41 GIRDLE CLASP with dragon head, mutton fat jade, Ch'ien-Lung.
42 GIRDLE CLASP, grey white jade with carved ornaments.
43 GIRDLE CLASP, white jade open-work carving, Ch'ien-Lung.
44 GIRDLE ORNAMENT, oblong shape white jadeite.
45 ORNAMENT, shape of a leaf with figure of a sleeping girl, mutton fat jade, Ch'ien-Lung.
46 FAN HANDLE in the shape of a flower bud, greenish jade, Ch'ien-Lung.
47 ORNAMENT representing the talon of a phoenix, white jade.
48 BRACELET, mutton fat jade, Sung.
49 BOTTLE, pebble shape, mutton fat jade.
50 SNUFF BOTTLE, white jade with engraved poem, Ch'ien-Lung.
51 SNUFF BOTTLE, white jade, plain.
52 PAIR OF VASES, greyishblue jasper, from Urals, presented by Tsar Nicholas I to the Governor of Lithuania, lathe turned.
53 TWIN SNUFF BOTTLE, gilded and enamelled bronze, Ch'ien-Lung.
54 SNUFF BOTTLE, double layer agate, figures carved in relief, Ch'ien-Lung.
55 BOTTLE, pumpkin shape, brownish jade.
56 SNUFF BOTTLE, turquoise matrix, Ch'ien-Lung.
57 SNUFF BOTTLE, hexangular shape, smoky crystal.
58 SCENT BOTTLE, grey white striated agate, Ming.
59 SCENT BOTTLE, shape of date fruit, brown agate, silver mounted stopper, Ch'ien-Lung.
60 FIGURE of "Heaven Watchdog" cut from an alloy of copper, silver and gold, Japanese.
61 SNUFF BOTTLE, gourd shape, calcedony, Ch'ien-Lung.
62 BOTTLE, rock crystal with engraved bats.
63 SNUFF BOTTLE in the shape of a pebble, as jade is found in the river beds. This pebble, through a small opening, has been hollowed out to a wall thickness of about ¼ inch. The technique for the finishing stages at least would be by using bent copper tools manipulated by hand and inserted with fine fragments of diamond or emery and using a constant filing movement. (The same technique would be used for Nos. 49 and 66). The material is greenish jade, Ch'ien-Hsi.
64 SNUFF BOTTLE, shape of a date, engraved inscription, brown agate, Ch'ien-Lung.
65 BOTTLE of yellow translucent calcedony.
66 BOTTLE, flat shape with fine geometrical ornament, rock crystal, Ch'ien-Lung.
67 SNUFF BOTTLE, rock crystal with amethyst stopper, engraved.

## Section IV. MEISSEN PORCELAIN

1 Two large round dishes and seven smaller dishes decorated with flower paintings from the "Royal Saxony" factory, Meissen. 18th century.

"FREE PRESS" CO. LTD., SPALDING.

*the position to do so and would like to know if you still desire it. There is furthermore another thought in my mind and it concerns the decision, which I will sooner or later have to make, where my own artistic works, bronzes and especially my collection of engravings in rock crystal and other precious stones shall find a lasting home, not to speak of all the rare and fine items, you will remember to have seen in the big showcase at my home. All this would go fine together with the collection now installed so excellently at your museum!*

By this time, however, Maples was too ill to send a reply, but it would also appear that there was some confusion as to whether Artur actually possessed a collection of precious stones for disposal or was merely in a position to acquire one. The finances of the Society had, however, already been stretched with the purchase of the collection of Chinese glass etc, so that no further action was taken and the matter was dropped. As for finding a final resting place for his own works and his other collections, a letter from Turner, dated 21 December 1949, put off making a decision due to Maples' ill health and the matter seems never to have been raised again by any of the parties involved.

One local person who befriended Artur and, while acting as his solicitor, helped him find accommodation and set himself up when he came to Lincoln, was James William Francis Hill, a well-known solicitor, alderman and avid historian. In 1948 Hill published the first volume of his outstanding four volume opus on the history of Lincoln, *Medieval Lincoln* (Oxford University Press, 1948). He also became Chancellor of Nottingham University the same year, and it may have been a combination of these two events that led to Artur producing a bronze portrait medal of Hill. The completed medal was exhibited at the Royal Academy, London, in 1949 and again in 1955 and received suitable praise. (A plaster cast is in a private collection, while a finalised bronze is in the collection of The Collection, Lincoln). Hill's appointment diaries record numerous meetings

*Fig.23. LOE233. A bronze portrait medal of Ashley Maples, Spalding, 1948. 195mm. 1:2. (The Spalding Gentlemen's Society, Spalding).*

with Artur during the year but unfortunately there is no detail as to the reasons. 1949 was the year in which Artur celebrated his seventieth birthday and to mark the occasion he sculpted a portrait of himself. Several examples of the subsequent medals in bronze have been traced and two have a green patina so as to resemble an ancient bronze coin (private collection, England, and The Collection, Lincoln), while one example lacks the patina and shows in clear detail what he was still able to achieve in portraiture (private collection, England).

Plaster casts of the mould and final design of a portrait of his friend Francis John Cooper dated 1948 survive in a private collection in England, although no bronze medal has been traced with this date. However, a bronze medal dated 1950 survives in a private collection in Canada. In 1948 Artur also produced yet another portrait of Einstein, who was celebrating his own seventieth birthday, and three examples in bronze have been found (private collection in England, the Ashmolean Museum and the Spalding Gentlemen's Society).

Artur continued to exhibit at the Royal Academy of Arts, showing eleven bronze plaquettes in 1948, eight portrait medals and one bronze plaque in 1949, and thirteen bronze medals and a plaque in 1950. The catalogue for the 1949 exhibition by the Lincolnshire Artists' Society fails to give much detail except for the subjects: Francis J. Cooper; Professor Albert Einstein; J. W. Francis Hill; Artur Loewental, self portrait; Ashley K. Maples; 'Hadassa'; 'A deer'; and 'A lioness'. The two animal plaques exhibited are unusual for Artur and his motivation for sculpting them is unknown. 1949 was also to bring the news of Einstein's *'Generalised Theory of Gravitation'* and in an interview with the *Lincolnshire Echo*, 9 January 1950, Artur recalled details of his 'close personal friend'. The wax portrait he produced to commemorate this achievement is now preserved at the Ashmolean Museum, framed as a medal and dated 1950. One other identified bronze portrait sculpted by Artur in 1950 is of the American James M. Efross (private collection, England). For the next three years no details of his work are known.

While living at West Parade Artur's GP was Dr Augustine Fennell. Dr Fennell, who was born in Eire, had purchased a medical practice at 129 Yarborough Road in Lincoln. They became friends and Fennell was a frequent visitor to the Loewental household on West Parade. Desmond Fennell, the doctor's son, recalled that the smell of Rosa's cooking always pervaded the house on these occasions. Artur produced two portrait medals of Dr Fennell, dated 1954, the difference between the two being the style of his hair, although it is not possible to say which was produced first. Artur also produced a portrait of Desmond Fennell in 1955 and a number of examples have been traced, both as plaster of Paris casts and the final bronze medal (private collection, England).

Artur again exhibited at the Lincolnshire Artists' Society exhibition in 1954, although this time, unusually, the catalogue states that none of the exhibits is for sale:

| | | |
|---|---|---|
| Francis J. Cooper | 1950 | Bronze medal |
| Professor Albert Einstein | 1950 | Bronze medal |
| Dr Augustine Fennell | | Bronze medal |
| Artur Loewental self portrait | 1949 | Bronze medal |
| Professor Max von Planck | | Plaster medal |

*Fig.24. LOE229. A bronze portrait medal of Alderman James William Francis Hill, Lincoln, 1948. 175mm. 1:2. (The Collection, Lincoln).*

*Fig.25. LOE230. A bronze self-portrait medal of the sculptor Artur Loewental to commemorate his 70th birthday, Lincoln, 1949. 140mm. 1:2. (The Fennell private collection).*

In 1955 a major Exhibition of European Medals 1930-1955, sponsored by the Royal Society of Arts in association with the Royal Numismatic Society and La Fédération des Éditeurs de Médailles, was held in London between 8 – 29 June. At its finish the promoters decided that the exhibition should travel around the country, and Lincoln was chosen as one of the venues. It was held at the Usher Art Gallery, Lincoln, in December that year and included in the official display case were the following five examples of Artur's work: (See page 44)

Fig.26. LOE250 (Above) A bronze portrait medal of Dr Augustine J. Fennell, Lincoln, 1954. 182mm. 1:2. (The Fennell private collection).

Fig.27. (Below) The display board of thirteen bronze medals exhibited at the Usher Art Gallery, Lincoln, 1955. (© Lincolnshire Illustrations Index, Lincoln).

Row 1 (From left to right): Dr Augustine Fennell, 1954 (LOE251); Professor Max von Planck, n.d. (LOE160); Professor Albert Einstein, 1950 (LOE249).

Row 2 (From left to right): 'Viel Glück', n.d. (LOE038); Sir Robert Abdy, n.d.(LOE173)

Row 3 (From left to right): 'Rosa Lavorosa', n.d. (LOE113); Winston Churchill, 1945 (LOE217); Artur Loewental, 1949 (LOE230).

Row 4 (From left to right): Dr Otto Braun, n.d. (LOE151); Sir George Franckenstein, 1946 (LOE222).

Row 5 (From left to right): Theodor Däubler, 1929 (LOE140); 'A Lioness', 1948 (LOE242); Francis J. Cooper, 1950 (LOE246).

| | | |
|---|---|---|
| Jean Babelon | 1937 | Bronze cast |
| Wilhelm von Bode | 1935 | Silver cast from a stone mould and hand engraved |
| Winston Churchill | 1945 | 'Silver' struck |
| Rosa Loewental ('Ida') | 1948 | Bronze cast |
| 'Tyrtaios' | 1949 | Bronze cast |

A photographic portrait of Artur, dated August 1955, may have been taken to coincide with the exhibition. It is now in the collection of The Collection, Lincoln. In addition to the official display case the gallery erected a display board on which thirteen bronze medals by Artur were mounted.

The *Lincolnshire Echo*, 26 April 1955, reported the death of Einstein and of his connection with Artur, yet Artur, surprisingly, does not appear to have produced a medal to commemorate the death of his friend. Perhaps advancing age was beginning to take its toll.

*Fig.29. LOE256. A bronze portrait medal of Sir Francis Hill, Lincoln, circa 1958. 175mm. 1:2. (Andrew & Company Limited LLP, Lincoln).*

For some years Artur had been pressing for reparations from Germany for the losses sustained due to the war, and in a letter to his nephew on 1 December 1957 he asked him if he could obtain a few days leave in order to accompany him to Berlin to progress his claims. Artur had already been granted a pension in the region of £50 a month but there was still an outstanding claim for DM250,000, which was in the hands of a Berlin lawyer. This visit appears never to have taken place and all that seems to have occurred were more legal fees.

On 30 January 1958, Artur's wife, Rosa, died aged 76. She had always had a volatile temperament and was to end her days in Bracebridge Heath Mental Hospital, close to Lincoln, in her final days even refusing to take food. The death certificate gave the cause of death as 'hypostatic pneumonia and cardio vascular degeneration'. She was buried in a double plot in Canwick Road Old Cemetery, Lincoln, on 5 February. The grave is delineated by a low stone kerb, and the tombstone reads 'Rosa Catharina Josepha Loewental 1881-1958 Requiescat in Pace'. In addition there is a small loose flower vase inscribed with the name 'Ida', the name by which Artur and the family had always known her. Despite the fact that Artur had asked his nephew Tony not to attend Rosa's funeral, he still wrote to him on 16 March that he would need to draw up a new will and that he would be 'Number One' in it. He also stated that reports from Berlin in connection with his claim for reparations were promising, although

*Fig.28. Artur Loewental and his wife, Rosa, probably taken at their home in West Parade, Lincoln, n.d. (The McNichol private collection).*

there seems to have been no further reports of progress and the matter was subsequently dropped.

On 10 June 1958 Francis Hill was knighted in the Queen's Birthday Honours List and, probably in recognition of the occasion, Artur produced a cast bronze medal using his existing 1948 portrait, but changing the legend to read 'Sir Francis Hill'. The medal is undated, has a black patina and is mounted on a square wood frame. It now hangs in the office of the senior partner at Andrew & Company Limited LLP, Lincoln.

In 1958 Artur also sold his *vasa murrina* to Mr C. F. Turner, who was at the time the chairman of the Spalding Gentlemen's Society, for about £2,000. Artur had previously written to Einstein in order to seek his backing for this sale but Einstein in his reply was reluctant to become involved and merely stated that he had admired it. Turner subsequently placed it on loan to the Society with the stated intention that it would be left to them when he died. This wish did not transpire; instead, it was eventually purchased by the National Art Collections Fund for £2,300, in 1971, a year after Turner's death, probably from his daughter. Later, it was presented to the British Museum to commemorate the Earl of Crawford and Balcarres, who had served as Chairman of the National Art Collections Fund for twenty-five years, and subsequently named 'The Crawford Cup'. It is a curious fact that the other item thought by Artur to have been found at the same time and with his *vasa murrina* was a

*Fig.30. The Loewental family grave, Canwick Road Old Cemetery, Lincoln, 2002.*

goblet carved from a similar feldspar material. This latter article found its way into the collection of the Swedish collector Baron Adolphe Stoclet.

Artur committed his thoughts to paper in an article for the Society for Roman Studies in 1949, which is still the only source of provenance for the two items. The goblet now resides in the Roman gallery of the British Museum, having been purchased by them with help from the British Museums Friends in 2004 for £25,000. It was named 'The Barber Cup' in honour of Nicholas Barber and now resides alongside the Crawford Cup.

# 6. RETIREMENT TO WELLINGORE

AFTER spending years ensuring that Rosa would be well provided for if he died first, her death left him devastated. Aware that Artur would be unable to cope living on his own at his home in West Parade, his nephew Tony Lucas offered to provide him with a home with his family in Leeds. With his changed circumstances Artur's friend Francis Cooper, who had helped him ever since his arrival in Lincoln, came to his aid once more and introduced him to his friend Dr Jacob Bauer of Wellingore as a potential lodger. In a letter to his nephew in February 1958 Artur mentions the great help given to him by Cooper, and thanked his nephew for the offer to move to Leeds, although for some reason this was never to occur.

Dr Bauer had studied medicine at Warsaw University, Poland, where he obtained his MD in 1926. After military service during the Second World War he had come to England in 1947, accompanied by his second wife Gizella and his son Ralph by his first wife. He travelled around the country trying to find a suitable position and his early attempts included Assistant Medical Superintendent at the Blencathra Sanitorium, Threlkeld, and Registrar at Preston Hall Hospital, near Maidstone. Finally, however, he found a position as Medical Director at the Lincolnshire Mass Radiography Unit of St George's Hospital, Lincoln, based at Lincolnshire Chest Unit in Mint Lane in the city, working under Dr Butcher, the Chief Medical Officer. Dr Bauer set up home in the small village of Wellingore, a few kilometres south of Lincoln, after a period at Spridlington Hall and at Wellingore Hall. However, in 1953 he was able to purchase the former vicarage at Wellingore from the Church Commissioners, which he renamed The Old Rectory, although it was in a very dilapidated condition.

For Dr Bauer the prospect of a paying lodger to help him finance the necessary restoration of The Old Rectory would have been a most welcome benefit. In addition to the financial contribution Artur agreed to pay towards his stay, the Bauers were also aware that he still hoped to receive a large sum from his claim for Jewish Reparations. At Whitsun 1958 Tony Lucas visited Branston, a village close to Lincoln, for his first meeting with Dr and Mrs Bauer, and by 11 November Artur informed his nephew that he was spending every second day at Wellingore, where he felt snug and well cared for. Once a satisfactory arrangement had been agreed upon, two upstairs rooms of the former nursery were converted for his use, while

the cellar was converted into a workshop to house his lathes and materials – Artur obviously did not intend to stop working! However, Artur was still deeply depressed at the loss of Rosa and even turned to spiritualism in order to contact his wife.

Sir Hugh Dowding, 1st Baron Dowding, had had a distinguished career in the Royal Air Force, advancing to the rank of Air Chief Marshal. Upon his retirement he had become actively interested in spiritualism, even going so far as to write to Artur suggesting he should attend a séance in London. Towards the end of June 1958 Artur requested the return of a green overcoat of Rosa's he had given to Mrs Cooper so that he might have something belonging to her to present at the séance, believing that he had already had some contact with his wife. Artur repeatedly asked Cooper to drive him down to London for a séance but when he had refused and tried to dissuade Artur from any further involvement, it was Dr Bauer who drove Artur to London shortly afterwards.

In a letter to his nephew dated 24 February 1959 Artur describes his apartment at The Old Rectory as luxurious, with his new stove burning day and night, making the room the cosiest he had ever enjoyed. In apparent appreciation of the help and support that the Bauers were giving him at this time Artur now made a new will, dated 3 June 1959, naming Dr Bauer's wife, Gizella, his sole beneficiary and leaving her

> ... the whole of my estate both real and personal and wheresoever situate unto the said Gizella Bauer for her own absolute use and benefit and I DECLARE that I do so because of her unfailing kindness and care for my welfare since the death of my wife and in recognition of the great happiness which she and her husband have given me.

Thus he cut out his nephew Tony Lucas. Artur's relationship with his nephew, the only relative he had living in England at this time, seems to have ebbed and flowed over the years, as is illustrated in their frequent correspondence, and ranged from promises to change his will making Tony his sole beneficiary (16 March 1958) to wishing to have no further contact with him (15 November 1962). Despite this variance Artur constantly tried to encourage his nephew to develop his artistic skills and to that end would send him valuable rare books of his own to be rebound.

Despite the trauma caused by the loss of his wife Artur was still able to accept an invitation from Dr Humphrey Sutherland of the Ashmolean Museum to contribute to the British section of the *Internationale Tentoonstelling Hedendaagse Penningkunst* exhibition held in Antwerp 27 June to 27 September 1959, with a display of nine of his bronze medals, all of which had been produced during his time in England. (See table below).

It was unfortunate that Dr Bauer died on 17 September 1961, about two years after Artur's arrival, thus depriving Gizella of her continual financial security, and with the heavy burden of looking after three children, a large house, and a lodger whose constant demands proved to be very tiring. Artur is said to have been a hearty eater, required his fire to be constantly stoked up and to be supplied with his daily bottle of Liebfraumilch, obtained from the local shop, so that little was left over financially from the contribution he was making. Artur's house on West Parade was let through solicitors, who acted as his agents. As things turned out this proved to be a bad move as the tenants caused such extensive damage to the property that builders had to be engaged to rectify it. In the end the solicitors sold the property to the builder who had carried out the repairs, and it is said that at the end of the day almost nothing remained financially for Artur himself.

It is clear that Artur was still concerned with the final resting place for his own works. In 1960 he travelled down to the Ashmolean Museum in Oxford with a gift of twenty examples of his work. This gift comprised nineteen bronze medals depicting:

| Rosa | Vienna | 1910 |
|---|---|---|
| Professor von Bode | Berlin | 1914 |
| Emperor Franz Joseph I and Kaiser Wilhelm II | Berlin | 1914 |
| General von Hindenberg | | 1914 |
| Kaiser Wilhelm II | | 1915 |
| Admiral von Tirpitz | | 1915 |
| Admiral von Tirpitz, uniface | | 1915 |
| General Litzmann | | 1915 |
| Otto Wolff | Berlin | 1916 |
| Adolph Donath | Berlin | 1926 |
| Charles Ahl | Berlin | 1928 |
| Dr Hopker-Aschoff | Berlin | 1929 |
| Dr Otto Braun | Berlin | 1930 |
| Dr Otto Merckens | Berlin | 1927 |
| Theodor Daubler | Berlin | 1931 |
| Dr Robert Schmidt | Berlin | 1932 |
| Jimmy Tennant | London | 1935 |
| Professor Albert Einstein | Lincoln | 1948 |
| Rufus Isaacs | | 1936 |

There was also a wax depicting Professor Albert Einstein, framed as a medal. This gift was followed by a further five examples in 1961 comprising four waxes depicting: Guido Henckel-Donnersmarck (1915); Theodor Daubler as a medal; Sir George Franckenstein (1934); and 'Cornelia' (Berlin 1933); plus a plaster of Paris cast of 'Cornelia' (Berlin 1933). These two gifts augmented the earlier gift made to the museum by Sir George Hill in 1946 of three bronze medals: Sir George Hill (1935); Sir George Hill, uniface (1936); and Winston Churchill (1945).

At some period Artur had presented many of his plaster of Paris casts to the Usher Art Gallery, Lincoln, which had previously stored many of them for him over the years. Artur did manage to produce some work during his stay at The Old Rectory, although it appears to have now been restricted to members of the Bauer household. His advancing years, Rosa's death and his failing eye-sight brought on mood swings and bouts of depression. He is said to have become more and more demanding, constantly banging on the floor with his walking stick

| **International Exhibition of Contemporary Medallic Art, Antwerp, 1959 Artur Loewental's Display of 9 Bronze Medals** | | |
|---|---|---|
| Jean Babelon | Bronze medal | 1937 |
| Professor Albert Einstein | Bronze medal | 1948 |
| Sir George Franckenstein | Bronze medal | 1946 |
| Sir George Hill | Bronze medal | 1936 |
| Rufus D. Isaacs | Bronze medal | 1936 |
| Artur Loewental, self portrait | Bronze medal | 1949 |
| Rosa Loewental ('Ida') | Bronze medal | 1948 |
| James Tennant, son of Lord Glenconnor | Bronze medal | 1935 |
| 'Tyrtaios' | Bronze medal | 1949 |

*Fig.31 (Above). Artur Loewental, probably taken at Wellingore, n.d. (The McNichol private collection).*

and having Gizella chasing up and down stairs fetching and carrying. In the end attempts were made to try and find him alternative accommodation but without success. He did continue to exhibit examples of his work, and displayed at the Brussels Exhibition of 1961.

No trace has so far been found of the portraits thought to have been made of Jacob and Gizella Bauer, but an undated plaster of Paris cast of the portrait medal of Ralph, Jacob's son by his first wife, has been found. Also bronze medals of Gizella's two sons: Gerard Miet Bauer, dated 1962, and what must have been his last sculpture, of Eran Nicodemus Bauer, dated 1963, the year before Artur died (all in a private collection in England). It is remarkable that this latter portrait, although produced in the year before his death when Artur was aged eighty-four, still displays much of the naturalistic style for which he was always renowned.

Artur's death was quite sudden and unexpected. In the November of 1964 he suffered a fall at The Old Rectory and fractured his pelvis, as a result of which he had to be transferred to St George's Hospital, Lincoln. He appeared to be recovering quite well but ten days later he suffered a heart attack and was returned to hospital. On 15 November his nephew Tony Lucas came up by train and was met at the railway station at Leadenham by Gizella who then drove him to The Old Rectory. After lunch they had what Tony described as 'a very animated conversation' on various topics concerned with Artur's health and affairs. One of the other topics discussed was whether the *vasa murrina* was a forgery executed by Artur himself.

This suggestion was no doubt occasioned by the working drawings that Artur had produced, in all probability in order to reproduce such a vessel and learn the techniques that would have been employed in the Roman period. Certainly it is entirely impossible that it could have been produced in Lincoln as Artur had brought it with him from Berlin in 1934. Another point of discussion was Artur's copy of Giodsenhoven's catalogue of the Adolphe Stoclet collection, published in 1956, which appears to be unique in having a dedication page bound into it stating that it was printed in honour of Professor A. Loewenthal. Tony visited Artur in hospital the next day and then returned to his home in Leatherhead.

At around 11am the following day, 17 November, he received a telephone call from Gizella informing him of his uncle's death. The death certificate, after a post mortem, states the cause of death as a coronary occlusion atheroma. Gizella registered the death on the 18th and made arrangements for the funeral. The funeral took place on the 19th and Artur was interred beside his beloved Rosa in Canwick Road Old Cemetery. It is recorded that at his own request there was no funeral service, instead prayers were said at the graveside by the Rev W. T. Price, a Methodist minister from the Central Methodist Church, Lincoln. The short time between his death and burial would account for the absence of representatives from the national museums and institutions, and even of his close friend Francis Cooper who had moved to Folkestone on his retirement. One surprising absence is Artur's solicitor and friend Sir Francis Hill. Among those who are recorded in the *Lincolnshire Echo* as having

*Fig.32 LOE261. A bronze portrait medal of Eran Bauer, Wellingore, 1963. 140mm. 1:2. (The Bauer private collection).*

attended the funeral were: Gizella Bauer and her step-son Ralph; Artur's nephew Tony Lucas; Mr Tom Baker, Director of Lincoln Libraries, Museum and Art Gallery, and Miss E. M. Jahn, Deputy Director; Miss M. L. Smith, Keeper of the Usher Gallery; and Mr and Mrs C. F. Turner, representing the Spalding Gentlemen's Society. A few private individuals were also listed: Mr and Mrs Roy Page; Miss D. Fenwick; Mr and Mrs R. Wakeling of Tumby; and Mr D. McLachlan. It is sad that the return correspondences received by Tom Baker in reply to his notifications of Artur's death to various heads of national museums and institutions were more concerned with the fate of the *vasa murrina* than with his death.

The terms of Artur's will, which left everything to Gizella Bauer, were hotly contested by Tony Lucas on behalf of the Loewental family, and three depositions were presented by him in support of his claim, dated 25 November and 30 December 1964, and 23 January 1965. He even evoked a caveat to stay the proceedings but, after a protracted and bitter legal battle, probate was finally granted to Gizella on 12 March 1965. The gross value of the estate was stated as £2520-11s. and the net value as £1900-11s. With Artur's death the large collection of his own works, together with his other personal possessions, were packed away and, remarkably, much of it still remains in storage some fifty years later. No headstone was ever erected in his memory.

Artur had had a lifetime's experience of working with hard gemstones and among his effects were found several boules of synthetic rubies and sapphires, one at least of which has been split longitudinally to reveal the strain developed during cooling. These boules would have been produced by the flame-fusion process of adding either chromium oxide or iron and titanium to aluminium oxide. Boules produced by this process are of gem quality and have a hardness next to diamond. If Artur produced these boules himself it is likely that it was in connection with the War Office position offered to him in 1940. Also surviving among Artur's effects are a number of trial plaster of Paris casts, curiosities for the most part except where they depict a medal for which no bronze casting has been traced. Some are rough casts made merely to give him an idea of the progress he was making on a particular portrait, while others have been coated so that they might be handled and would be used so show to the clients for their approval.

So ended the life of a highly skilled sculptor, gem engraver and medallist, who achieved an international reputation, but who was to be buried in an unmarked grave far away from his place of birth. Many questions still remain to be answered. What are the details of his early life? Did he undertake further commissions for people in Lincolnshire? Many of his medals are unsigned so examples of his work no doubt still lurk in private collections and museums. It is a pity that the greatest British tribute to Artur's sculpting skills should occur within a few weeks of his own death, with the death of Sir Winston Churchill on 24 January 1965. B. A. Seaby Limited, coin dealers, London, who had handled the sale of his 1945 Churchill medals, chose to reproduce an exact copy of Artur's Victory medal at a slightly reduced diameter, merely adding the legend 'OB 24.JAN.1965' beneath the truncation, as a commemorative medal. In their Bulletin Seaby's described Artur's portrait as 'one of the finest portraits of Churchill', praise indeed from one of the most respected dealers in coins and medals in England at that time. The resulting medal was struck in bronze, silver and two standards of gold by John Pinches (Medallists) Limited, London. These medals now form a lasting memorial to a dedicated and highly skilled sculptor, and for which he is perhaps best known outside Central Europe. Fortunately, on completion of

*Fig.33.LOE267. The general issue death medal depicting Sir Winston Churchill, struck in bronze, silver and gold, 1965. 50mm. 1:1.*

the striking of these medals, the steel dies and puncheons used were presented to the British Museum.

In the years following Artur's death little reference to his life in England has been published, although more of his works are beginning to surface. In 1974 Sir Francis Hill made a gift of his valuable coin collection to the City of Lincoln. In order to house this collection a special strong room was subsequently installed in the Curtois wing of the now renamed Usher Gallery in 1976. In addition to Hill's collection of coins a display of eleven of Artur's medals were also shown (all subsequently put into storage):

| | | |
|---|---|---|
| Evelyn Baring | Bronze plaque | |
| Winston Churchill | Plaster medal | 1944 |
| Winston Churchill | Bronze medal | 1944 |
| Sir George Franckenstein | Plaster medal | 1941 |
| Sir George Franckenstein | Bronze medal | 1935 |
| Franz Joseph and Wilhelm II | Bronze medal | 1915 |
| Francis Hill | Bronze medal | 1948 |
| Rufus D. Isaacs | Bronze medal | 1935 |
| Artur Loewental, self portrait | Bronze medal | |
| Countess Mengerson | Bronze medal | 1916 |
| 'Rosa Lavorosa' | Bronze medal | |

In 1980 much of the content of The Old Rectory was sold off and included in the subsequent sale held by Henry Spencer & Son, Retford, on 28 and 29 October 1980 were some of Artur's effects, including eight examples of his sculptures:

Lot 324   A fine rock crystal circular bowl, intaglio carved with a naked athlete holding a flaming torch, within a circular panel, the rim carved with flaming torches. 180mm diameter.

Lot 347   Three bas-relief plaques, two of an elderly gentleman and a lady, one of a young lady. Signed and dated 1903 and 1924. 140mm x 130mm.

Lot 366   A bronze bas-relief plaque of Rufus, Marquis of Reading, 230mm diameter.

Lot 383   A bas-relief plaque entitled *Studie*, dated 1901. A bas-relief plaque of an elderly lady. A bas-relief plaque of a leopard, dated 1949.

Only the purchaser of Lot 347 has been traced and the lot actually comprised: a bronze plaque depicting Antonia Loewental, 1924; a bronze plaque of the musician Gärtner, 1901; and a bronze medal of Lady Betty Hambro, n.d. (private collection, England).

Two books formerly belonging to Artur were sold by Seaby (Rare Books) Limited in 1981. One was a presentation volume dated 1907 presented by the author Karl Domanig, while a second volume was presented by Sir George Hill of one of his own works. When Sir Francis Hill died in 1980 he bequeathed his extensive collections to the City of Lincoln. The Usher Gallery subsequently held an exhibition entitled The Collection of the Late Sir Francis Hill 1899-1980. Included in the exhibition was Artur's panther vase, carved in rock crystal, which Hill had presented to the Gallery in 1976 after it had been on loan to the Gallery since 1952. Also exhibited was the 1948 bronze portrait medal of Hill. Several modern reproductions of this medal have been found and it is probable that they were produced by the Gallery at this time to coincide with the exhibition.

# A SELECT CATALOGUE
# OF ARTUR LOEWENTAL'S SCULPTED WORKS

NO COMPLETE listing of Loewental's works will ever be possible. No record appears to have been kept by the sculptor himself, and the losses due to World War Two also preclude such a listing. There is little doubt that over future years many more examples of his work will surface as family estates are wound up and museums and art galleries catalogue their collections, hopefully prompted by this initial brief biography. The listing that follows concentrates, for the most part, on examples in collections outside Germany and Austria. It is intended to give an overview of his sculptural style. Many more examples survive in the museums and private collections of the latter two countries, but most of the items in the following listing are either examples that he brought with him when he fled Berlin and came to England in 1934 and subsequently exhibited, or that he sculpted during his later years living in this country between 1934 and 1964.

All of the illustrations have been reduced to a common size, as the originals vary considerably from 32mm to 406mm diameter. The illustrations themselves have been obtained from a wide variety of sources: professional, published and private, and the reproduction quality in some instances, therefore, reflect this variation. Many of the 'NOT LOCATED' examples are known only from exhibition catalogues and other publications, but have nevertheless been listed for comprehensiveness.

The listing is in date order, where this is known, although many of Loewental's portraits are undated. However, an attempt has been made to place these undated portraits roughly in their correct sequence. Where an example is undated but a date is known from an exhibition catalogue or other record, that date has been included in brackets. A further problem has been that a portrait sculpted and issued in a particular year was quite often recast in subsequent years, for example in the case of the 'Rosa Lavorosa' medal, which is believed to have been originally sculpted *circa* 1925, but continued to be reissued up to

1936. Only the diameter of a struck medal can be given with any degree of accuracy. The dimensions of cast medals and plaques, which often have a sloping edge, may vary between one casting and another and also depend on where the measurement is taken. This has meant that in some instances a compromise has had to be reached in the following listing. The legends on repeat castings, often incised at the last moment before pouring the liquid metal, may also vary between individual casts from the same master mould; these small variations in legends have for the most part been ignored. The term 'bronze' has been used except where a medal is definitely known to be made in brass, as often the dark patina hides the true nature of the material.

Many of the examples listed are unique and fall into the following general categories. (1) Wax models. The beeswax that Loewental used for his models was usually melted down and reused, thus few examples of his wax models have survived in England. The Ashmolean Museum, Oxford, has five examples that were donated by Loewental himself, although other examples may survive elsewhere. (2) Plaster casts. During the development of the master model, casts in plaster of Paris were periodically taken and may be divided into two categories: (a) Trial casts taken periodically at various stages as the work progressed, both of the master die and the subsequent mould. As would be expected very few of these have survived and all traced examples are included in Loewental's effects; (b) Casts taken of what was expected to be the final design: these were sealed and intended for the approval of the sitter prior to the final casting in bronze. Only a few are known to survive. (3) Cast medals and plaques. The finished cast medal or plaque in bronze etc., polished and occasionally with an added patina.

Almost all of Loewental's output was from private commissions, with only a few examples being produced in the hope of commercial sales. Thus most portrait medals and plaques are unique, or almost so. An exception is the well known series of commemorative medals that he was commissioned to produced while trapped in Berlin during the First World War – see Steguweit (1998) and Zetzmann (2002) for illustrations of many of the examples in this series. Most of the examples illustrated have not been published previously and it is hoped that their publication will help museums, collectors and dealers identify other examples of his work – many of which will be unsigned. There are two important collections of Loewental's works in England. The collection of The Collection, Lincoln, is extensive and has been formed from a combination of examples purchased from Loewental himself, supplemented by gifts that he made of his work, previously stored by the Usher Art Gallery, Lincoln, during his lifetime. By far the largest collection of Loewental's work in England is, however, in a private collection and represents the remnants of the effects left by Loewental in his will. Unfortunately much of this latter extensive collection is still in storage and its full extent has yet to be revealed. The many objects engraved by Loewental in such materials as ivory, gemstones, rock crystal, and other hard materials have been excluded, although some are mentioned in the main text. This also applies to the small statuettes in bronze he produced in his early years. Most of such objects are unsigned and almost impossible to identify without a known provenance.

**LOE001  1898  MARK TWAIN** (1835–1910) (Pseudonym of Samuel Langhorne Clemens)
American humorist, writer and lecturer.
**Obv:** The profile portrait of a man, facing left.
Legend in relief around the rim: **MARK TWAIN**
Incised in three lines in field beneath chin: **M / DCCC / XCVIII**
Incised below date: **AL** within circle
**Rev:** Uniface
**[A] Cast bronze medal   90mm diameter**
      (1) The Nationalmuseum, Vienna, Austria
      (2) The Mark Twain House and Museum, Hartford, USA  70.6.DUP16

LOE001

**LOE002  1898  MORIZ KANITZ**
**Portrait**  No other details
      Reference: **Friedenberg, Daniel M., 1976** *Jewish minters and medalists*
      (Philadelphia: The Jewish Publication Society of America)

**LOE003  1899  WILHELM TRINKS**  Famous Viennese numismatist.
**Portrait**  No other details
**[A] Wax model on slate**
      Exhibited at the Usher Art Gallery, Lincoln, 1941/2.
      Returned to Loewental by the Usher Art Gallery, Lincoln, in 1952.
**NOT LOCATED**

**LOE004  1899  WILHELM TRINKS**
**Portrait**  No other details
**[A] Lithographic stone matrix**
      Returned to Loewental by the Usher Art Gallery, Lincoln, in 1952.
**NOT LOCATED**

**LOE005  1899  AUGUST RITTER VON LOEHR**  President of first camera club in Austria
**Obv:** The profile head and shoulders portrait of a bearded man, facing left.
Legend in relief around the rim: **AVGVST · RITTER · V · LOEHR : V · PRAESIDENT · D
· CAMERA CLVB**
In relief in two lines in field to right of portrait: **MDCCCIC / LOEWENTHAL**
**Rev:** Uniface
**[A] Soapstone medal   81mm diameter**
      Exhibited at the Usher Art Gallery, Lincoln, in 1941/2.
      (1) The Collection, Lincoln  LCNUG:1927/2059
      Presented by Loewental.

LOE005

**LOE006  1900  EDUARD GAERTNER**  Austrian singer of light opera.
**Obv:** The profile head and shoulders portrait of a man, facing left.
Legend in relief in three lines in field to right of portrait: **EDUARD / GAERTNER · / 1900**
In relief in field to lower left: **· LÖWENTHAL ·**
**Rev:** Uniface
**[A] Cast bronze medal   144mm diameter**
      Reference: **Svarstad, Carsten, 1963** *Medals of actors, singers & dancers*
      London: Spink & Son Ltd.

**LOE007  n.d. (1900)  RUDOLPH ALTER VON WALDHOF**  Chief of Austrian judiciary
**Obv:** The profile head and shoulders portrait of a man, facing left. No legend.
Incised in field to right of portrait: **ALÖWENTHAL**
**Rev:** Uniface
**[A] Cast bronze plaque   122mm x 156mm**
      Exhibited at the Usher Art Gallery, Lincoln, in 1941/2.
      (1) The Collection, Lincoln LCNUG:1927/1879
      Purchased from Loewental in 1948.

LOE007

**LOE008**

**LOE008 1901 GÄRTNER** Musician.
**Obv:** Profile head and shoulders portrait of a man, facing left, no legend.
Incised in two lines in field to left of portrait: **ALÖWENTHAL · F / 1901**
**Rev:** Uniface
**[A] Cast bronze plaque   114 x 172mm**
       (1) The Jackson private collection, England
      Purchased at the 1980 Bauer sale.

**LOE009 n.d. (1901) SALO COHEN** (1842–1917) Director of the Jewish community
in Vienna
**Portrait** No other details
      Reference: **Friedenberg, Daniel M., 1976** *Jewish minters and medalists*
      (Philadelphia: The Jewish Publication Society of America).
      Reference: **Singer, Isidore & Cyrus Adler, (eds), 1901-06** *The Jewish Encyclopedia*
      (New York: Funk and Wagnall).

**LOE010 1901 'PORTRAIT OF AN OLD GENTLEMAN'**
**Portrait** No other details
**[A] Bronze**
      Exhibited at the Beaux Arts Gallery, London, in 1935.
      Exhibited at the Usher Art Gallery, Lincoln, in 1941/2.   **NOT LOCATED**

**LOE011**

**LOE011 1901 'FELIX'** Silk merchant?
**Obv:** The profile head and shoulders portrait of a man, facing left.
Legend in relief in exergue between two mulberry leaves, each with a silk worm across it;
the 'X' of Felix being formed by two crossed silk worms: **FELIX**
Incised in two lines in field to right of portrait: **ALÖWENTHAL / · 1901 ·**
**Rev:** Uniface
**[A] Cast bronze plaque   104mm x 168mm**
      (1) The Rezak private collection, USA

**LOE012 1902 MRS LEWIS OF VIENNA**
**Portrait** No other details
**[A] Bronze**
      Exhibited at the Usher Art Gallery, Lincoln, in 1941/2.   **NOT LOCATED**

**LOE013 1902 DR ADOLPH HOFFMANN**
**Portrait** No other details
      Reference: **Friedenberg, Daniel M., 1976** *Jewish minters and medalists*
      (Philadelphia: The Jewish Publication Society of America).
      Reference: **Singer, Isidore & Cyrus Adler (eds), 1901–06** *The Jewish Encyclopedia*
      (New York: Funk and Wagnall).
      Reference: **Forrer, L., 1923,** *Biographical dictionary of medallists: coin, gem, and*
      *seal-engravers, mint masters, &c., ancient and modern, with references to their works*
      *B.C.500-A.D.1900,* VolumeVII supplement (A-L, London: Spink & Son Ltd).

**LOE014**

**LOE014 1902 DR V. W. RUSS** Member of the Austrian parliament
**Obv:** The profile head and shoulders portrait of a bearded, bespectacled man, facing left.
Legend in relief in two lines in field to left of portrait: **DR · V · W · / RUSS**
Incised in two lines in field to right of portrait: **ALÖWENTHAL · / 1902 ·**
**Rev:** Uniface
**[A] Cast bronze medal   175mm diameter**
      An example exhibited at the Usher Art Gallery, Lincoln, in 1941/2.
      (1) The Rezak private collection, USA

**LOE015 1903 BARONESS NEWLINSKI**
**Portrait** No other details
**[A] Bronze**
      Exhibited at the Usher Art Gallery, Lincoln, in 1941/2.   **NOT LOCATED**

**LOE016  1903  'TITY', A CHILD**
**Portrait**  No other details
**[A] Bronze**
Exhibited at the Usher Art Gallery, Lincoln, in 1941/2.  **NOT LOCATED**

**LOE017  1904  WILHELM LICHTENSTERN**  An advocate.
**Portrait**  No other details
Reference: **Friedenberg, Daniel M., 1976** *Jewish minters and medalists.*
(Philadelphia: The Jewish Publication Society of America).

LOE018

**LOE018  1904  DR FRANZ HARTMANN** (1838–1912) German theosopher and author.
**Obv:** The profile head and shoulders portrait of a man, facing left.
Legend in relief on bottom border, in Art Nouveau lettering and design against background
of sun rising over waves, and with flowers at either end: **DR · FRANZ · HARTMANN**
Incised in two lines in field to left of portrait: **ALÖWENTHAL / 1904**
**Rev:** Uniface
**[A] Cast bronze plaque   211mm x 285mm**
Exhibited at the Usher Art Gallery, Lincoln, in 1941/2.
(1) The British Museum, London  BM1981-8-17-1

**LOE019  1904  DR H. STIASSING**  A lawyer from Prague.
**Obv:** The profile head and shoulders portrait of a bearded, bespectacled man, facing left.
No legend.
Incised in two lines in field below chin: **ALÖWENTHAL · / 1904**
**Rev:** Uniface
**[A] Cast bronze plaque   130mm x 185mm**
(1) The Bauer private collection, England
A handwritten note attached to the reverse reads: 'Dr. H. Stiassing, lawyer, Prag.'.

LOE019

**LOE020  1905  UNIDENTIFIED SITTER**
**Obv:** The profile head and shoulders portrait of a bearded man, facing right. No legend.
Incised in two lines in field to left of portrait: **ALÖWENTAL · F · / 1905**
**Rev:** Uniface
**[A] Cast bronze medal   165mm diameter**
(1) The Bauer private collection, England

**LOE021  1905  PRINCESS ADELGUNDE OF BAVARIA** (1823–1914)  Née Adelgunde
Auguste Charlotte Caroline Elisabeth Amalie Marie Sophie Luise von Bayern. Consort
Duchess of Modena, Italy, by her marriage to Francis V, Duke of Modena. (To celebrate
Christmas 1905).
**Obv:** The head and shoulders portrait of an elderly bejewelled lady, facing left.
Legend in relief in two lines at top left hand corner: **WEIHNACHTEN / 1905**
In relief in field to right of portrait: **ALÖWENTAL**
**Rev:** Uniface
**[A] Bronze plaque   40mm x 52mm**
(1) Example offered for sale by Artemide Aste, San Marino, 2010
(Illustration in  sale catalogue)

LOE020

**LOE022  n.d. (1905)  ALEXANDER GIRARDI** (1850–1918)  Austrian singer of light opera
**Obv:** The profile head and shoulders portrait of a man, facing left.
Legend in relief below portrait: **ALEXANDER GIRARDI**
**Rev:** Uniface
**[A] Bronze plaque   80 x 58mm**
Reference: **Loewental, Artur, 1928/29** Wie ich Girardi porträtierte.
In *Der Kunstwanderer*, (1928/9). (Berlin: "Der Kunstwanderer" G.m.b.H.), pp458-9.
Reference: **Svarstad, Carsten, 1963**, *Medals of actors, singers & dancers.* (London:
Spink & Son Ltd). **(Illustration)**

**LOE023**

**LOE027**

**LOE028**

**LOE029**

**LOE023 n.d. [1906] EVELYN BARING, 1ST EARL OF CROMER** (1841-1917). British diplomat and administrator. Consul General and virtual ruler of Egypt between 1883 and 1907.
**Obv:** The head and shoulders portrait of a man. facing forward.
No legend.
Incised in field to right of portrait: Conjoined **AL** within circle
**Rev:** Uniface
**[A] Cast bronze plaque   126mm x 191mm**
  Exhibited at the Beaux Arts Gallery, London, in 1935.
  Exhibited at the Usher Art Gallery, Lincoln, in 1941/2.
  **(1) The Collection, Lincoln LCNUG:1927/1868**
  Purchased from Loewental in 1948.

**LOE024  1906  DR ALFRED HOFFMANN**
**Obv:** No other details
**Rev:** Uniface
**[A] Cast bronze medal   64mm diameter**
  **(1) Ex Friedenberg private collection, USA**
  **NOT LOCATED**

**LOE025  1910  ADOLF LOOS** (1870-1933). Austrian architect whose planning of private residences strongly influenced European Modernist architects after World War One.
**Portrait bust**  No other details
**[A] Plaster of Paris cast bust**
  **(1) The Kunsthistorisches Museum, Vienna, Austria**
  Reference: ----------, 1985, *Traum und Wirklichkeit. Wien 1870-1930.*
  (Vienna: Historisches Museum der Stadt Wien). **(Illustration)**

**LOE026  1910  ADOLF LOOS**
**Portrait bust**  No other details
**[A] Cast bronze bust**
  Reference: Vollmer, Hans, c.1930, *Allgemeines Lexikon der Bildenden Künstler*
  *von der Antike bis zur Gegenwart, Dreiundzwanzigster Band.*
  (Leipzig: E. A. Seemann Verlag).

**LOE027  1910  UNIDENTIFIED SITTER**
**Obv:** The profile head and shoulders portrait of a bespectacled man, facing left. No legend.
Incised in two lines in field to right of portrait: **ALOEWENTAL · / 1910**
**Rev:** Uniface
**[A] Struck bronze plaque   48mm x 64mm**
  **(1) The Rezak private collection, USA**

**LOE028  1910  ROSA KATHARINA JOSEPHA LOEWENTAL** (1881-1958). The wife of the sculptor Artur Loewental.
**Obv:** The profile head and shoulders portrait of a lady, facing left. No legend.
Incised in two lines in field to right of portrait: **ALOEWENTAL / 1910**
**Rev:** Uniface
**[A] Cast bronze medal   186mm diameter**
  **(1) The Bauer private collection, England**

**LOE029  n.d. (1910)  ROSA KATHARINA JOSEPHA LOEWENTAL**
**Obv:** The profile head and shoulders portrait of a lady, facing left. No legend. No artist's signature or date.
**Rev:** Uniface
**[A] Cast bronze medal   191mm diameter**
  **(1) The Ashmolean Museum, Oxford**
  Presented by Loewental 15 December 1960.

**LOE030  1910  'DANCING GIRL'**
Obv: The full-length figure of a dancing girl, facing left.
Incised in two lines at bottom right: ALÖWENTAL · F · / 1910 ·
Rev: Uniface
[A] Cast brass plaque   125mm x 182mm
　　　(1) The Turner private collection, England

LOE030

**LOE031  1912  PROFESSOR FRITZ KREISLER AND HIS WIFE, HARRIET WOERZ (née LIES) (1875-1962).** Austrian-born violinist and composer. One of the most accomplished violinists of his time.
Portrait medal  No other details
[A] Silver
　　　Exhibited at the Usher Art Gallery, Lincoln, in 1941/2.  **NOT LOCATED**

**LOE032  1912  LUDWIG VAN BEETHOVEN (1770-1827).** German composer, considered one of the greatest musicians of all time.
Portrait mask  No other details
[A] Cast bronze mask
　　　Exhibited at the Beaux Arts Gallery, London, in 1935.  **NOT LOCATED**

**LOE033  n.d. (1912)  LUDWIG VAN BEETHOVEN**
Descr: A life-size portrait bust of a man, looking slightly downwards.
Incised at the base of the collar, at the rear: ALOEWENTAL
[A] Cast bronze bust   380mm high
　　　Exhibited at the Beaux Arts Gallery, London, in 1935.
　　　(1) The Collection, Lincoln LCNUG:1927/901
　　　Black patina and mounted on a wood base.
　　　Purchased from Loewental in 1942.

LOE033

**LOE034  n.d. (1912)  LUDWIG VAN BEETHOVEN**
Descr: A life-size portrait bust of a man, looking slightly downwards.
[A] Carved marble bust   415mm high
　　　(1) The Beethoven Haus, Bonn, Germany P36 (Illustration on website)
　　　Purchased at auction, Hauswedell, Hamburg, Germany, 1969.

**LOE035  n.d. (c.1912)  LUDWIG VAN BEETHOVEN**
Descr: A life-size portrait bust of a man, looking slightly downwards.
[A] Carved marble bust   330mm high
　　　(1) The Beethoven Haus, Bonn, Germany P25 (Illustration on website)
　　　Gifted by Frau Windthoest, 1918.

**LOE036  n.d.  MARIA CANDIDA**
Portrait  No other details
[A] Bronze
　　　Exhibited at the Usher Art Gallery, Lincoln, in 1941/2.  **NOT LOCATED**

**LOE037  n.d.  'VIEL GLÜCK'**
Obv: A small naked boy striding to the left but looking to the right, carrying a cornucopia in each arm.
In relief in field to each side of figure: VIEL GLÜCK
Rev: Uniface
[A] Lithographic stone matrix  No other details
　　　Returned to Loewental by the Usher Art Gallery, Lincoln, 1952.  **NOT LOCATED**

**LOE038 n.d. 'VIEL GLÜCK'**
**Obv:** A small naked boy striding to the left but looking to the right, carrying a cornucopia in each arm.
In relief in field to each side of figure: **VIEL GLÜCK**
**Rev:** Uniface
**[A] Bronze medal** *c.*56mm diameter
      Exhibited at the Usher Art Gallery, Lincoln, in 1941/2.
      Exhibited at the Usher Art Gallery, Lincoln, in 1955.
      **(Illustration on photograph of display) NOT LOCATED**

**LOE39 n.d (c.1914) ÖSTERREICHISCHEN AERO-CLUB** Award medal.
**Obv:** Ikarus in front of sunrise.
Legend in two lines relief in field to right of Icarus: **AD / ASTRA**
**Rev:** Female winged guardian spirit with right arm stretched out above view of the city of Vienna and laurel wreath in each hand.
Legend in relief in seven lines in field to left had side: **DER / OESTER- / REICHISCHE / AEROCLVB / DEN / EROBERERN / DER LVFT**
Beneath legend engraved name of recipient: **ERNST VON LÖSSE**
Sculptor's details incised along right hand side rim but undecipherable from illustration.
Award details engraved in exergue.
**[A] Struck bronze medal, gold plated 63.2mm diameter**
      **(1) Offered at auction by A. Button, 1979 (Illustration on website)**

LOE040

**LOE040 1914 DR KARL DOMANIG** (1850–1913) Director of the Vienna Münzkabinetts
**Obv:** The profile head and shoulders portrait of a bearded bespectacled man, facing left.
Legend in relief around the rim: **REGIERUNGSRAT · DR · KARL DOMANIG · GEB · 1850 GEST · 1913**
Incised in two lines in field to right of portrait: **A · LOEWENTAL · F / 1914 ·**
**Rev:** Uniface
**[A] Cast bronze medal 176mm diameter**
      Exhibited at the Usher Art Gallery, Lincoln, in 1941/2.
      **(1) The British Museum, London BM1984-11-1-1**

**LOE041 1914 PROFESSOR VON SCHMOLLER** Scientist and political economist.
**Portrait** No other details
**[A] Bronze**
      Exhibited at the Beaux Arts Gallery, London, in 1935.
      Exhibited at the Usher Art Gallery, Lincoln, in 1941/2. **NOT LOCATED**

**LOE042 1914 ROSA KATHARINA JOSEPHA LOEWENTAL** (1881–1958). The wife of the sculptor Artur Loewental.
**Portrait** No other details
**[A] Bronze**
      Exhibited at the Usher Art Gallery, Lincoln, in 1941/2. **NOT LOCATED**

**LOE043 1914 PAUL LUDWIG HANS ANTON VON BENECKENDORFF UND VON HINDENBURG** (1847–1934). German general and field marshal who scored a notable victory at Tannenberg in August 1914. To commemorate his victory at Tannenberg. Commissioned by Grünthal.
**Obv:** The head and shoulders portrait of a man in uniform, facing forward and slightly to the left.
Legend in relief around the rim: **GENERALOBERST VON · HINDENBURG**
Incised below bust: **GR[ÜNTHAL]**
**Rev:** A knight striding to the right wielding a sword.

Legend in relief around rim: DER · RUSSEN · BEZWINGER OSTPREUSSENS · BEFREIER

Incised in three lines in field to either side of figure and between legs: TANNEN / BERG ORTELS / BURG / 1914

Incised at base: ALOEWENTAL

(Illustration in Zetzmann 2002, 4025)

[A] Struck gold medal   33mm diameter   General Issue
    (1) Sold by Numismatik Lanz, Germany, 2008   Location unknown

[B] Struck silver medal   33mm diameter   General issue
    A medal in silver of the reverse exhibited at the Usher Art Gallery, Lincoln, 1941/2. **NOT LOCATED**
    (1) The American Numismatic Society, New York, USA 2000.1.109

[C] Struck silver-gilt medal   32mm diameter   General issue
    (1) The British Museum, London BM1919-8-17-148

[D] Struck bronze medal   33mm diameter   General issue
    (1) The Ashmolean Museum, Oxford
    Presented by Loewental 15 December 1960.

[E] Struck war metal medal   38mm diameter   General issue
    (1) The American Numismatic Soceity, New York, USA 2000.1.110

[F] Struck white metal medal   35mm diameter   General issue
    (1) The American Numismatic Society, New York, USA 1916.187.26


## LOE044  1914  PAUL LUDWIG HANS ANTON VON BENECKENDORFF UND VON HINDENBURG

Commissioned by Grünthal

**Obv:** The head and shoulders portrait of a man in uniform, facing forward and slightly to the left.

Legend in relief around the rim: GENERALOBERST VON · HINDENBURG

Incised below bust: GRÜNTHAL

**Rev:** A knight striding to the right wielding a sword, within beaded border. (Revised reverse).

Legend in relief around the rim: DER · RUSSEN · BEZWINGER OSTPREUSSENS · BEFREIER

In relief in three lines in field to either side of figure and between legs: TANNEN / BERG ORTELS / BURG / 1914

Incised at base: ALOEWENTAL

[A] Struck silver medal   34.5mm diameter   General issue
    (1) Offered by auction by Fritz Rudolf Künker GmbH & Co., Germany, 12 March 2009 (Illustration on website)


## LOE045  1914  PAUL LUDWIG HANS ANTON VON BENECKENDORFF UND VON HINDENBURG

Commissioned by Grünthal

**Obv:** The head and shoulders portrait of a man in uniform, facing forward and slightly to the left.

Legend in relief around the rim: GENERALOBERST VON · HINDENBURG

Incised below bust: GRÜNTHAL

**Rev:** A knight striding to the right wielding a sword, within beaded border. (Revised reverse).

Legend in relief around the rim: DER · RUSSEN · BEZWINGER OSTPREUSSENS · BEFREIER

In relief in three lines in field to either side of figure and between legs: TANNEN / BERG ORTELS / BURG / 1914

Incised at base: ALOEWENTAL ·

[A] Struck silver medal   34mm diameter   General issue
    (1) Offered for sale by Medaillenhandlung Annette Hossfeld, Germany, 2010 (Illustration on website)

**LOE046** 1914 PAUL LUDWIG HANS ANTON VON BENECKENDORFF UND VON HINDENBURG  Commissioned by Grünthal
**Obv:** Head and shoulders portrait of a man in uniform, facing forward and slightly to left.
Legend in relief around the rim: GENERALOBERST VON · HINDENBURG
Incised below bust: GRÜ....
**Rev:** A knight striding to the right wielding a sword.
Legend in relief around the rim: DER · RUSSEN · BEZWINGER OSTPREUSSENS · BEFREIER
Incised in field in three lines to either side of figure and between legs: TANNEN / BERG ORTELS / BURG / 1914
Incised in two lines at base: BALL'S NACHFOLGER / ALOEWENTAL
[A] Cast bronze medal   105mm diameter
     (1) The Deutsches Historisches Museum, Berlin, Germany  XY001098
     (2) The American Numismatic Society, New York, USA
[B] Cast bronze medal   110mm diameter
     (1) Sold by Auktionshaus für Historica, Germany, 2008 (Illustrated on website)
[C] Cast bronze medal   114mm diameter
     (1) Ex Friedenberg private collection, New York, USA   Sold   NOT LOCATED
[D] Cast iron medal   105mm diameter
     (1) The Imperial War Museum, London MED45
[E] Cast iron medal   114mm diameter
     (1) The British Museum, London BM1916-7-5-4


**LOE047** 1914 PAUL LUDWIG HANS ANTON VON BENECKENDORFF UND VON HINDENBURG  To commemorate his victory at Tannenberg. Commissioned by Grünthal.
**Obv:** A knight striding to the right wielding a sword.
Legend in relief around the rim: DER · RUSSEN · BEZWINGER OSTPREUSSENS · BEFREIER
Incised in field in three lines to either side of figure and between legs: TANNEN / BERG ORTELS / BURG / 1914
Incised in two lines at base: BALL'S NACHFOLGER / ALOEWENTAL
**Rev:** Uniface
[A] Plaster of Paris cast?   104mm diameter
     (1) The Ashmolean Museum, Oxford


**LOE048** 1915 PAUL LUDWIG HANS ANTON VON BENECKENDORFF UND VON HINDENBURG
**Obv:** The portrait of a man in uniform, facing forward and slightly to the left.
Legend in relief around the rim: FELDMARSCHALL VON · HINDENBURG
**Rev:** Siegfried taming the Russian Bear.
Legend in relief around the rim: WIE · SIEGFRIED DER HELD · DEN · BAEREN · BAND
In relief in centre field: 1915
In relief on bottom rim: LÖWENTAL · FEC ·
(Illustration in Steguweit 1998, 104; Zetzmann 2002, 4074)
[A] Tin two-sided model
     (1) Der Königlichen Museen zu Berlin, Germany
[B] Struck silver medal   33mm diameter   General issue
     An example was exhibited at the Beaux Arts Gallery, London in 1935.
     (1) The British Museum, London. BM1919-8-17-147
[C] Struck white metal medal   34mm diameter  General issue
     (1) Der Königlichen Museen zu Berlin, Germany  MKB344/1916
[D] Cast bronze medal   104mm diameter
     (1) The Kadman Numismatic Pavilion, Tel-Aviv, Israel  K66934
     (2) Der Königlichen Museen zu Berlin, Germany  MKB  without number

**LOE049  1914  RUDOLPH HERZOG** (1869–1943) German writer, journalist, poet and story teller.

Obv: The profile head and shoulders portrait of a man, facing left.
Legend in relief along left hand rim: **RUDOLPH HERZOG**
In relief in field to right of portrait: **1914**
Incised on truncation: **A · LÖWENTAL · F ·**
Rev: The naked figure of a man striding to the right, playing a lyre.
In relief in field to left of figure: **TYRTAIOS**
**(Illustration in Steguweit 1998, 121)**
[A] Cast bronze medal   87mm diameter
　　　An example of the reverse exhibited at the Beaux Arts Gallery, London, in 1935.
　　　**NOT LOCATED**
　　　An example exhibited at the Beaux Arts Gallery, London, in 1935.
　　　An example exhibited at Usher Art Gallery, Lincoln, in 1941/2.
　　　**NOT LOCATED**
　　　**(1) Der Königlichen Museen zu Berlin, Germany MKB321/1916**

**LOE050  n.d. (1914)  PROFESSOR WILHELM VON BODE** (1845–1929). German art historian. He became General Director of German Museums in 1905.

Obv: The profile head of a man, facing left.
Legend in relief in field to right of head: **BODE**
In relief below truncation: **ALÖWENTAL**
Rev: Uniface
[A] Cast bronze medal   55mm diameter
　　　**(1) The Ashmolean Museum, Oxford**
　　　Presented by Loewental 15 December 1960.

**LOE050**

**LOE051  n.d 'NACH WALHALL'**
Obv: Mounted Valkyrie carries fatally wounded warrior to Valhalla.
Legend in relief in two lines in field to left of rider: **NACH / WALHALL**
Rev: Symbolic portrayal of consecration of weapons.
Legend in relief around the rim: **EHRE · UNSERN HELDEN · ALLEZEIT ·**
Incised at right hand edge: **A · LOEWENTAL · F ·**
**(Illustration in Steguweit 1998, 105; Zetzmann 2002, 6013)**
[A] Struck silver medal   50mm diameter   General issue
　　　**(1) The British Museum, London  BM1919-8-17-211**
　　　**(2) Der Königlichen Museen zu Berlin, Germany  MKB349/1916**
　　　**(3) The American Numismatic Society, New York, USA  0000.999.42000**
[B] Cast bronze medal (Uniface)   109mm diameter
　　　**(1) Der Königlichen Museen zu Berlin, Germany  MKB141/1916**
[C] Cast bronze medal (Uniface)   170mm diameter
　　　**(1) Der Königlichen Museen zu Berlin, Germany MKB144/1916**

**LOE052  1915  'NACH PARIS', reverse**
Obv: Uniface
Rev: A naked Amazon on horseback holding a lighted torch in each hand, riding to the left. A town in flames in background.
Legend in relief in two lines in field to left of rider: **NACH / PARIS**
In relief in field to right of rider: **1914**
Incised on rim at base: **ALÖWENTAL · F · 1915 ·**
[A] Plaster of Paris cast   154mm diameter
　　　**Exhibited at the Usher Art Gallery, Lincoln, in 1941/2**
　　　**(1) The Collection, Lincoln  LCNUG:1927/2053**
　　　Presented by Loewental.

**LOE052**

**LOE053 1915 'NACH PARIS', ALEXANDER HEINRICH RUDOLPH VON KLUCK**
(1846-1934). German field commander who led the First Army in the opening campaigns of the Western Front from August 1914. He was almost successful in defeating France, his forces being halted 13 miles from Paris in September 1914.

**Obv:** The head and shoulders portrait of a man in uniform, facing forward and slightly to right.

Legend in relief around the rim: **GENERALOBERST VON · KLUCK · 1914 · 1915**

**Rev:** A naked Amazon on horseback holding a lighted torch in each hand, riding to the left. A town in flames in background.

Legend in relief in two lines in field to left of rider: **NACH / PARIS**

In relief in field to right of rider: **1914**

Incised on rim at base: **ALÖWENTAL · F · 1915**

**(Illustration in Zetzmann 2002, 4105)**

[A] Struck silver medal   29mm diameter   General issue
       Exhibited at the Usher Art Gallery, Lincoln, in 1941/2
       (1) The British Museum, London  BM1916-8-14-3
[B] Struck silver medal   35mm diameter   General issue
       (1) The American Numismatic Society, New York, USA 1916.187.19
[C] Cast iron medal   95mm diameter
       (1) Ex Friedenberg private collection, USA   NOT LOCATED

**LOE054 1915 ALEXANDER HEINRICH RUDOLPH VON KLUCK**

**Obv:** The head and shoulders portrait of a man in uniform, facing forward and slightly to the right.

Legend in relief around the rim: **V · KLUCK 1914 · 15**

**Rev:** A naked Amazon on horseback holding a lighted torch in each hand, riding to the left. A town in flames in background.

Incised on the bottom rim: **ALÖWENTAL · F · 1915**

[A] Struck silver medal   34mm diameter   General issue
       An example exhibited at the Beaux Art Gallery, London, in 1935.
       (1) The Kadman Numismatic Pavilion, Tel-Aviv, Israel  K67064

**LOE054**

**LOE055 1915 'THE DRIVE ON PARIS', September 1914, ALEXANDER HEINRICH RUDOLPH VON KLUCK**

**Obv:** The profile head and shoulders portrait of a man in uniform, facing right.

Legend in relief in four lines in field to right of portrait: **GENERAL / OBERST / VON / KLUCK**

Dates in relief in two lines in field to left of portrait: **1914- / 1915**

**Rev:** Eagle perched on a gun-emplacement, gazing at a distant view of Paris.

Legend in relief in field to right of scene: **PARIS**

Incised on walling: **ALOEWENTAL**

**(Illustration in Steguweit 1998, 113)**

[A] Bronze two-sided model
       (1) Der Königlichen Museen zu Berlin, Germany
[B] Struck iron medal   45mm diameter   General issue
       (1) Der Königlichen Museen zu Berlin, Germany  MKB1231/1914.
[C] Cast iron medal  89mm diameter  General issue
       (1) The Imperial War Museum, London  MED493
       (2) The British Museum, London  BM1917-11-6-1
       (3) The Kadman Numismatic Pavilion, Tel-Aviv, Israel  K66975
       (4) Der Königlichen Museen zu Berlin, Germany  MKB323/1916

**LOE056 1915 KAISER WILHELM II** (1859–1941) Kaiser of Germany and King of Prussia.
**Obv:** The profile portrait of a man, facing left.
Legend in relief along left hand rim: WILHELM · II ·
Incised on truncation: LÖEWENTAL · F
**Rev:** Altar on a double plinth with flames issuing from the top. Outer double ring of oak leaves.
Legend in relief in five lines on side of altar: MIT GOTT / FÜR / KAISER / UND / REICH
Dates in relief either side of altar: **1914 1915**
[A] **Bronze medal   59mm diameter   General issue**
    (1) The Ashmolean Museum, Oxford
    Presented by Loewental 15 December 1960.
[B] **Iron medal   58mm diameter   General issue**
    (2) The Kadman Numismatic Pavilion, Tel-Aviv, Israel  K66720
    (3) Der Deutsches Historisches Museen, Berlin, Germany  N1001264

LOE056

**LOE057 n.d. (1915) KAISER WILHELM II**
**Obv:** The profile portrait of a man wearing a steel helmet of the Garde du Corps with links, facing left. No legend.
Incised below truncation: LÖWENTAL
**Rev:** The head of an eagle with laurel branch below.
Legend in relief in two lines in field below beak: WILHELM / II
[A] **Bronze medal   67mm diameter.**
    (1) Münzkabinett, Staatliche Museen zu Berlin, Germany 18205775
    (Illustration on website)

**LOE058 n.d. (1915)  ALFRED VON TIRPITZ** (1849-1930) German Grand Admiral and Secretary of State of the Imperial Naval Office.
**Obv:** The profile head and shoulders portrait of a bearded man in uniform, facing left. No legend
Facsimile of Tirpitz's signature incised in field to right of portrait.
**Rev:** The rear view of a naked male archer aiming to the left.
Legend in relief around the rim: ZIEL · ERKANNT KRAFT · GESPANNT
Incised on bottom rim: ALÖEWENTAL · F ·
**(Illustration in Steguweit 1998, 128)**
[A] **Cast bronze medal  73mm diameter  General issue**
    (1) The Kadman Numismatic Pavilion, Tel-Aviv, Israel  K67162
[B] **Cast iron medal  73mm diameter  General issue**
    (1) Der Königlichen Museen zu Berlin, Germany  MKB446/1919
    (2) British Museum, London  BM1919-6-10-37
    (3) Imperial War Museum, London  MED550
[C] **Cast iron medal, silver plated  73mm diameter  General issue**
    (1) Sold by Leipziger Munzhandlung und Auktion Heidrun Höhn, 2007
[D] **Cast bronze model of obverse  145mm diameter**
    (1) Der Königlichen Museen zu Berlin, Germany  MKB140/1916

**LOE059 1915 THE 1915 SUBMARINE BLOCKADE OF BRITAIN, ALFRED VON TIRPITZ**
**Obv:** The head and shoulders portrait of a bearded man in uniform, facing forward and slightly to the left.
Legend in relief around the rim: GROSSADMIRAL VON · TIRPITZ
**Rev:** Neptune rising from sea with a trident in his right hand and blowing a conch shell. A submarine approaches the English coast in the background with lighthouse in the distance.
Legend in relief around top rim: GOTT STRAFE ENGLAND
In relief in three lines in field to left of Neptune: **18 / FEBRUAR / 1915**
Incised along right hand side rim: A · LÖWENTAL · F
**(Illustration in Zetzmann 2002, 2117)**

[A] Struck silver medal   34mm diameter   General issue
     (1) An example sold by Chris Balm, England, 2006
     (2) The American Numismatic Society, New York, USA  2000.1.99
     (3) The National Maritime Museum, Greenwich, England  MEC2449
     Described as 'frosted silver', 35mm diameter.
[B] Struck silver medal  49mm diameter  General issue
     (1) British Museum, London  BM1916-7-7-10
     (2) Imperial War Museum, London  MED54
     (3) National Maritime Museum, Greenwich, England  MEC2450
[C] Struck bronze medal   48mm diameter   General issue
     (1) British Museum, London  BM1919-8-17-111
[D] Cast bronze medal  105mm dimater
     (1) The Ashmolean Museum, Oxford
     Presented by Loewental 15 December 1960.
[E] Struck iron medal   47mm diameter   General issue
     (1) The American Numismatic Society, New York, USA  1919.6.5

LOE060

### LOE060 n.d. (1915)  ALFRED VON TIRPITZ
**Obv:** The head and shoulders profile portrait of a bearded man in uniform, facing left.
Facsimile of Turpitz's signature incised in field to right of portrait.
Incised below portrait: **ALOEWENTAL · FECIT ·**
**Rev:** Uniface
[A] Cast bronze medal  74mm diameter
     (1) The Ashmolean Museum, Oxford
     Presented by Loewental 15 December 1960.

### LOE061 1915  COUNT ARTHUR VON POSADOWSKY-WIEHNER (1845–1932)
Minister of state
**Obv:** The profile head and shoulders portrait of a bearded man, facing right.
Legend in relief along right hand side rim: **POSADOWSKY**
In relief in two lines in field to left of portrait: **ALOEWENTAL · / 1915**
**Rev:** Uniface
(Illustration in Steguweit 1998, 111)
[A] Cast bronze medal   175mm diameter
     An example was exhibited at the Usher Art Gallery, Lincoln, in 1941/2.
     **NOT LOCATED**
     (1) Der Königlichen Museen zu Berlin, Germany  MKB135/1916

### LOE062 1915  ALEXANDER GIRARDI (1850-1918) Austrian singer of light opera.
**Portrait**  No other details
[A] Bronze
     Exhibited at the Beaux Art Gallery, London, in 1935.
     Exhibited at the Usher Art Gallery, Lincoln, in 1941/2.
     **NOT LOCATED**

### LOE063 1915  PROFESSOR ADOLPH WAGNER (1835–1917) Economist and financier,
professor of political science at Berlin University.
**Obv:** The profile head and shoulders portrait of a man, facing left.
Legend in relief in two lines in field below chin: **ADOLPH / WAGNER**
Incised in two lines in field to right of portrait: **ALÖWENTAL / 1915**
**Rev:** Uniface
(Illustration in Steguweit 1998, 110)
[A] Wax model on slate

(1) Der Königlichen Museen zu Berlin, Germany  MKB  without number
[B] Tin model
(1) Der Königlichen Museen zu Berlin, Germany  MKLB  without number
[C] Cast bronze medal  175mm diameter
(1) Der Königlichen Museen zu Berlin, Germany  MKB134/1916
(2) Der Königlichen Museen zu Berlin, Germany  MKB  without number


**LOE064 n.d. (1914) 'AUSTRO-GERMAN ALLIANCE', EMPEROR FRANZ JOSEPH I and KAISER WILHELM II**
**Obv:** The jugate profile head and shoulders portraits of two men in uniform, facing left.
Legend in relief around the rim: **FRANZ · IOSEF · I · WILHELM · II ·**
**Rev:** Two naked male warriors fighting Hydra.
Legend in relief around the rim: **EIN ENDE ALLER TÜCKE**
Incised at base: **A · LOEWENTAL · F ·**
Note: 'crossed ovals' monogram to left of signature on 34mm and 50mm diameter medals.
**(Illustration in Zetzmann 2002, 3011)**
[A] Struck silver medal  34mm diameter  General issue.
(1) The Jewish Museum, New York, USA  FB/LOWN-1
[B] Struck bronze medal  34mm diameter  General issue
(1) The Ashmolean Museum, Oxford
Presented by Loewental 15 December 1960.
[C] Struck silver medal  50mm diameter  General issue
An example exhibited at the Usher Art Gallery, Lincoln, in 1941/2.
(1) The British Museum, London BM1919-4-4-8
(2) The Imperial War Museum, London MED27
(3) The American Numismatic Society, New York, USA 2000.1.113
[D] Cast bronze medal  124mm diameter  General issue
An example of the reverse exhibited at the Usher Art Gallery, Lincoln, in 1941/2.
**NOT LOCATED**
(1) The Collection, Lincoln  LCNUG:1927/1876
Purchased from Loewental in 1948.
(2) Münzkabinett, Staatliche Museen zu Berlin, Berlin, Germany
120mm diameter


**LOE065 1915 WALTER FRIEDENSBURG** German naval lieutenant.
**Obv:** The profile head and shoulders portrait of a man in uniform, facing left.
Legend in relief around the rim: **OBERLEUTNANT ZUR SEE WALTER ·**
**FRIEDENSBURG**
Incised in two lines in field to right of portrait: **ALOEWENTAL · / 1915**
**Rev:** An eagle swoops to catch a fish from the sea.
Dates in relief in two lines in field to right of scene: **1914 / 1915**
Incised along left rim: **ALOEWENTAL**
**(Illustrated in Steguweit 1998, 114)**
[A] Cast bronze medal  90mm diameter  General issue
(1) The Königlichen Museen, Berlin, Germany MKB308/1916


**LOE066 n.d. (1915) 'THE DESTRUCTION OF THE U29, OTTO WEDDIGEN** (1882–1915) German submarine commander. He was killed with all hands in March 1915 when the new U-boat U-29, which he was commanding, sank after being rammed by the British battleship HMS Dreadnought. To commemorate his death.
**Obv:** The head and shoulders portrait of a man in uniform, facing forward and slightly to the left.
Legend in relief in two lines in field to left of portrait: **OTTO / WEDDIGEN**
Legend in relief in four lines in field to right of portrait: **KOMMAN / DANT · / AUF / „U29"**

Incised to left of portrait near the rim: Conjoined **AL** within a circle.

**Rev:** A Viking man standing in the stern of a sinking boat looking up at seagulls flying overhead.

Legend in relief around the rim: ·· EWIG · UNVERGESSEN · BLEIBE – KÜHNER · WIKING – DEINE · TODESFART

(Bold Viking, may thy death cruise remain for ever unforgotten)

Incised at left rim: **A · LÖWENTAL ·**

**(Illustration in Steguweit 1998, 107)**

**[A] Two-sided tin model**
> (1) Der Königlichen Museen zu Berlin, Germany

**[B] Struck silver medal  50mm diameter  General issue?**
> (1) Der Königlichen Museen zu Berlin, Germany  MKB  without number

**[C] Cast bronze medal  115mm diameter  General issue**
> (1) Der Königlichen Museen zu Berlin, Germany  MKB301/1916
> **114mm diameter**
> (2) The Kadman Numismatic Pavilion, Tel-Aviv, Israel  K67207
> (3) The National Maritime Museum, London  MEC2359

**[D] Cast iron medal  115mm diameter  General issue**
> (1) The Collection, Lincoln  LCNUG:1982/44
> (2) The Imperial War Museum, London  MED82
> (3) Der Königlichen Museen zu Berlin, Germany  MKB  without number
> **114mm diameter**
> (4) Ex Friedenberg private collection, USA. Sold, NOT LOCATED

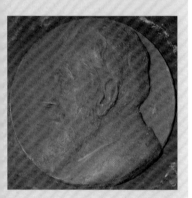

LOE068

**LOE067 n.d.  'TRIBUTE TO WOMEN IN AGRICULTURE'**

**Obv:** A peasant woman sowing. Lighthouse in left background.

Legend in relief around the rim: **TRAGE – TRAGE – REICHE – FRÜCHTE – DEUTSCHE – ERDE**

Incised at bottom right hand rim: **ALOEWENTAL**

**Rev:** An army man leaning on his rifle, his left foot on a rock, and smoking a pipe. Pines to left and church in background to right.

Incised at bottom left hand rim: **ALOEWENTAL**

**(Illustrated in Steguweit 1998, 116)**

**[A] Cast bronze medal  99mm diameter  General issue**
> An example exhibited at the Usher Art Gallery, Lincoln, in 1941/2.
> (1) The Königlichen Museen, Berlin, Germany  MKB315/1916

**LOE068 n.d. (1915)  PRINCE GUIDO HENCKEL VON DONNERSMARCK**

(1830–1916) Major Silesian industrialist and landowner. Member of the Prussian Upper Chamber.

**Obv:** The profile head and shoulders portrait of a bearded man, facing left.

Legend incised around the rim: **GUIDO · GRAF · HENCKEL · FÜRST VON DONNERSMARCK**

Incised in field to right of portrait: **A over L**

**Rev:** Uniface

**[A] Wax medal on slate  80mm diameter**
> (1) The Ashmolean Museum, Oxford
> Presented by Loewental in June 1961.

**LOE069  1915  PRINCE GUIDO HENCKEL VON DONNERSMARCK**

**Obv:** The profile head and shoulders portrait of a bearded man, facing left.
Legend in relief around the rim: **GUIDO · GRAF · HENCKEL · FÜRST VON DONNERSMARCK**
Date in relief in field to right of portrait: **1915**
Incised below date: **ALOEWENTAL**

**Rev:** Symbolic portrayal of blessing of mining. Fortune to right empties cornucopia of ore into a font. On the left a miner holds a sample. Coat of arms above. No legend.

[A] Uniface tin model of obverse   120mm diameter
      (1) Der Königlichen Museen zu Berlin, Germany  MKB139/1916

[B] Cast bronze medal   78mm diameter
      (1) The British Museum, London  BM1980-5-4-18
      (2) Der Königlichen Museen zu Berlin, Germany  MKB342/1916

LOE069

**LOE070  n.d. (1915)  COUNT FERDINAND ALBERT ALEXIS VON HAESELER** (1836–1919) German General Field Marshal. (Reverse of medal)

**Obv:** Chiron and Achilles.
Legend in relief around rim: **CHIRON ACHILL**
Incised along lower right rim: **ALOEWENTAL**

**Rev:** Uniface

(Illustration in Steguweit 1998, p.22)

[A] Stone model of reverse   113mm x113mm
      (1) Der Königlichen Museen zu Berlin, Germany  MKB  without number

**LOE071  1915  COUNT FERDINAND ALBERT ALEXIS VON HAESELER**

**Obv:** The profile head and shoulders portrait of a man in uniform and wearing a helmet, facing right.
Legend in relief around the rim: **FELDMARSCHALL GRAF · VON · HAESELER -1915 -**

**Rev:** Chiron and Achilles
Legend in relief around rim: **CHIRON ACHILL**
Incised along lower right rim: **ALOEWENTAL**

(Illustration in Steguweit 1998, 109)

[A] Cast bronze medal   100mm diameter  General issue
      An example exhibited at the Usher Art Gallery, Lincoln, in 1941/2.
      (1) Der Königlichen Museen zu Berlin, Germany  MKB  without number

[B] Cast iron medal   102mm diameter  General issue
      (1) The Imperial War Museum, London  MED255

**LOE072  1915  'THE GALICIAN OFFENSIVE', AUGUST VON MACKENSEN** (1849–1945) Considered one of the best commanders of the German Army during World War One. Promoted to Field Marshal in 1915.

**Obv:** A male nude holds down a buffalo by its horns
In relief in two lines in exergue: **GALIZIEN / 1915**
Incised in two lines in field below figure: **ALOEWENTAL / 1915**

**Rev:** Uniface

[A] Stone model of reverse
      (1) Der Königlichen Museen zu Berlin, Germany  MKB?

**LOE073 1915 'THE GALICIAN OFFENSIVE', AUGUST VON MACKENSEN**
**Obv:** The head and shoulders portrait of a man in uniform, facing forward.
Legend in relief around the rim: FELDMARSCHALL VON · MACKENSEN
**Rev:** A male nude holds down a buffalo by its horns.
In relief in two lines in exergue: GALIZIEN / 1915
Incised in two lines in field below figure: ALOEWENTAL / 1915
**(Illustrated in Steguweit 1998, 108; Zetzmann 2002, 4104)**
[A] Struck silver medal 50mm diameter General issue
    (1) Sold by Fritz Rudolf Künker GmbH & Co., Germany, 2007
[B] Struck bronze medal 50mm diameter General issue
    (1) The Imperial War Museum , London MED265
    (2) The Kadman Numismatic Pavilion, Tel-Aviv, Israel K66956
[C] Struck bronze medal, silver plated 50mm diameter General issue
    (1) Der Königlichen Museen zu Berlin, Germany MKB357/1916
[D] Cast bronze medal 100mm diameter General issue
    (1) Der Königlichen Museen zu Berlin, Germany MKB302/1916
[E] Cast bronze medal 110mm diameter General issue
    (1) The Kadman Numismatic Pavilion, Tel-Aviv, Israel K66961
    (2) The American Numismatic Society, New York, USA 2000.1.482


**LOE074 n.d. (1915) 'THE FALKLANDS WAR', COUNT MAXIMILIAN JOHANNES MARIA HUBERTUS VON SPEE (1861–1914). German Vice Admiral.**
At the Battle of the Falklands, 8 December 1914, heavily outgunned, six German ships, including Spee's own flagship were sunk, with some 2,200 sailors drowned, including Spee himself.
**Obv:** The head and shoulders portrait of a bearded man in uniform, facing forward and slightly to the right.
Legend in relief around the rim: VICEADMIRAL GRAF VON SPEE
Note: monogram of crossed elongated 'O's above shoulder on left side, on 50mm diameter medals only.
**Rev:** Nude female figure kneeling on a rock with eyes covered in grief by her right arm. A ship sinks in the background. Crescent moon above. No legend.
Incised below the rock: ALÖWENTAL
**(Illustration in Steguweit 1998, 106)**
[A] Two-sided bronze model
    (1) Der Königlichen Museen zu Berlin, Germany without number
[B] Struck silver medal 50mm diameter General issue
    (1) The British Museum, London BM1919-8-17-193
    (2) The Kadman Numismatic Pavilion, Tel-Aviv, Israel K67186
    (3) The American Numismatic Society, New York, USA 1916 189.2
    (4) The National Maritime Museum, Greenwich, England MEC 2440
[C] Cast bronze medal 98mm diameter General issue
    (1) The British Museum, London BM1993-8-25-3
    (2) The Kadman Numismatic Pavilion, Tel-Aviv, Israel K67191 99mm diameter
    (3) Der Königlichen Museen zu Berlin, Germany MKB without number
[D] Struck in iron 50mm diameter General issue
    (1) Der Königlichen Museen zu Berlin, Germany MKB352/1916
[E] Cast in iron 98.5mm diameter General issue
    (1) Der Königlichen Museen zu Berlin, Germany MKB295/1916
    (2) The National Maritime Museum, Greenwich, England MEC 2348
      99mm diameter

**LOE075 n.d. AUGUST VON MACKENSEN and PAUL VON HINDENBURG**
**Obv:** The jugate profile head and shoulder portraits of two men in uniform, facing left.
Legend in relief around the rim: MACKENDEN HINDENBURG
No artist's monogram.
**Rev:** No details. (Elchjagd in Poland).
**(Illustration in Steguweit 1998, 119)**
**[A] Plaster of Paris cast of obverse   123mm diameter**
      (1) Der Königlichen Museen zu Berlin, Germany (lost)
**[B] Cast bronze medal   123mm diameter**
      (1) Der Königlichen Museen zu Berlin, Germany  MKB338/1916

**LOE076 1916 GUSTAV KRUPP VON BOHLEN UND HALBACH** (1870–1950).
Major German industrialist. The Krupp field gun 'Big Bertha' played a vital role in the
German advance in 1914 and at Verdun in 1916.
**Obv:** The profile head and shoulders portrait of a man, facing left.
Legend in relief around the rim: GUSTAV KRUPP VON BOHLEN UND HALBACH 1916
In relief in field to right of portrait: ALOEWENTAL · F ·
**Rev:** Uniface
**(Illustration in Steguweit 1998, 122)**
**[A] Cast bronze medal   145mm diameter**
      An example exhibited at the Beaux Art Gallery, London, in 1935
      An example exhibited at the Usher Art Gallery, Lincoln, in 1941/2
      NOT LOCATED
      (1) Der Königlichen Museen zu Berlin, Germany  MKB142/1916

**LOE077 1916 MARGARETHE KRUPP** (1854–1931). The wife of Friedrich Alfred Krupp.
Daughter of the Prussian Baron August von Ende. She was involved in the planning and
building of the Margarethenhöhe housing estate, which, like the other company benefit
schemes, became a lifetime commitment.
**Obv:** The profile head and shoulders portrait of a lady, facing left.
Legend in relief around the rim: MARGARETHE KRUPP GER FREUN VON ENDE
In relief in two lines in field to right of portrait: 1916 / ALOEWENTAL · F ·
**Rev:** A kneeling female nude holding a cornucopia. A small roundel at the top with the
profile portrait of a bespectacled man, facing right. A scene with buldings.
Legend in relief in five lines in centre field: DES GATTEN / GEDAECHTNIS EHRT /
LEBENDES WEITER= / WIRKEN IN SEINEM / SINNE
Incised in two lines in exergue: MARGARETHEN = / HÖHE
Incised at left hand rim: ALOEWENTAL · FEC ·
**[A] Bronze medal   88mm diameter**
      Exhibited at the Beaux Art Gallery, London, in 1935.
      An example of the obverse exhibited at the Usher Art Gallery, Lincoln, in 1941/2.
      An example of the reverse exhibited at the Usher Art Gallery, Lincoln, in 1941/2.
      (1) The Collection, Lincoln  LCNUG:1982/42
      Purchased by the museum in 1981.
      (2) The American Numismatic Society, New York, USA  2000.1.454

LOE077

**LOE078 1916 MARGARETHE KRUPP**
No other details
**[A] Cast bronze medal   155mm diameter**
      (1) Ex Friedenberg private collection, USA   NOT LOCATED

**LOE079**

**LOE079 n.d. ALFRIED KRUPP VON BOHLEN UND HALBACH** (1907–1967).
Eldest son of Gustav Krupp von Bohlen und Halbach.
**Obv:** The profile head and shoulders portrait of a young boy, aged eight, facing left. To celebrate his 8th birthday.
Legend in relief in field to right of portrait: **ALFRIED**
In relief in two lines in field below chin: **AET · S · AO = / VIII ·**
Incised along right hand lower rim: **ALOEWENTAL · FEC ·**
**Rev:** Uniface
**[A] Cast bronze medal   114mm diameter**
      Exhibited at the Beaux Art Gallery, London, in 1935.
      Exhibited at the Usher Art Gallery, Lincoln, in 1941/2.
      (1) The Lee private collection, England

**LOE080 1916 CLAUS ARTHUR ARNOLD (KRUPP) VON BOHLEN UND HALBACH**
(1910–1940). Son of Gustav Krupp von Bohlen und Halbach.
No other details
**[A] Bronze**
      Exhibited at the Beaux Art Gallery, London, in 1935.
      Exhibited at the Usher Art Gallery, Lincoln, in 1941/2.   **NOT LOCATED**

**LOE081**

**LOE081 1916 'DER ERSTE GAST AUF DER MESSE ZU LYON'** Satirical of Edward Herriot, Mayor of Lyon and French Minister of Transport and Supply.
**Obv:** A man drives a donkey over a three-arched bridge.
Legend in relief around the rim: **·· DER · ERSTE · GAST · AVF · DER · MESSE · ZV · LYON · 1916**
Incised near base: **ALOEWENTAL**
**Rev:** Legend in relief in eight lines within a double beaded border: **HERRIOT / DEM / BÜRGERMEISTER / VON LYON / ALS ERSATZ / FÜR DEN / ALTEN SIEGEL = / STEMPEL**
**[A] Two-sided bronze model**
      (1) Der Königlichen Museen zu Berlin, Germany. Without number
**[B] Cast iron medal   73mm diameter   General issue**
      (1) The British Museum, London  BM1919-6-10-45
      (2) The Imperial War Museum, London  MED771
      (3) Der Königlichen Museen zu Berlin, Germany  MKB724/1922
      (4) The Rezak private collection, USA

**LOE082 1916 'BRITISCHE VERTRAGSTREUE'** Satirical of Asquith.
**Obv:** British bulldog tearing up document.
Legend in relief around the rim, terminating in an olive twig: **BRITISCHE VERTRAGSTREUE**
In relief in exergue: **ALOEWENTAL**
**Rev:** Legend in relief in border garter: **HONI SOIT QVI MAL Y PENSE**
Legend in relief in eight lines within garter: **DEM / „EHRENWERTEN" / HERRN / ASQVITH / ERNEUERT / NACH / DENON-GEVFFROY / 1916**
**[A] Cast iron medal   73mm diameter   General issue**
      (1) The British Museum, London  BM1919-6-10-33
      (2) The Imperial War Museum, London  MED485
      (3) Der Königlichen Museen zu Berlin, Germany  MKB without number
      (4) The Rezak private collection, USA

**LOE082**

**LOE083** 1916 BARON MORITZ FERDINAND VON BISSING (1844–1917) Former Prussian General der Kavallie. Appointed Governor General of occupied Belgium in 1914 until his death.

**Obv:** The profile head and shoulders portrait of a man in uniform, facing left. No legend. In relief in three lines in field to right of portrait: **ALOEWENTAL / BRÜSSEL / 1916** Facsimile of Bissing's signature incised in field below chin.

**Rev:** Uniface

(Illustration in Steguweit 1998, 129)

[A] Cast bronze model   146mm diameter
         (1) Der Königlichen Museen zu Berlin, Germany  MKB422/1919


**LOE084** 1916 BARONESS ALICE VON BISSING, née COUNTESS KÖNIGSMARCK
The wife of Baron Moritz Ferdinand von Bissing.

**Obv:** The profile head and shoulders portrait of a lady, facing left.
Legend in relief around the rim: **ALICE · FREIIN · VON · BISSING · GEBORENE · GRAEFIN · KÖNIGSMARCK**
Date in relief in field to right of portrait: **1916**
Incised in two lines below date: **ALOEWENTAL / F**

(Illustration in Steguweit 1998, 130)

[A] Cast bronze model   142mm diameter
         An example exhibited at the Beaux Art Gallery, London, in 1935.
         An example exhibited at the Usher Art Gallery, Lincoln, in 1941/2.
         (1) Der Königlichen Museen zu Berlin, Germany  MKB423/1919


**LOE085** n.d. (1916) OTTO WOLFF Steel industrialist of Cologne.
**Obv:** The profile portrait of a man, facing left. No artist's signature.
Legend in relief in two lines at lower right hand corner: **OTTO / WOLFF**
**Rev:** Uniface
[A] Cast bronze plaque  165 x 197mm
         (1) The Ashmolean Museum, Oxford
         Presented by Loewental 15 December 1960.

LOE085


**LOE086** 1916 ALEXANDRA VIKTORIA VON SCHLESWIG-HOLSTEIN-SONDERBURG-GLÜCKSBURG (PRINCESS AUGUST WILHELM OF PRUSSIA) (1887–1957)
**Obv:** The profile head and shoulders portrait of a lady, facing left.
Legend in relief in two lines in field beneath chin: **ALEXANDRA / VIKTORIA**
In relief in two lines in field to right of portrait: **ALOEWENTAL / 1916**
**Rev:** Uniface
(Illustration in Steguweit 1998, 115)
[A] Cast brass medal  158mm diameter
         (1) Der Königlichen Museen zu Berlin, Germany  MKB138/1916


**LOE087** 1916 PRINCE GUIDO HENCKEL VON DONNERSMARCK (1830–1916).
Major Silesian industrialist and landowner. Member of the Prussian Upper Chamber.
No other details
[A] Stone die of reverse
         Exhibited at the Usher Art Gallery, Lincoln, in 1941/2.  **NOT LOCATED**

**LOE088 1916 PRINCE GUIDO HENCKEL VON DONNERSMARCK**
No other details
[A] **Bronze of reverse**
>    Exhibited at the Beaux Art Gallery, London, in 1935.
>    Exhibited at the Usher Art Gallery, Lincoln, in 1941/2. **NOT LOCATED**

**LOE089 1916 COUNT ANDREAS MALTZAN**
No other details
[A] **Bronze**
>    Exhibited at the Usher Art Gallery, Lincoln, in 1941/2. **NOT LOCATED**

**LOE090 1916 KARL VON BÜLOW** (1846–1921) German Field Marshal who
commanded the German 2nd Army during World War One from 1914-1916.
**Obv:** The profile head and shoulders portrait of a man in uniform, facing left.
Legend in relief around left hand rim: **GENERALFELDMARSCHALL · V · BÜLOW**
In relief in two lines in field to right of portrait: **ALOEWENTAL / 1916**
**Rev:** A male nude fights with a lion
Legend in relief in three lines in field to left of scene: **DEM / SIEG - / ER**
Legend in relief in three lines in field to right of scene: **VON / ST · / QVENTIN**
Incised on exergue: **ALOEWENTAL · Fec**
**(Illustrated in Steguweit 1998, 112)**
[A] **Two-sided bronze model**
>    (1) **Der Königlichen Museen zu Berlin, Germany**
[B] **Cast bronze medal 82mm diameter General issue**
>    (1) **The Kadman Numismatic Pavilion, Tel-Aviv, Israel K66995**
[C] **Cast iron medal 82mm diameter General issue**
>    (1) **Der Königlichen Museen zu Berlin, Germany MKB340/1916**
[D] **Cast bronze medal of obverse 175mm diameter**
>    (1) **Der Königlichen Museen zu Berlin, Germany MKB136/1916**

**LOE091 1916 COUNT NIKOLAUS PAUL RICHARD ZU DOHNA-SCHLODIEN**
(1879–1956) German naval officer and author. Commandant of the minelayer and armed
merchantman *Möwe* (*Seagull*).
**Obv:** The profile portrait of a man, facing left
Legend in relief around the rim: **GRAF · DOHNA-SCHLODIEN · KOMMANDANT ·
DER · MOEWE 1916**
In relief in field to right of portrait: **A over L**
**Rev:** A Centaur riding the crest of a wave, holding aloft a large sea shell.
Incised along right hand side rim: **ALOEWENTAL**
**(Illustrated in Steguweit 1998, 131)**
[A] **Cast bronze medal 98mm diameter General issue**
>    (1) **The Collection, Lincoln LCNUG:1982/43**
>    Purchased by the museum in 1981.
>    (2) **Der Königlichen Museen zu Berlin, Germany MKB339/1916**
>       **100mm diameter**

LOE092

**LOE092 1916 COUNTESS MENGERSON** German head of the Red Cross in Belgium.
**Obv:** The profile portrait of a lady, facing left, pinned up hair and wearing a pearl earring.
Legend in relief in two lines in field to right of portrait: **BRÜSSEL / 1916 ·**
In relief on truncation: **ALOEWENTAL · F ·**
**Rev:** Uniface
[A] **Cast bronze medal 154mm diameter**
>    Exhibited at the Beaux Art Gallery, London, in 1935.
>    Exhibited at the Usher Art Gallery, Lincoln, in 1941/2.
>    (1) **The Collection, Lincoln LCNUG:1927/1871**
>    Purchased from Loewental in 1948.

**LOE093 n.d PROFESSOR FRITZ RAUSENBERGER** (1868–1926).
Professor at the Militärtechn. Akademie in Charlottenburg.
**Obv:** Portrait
**Rev:** Archimedes.
No other details
   **Reference:** Steguweit 1998, 123


**LOE094 1916 PROFESSOR BARON EMMO FRIEDRICH RICHARD ULRICH VON WILAMOWITZ-MOELLENDORFF** (1848–1931) Greek historian and rector of the University of Berlin. **Obverse only**
**Obv:** The profile head and shoulders portrait of a man, facing left.
Legend in relief around the rim: **ULRICII VON WILAMOWITZ-MOELLENDORFF**
In relief in two lines in field to right of portrait: **ALOEWENTAL / 1916**
**Rev:** Uniface
(Illustration in Steguweit 1998, 124)
[A] **Uniface bronze model   158mm diameter**
  (1) Der Königlichen Museen zu Berlin, Germany  MKB141/1916
[B] **Cast brass medal   79mm diameter**
  (1) Der Königlichen Museen zu Berlin, Germany  MKB734/1922


**LOE095 1916 PROFESSOR BARON EMMO FRIEDRICH RICHARD ULRICH VON WILAMOWITZ-MOELLENDORFF Reverse only**
**Obv:** An Athenian head looking to the right. Below a laurel bush.
Legend in relief in two lines across the centre field: **ΟΥΓΑΥΣΟΜΛΙΤΛΣΧΑΡΙΤΛΣ / ΜΟΥΣΛΣΣΥΝΚΑΤΑΜΕΙΓΝΥΣ**
**Rev:** Uniface
(Illustration in Steguweit 1998, 124)
[A] **Cast brass medal   85mm diameter**
  (1) Der Königlichen Museen zu Berlin, Germany  MKB304/1923


**LOE096 1916 KAISER WILHELM II** (1859–1941) Kaiser of Germany and King of Prussia.
**Obv:** The profile portrait of a man, facing left. An oak leaf below truncation.
Legend in relief around the rim: **WILHELM II · DEUTSCHER KAISER · 1916 ·**
**Rev:** The Kaiser in armour riding a horse to the left. Sword in right hand and lance in left, which has a banner reading: **PRO DEO**
Legend in relief in three lines in field to left of rider: **HIE GUT / ZOLLERN / ALLE WEGE**
In relief in exergue: **ALOEWENTAL ·**
(Illustration in Steguweit 1998, 127)
[A] **Cast bronze medal  91mm diameter  General issue**
  (1) Der Königlichen Museen zu Berlin, Germany  MKB326/1916
  (2) Der Königlichen Museen zu Berlin, Germany  MKB453/1919
  (3) Das Münzkabinett, Staatliche Museen zu Berlin, Germany  18214555
   92mm diameter


**LOE097 1916 'THE MEETING AT NISCH', KING FERDINAND OF BULGARIA and KAISER WILHELM II**
**Obv:** The profile portraits of two men, facing each other. A crowned eagle flies above. The town crest of Nisch at base.
In relief around the town crest: **19 NISCH 16**
**Rev:** A Viking warrior, with a spear in his right hand and his left foot on a boar, blows his horn. Scene of Egyptian pyramids and sphinx with crescent moon to right and St Sophia, Turkey, to the left.

Incised along left hand rim: ALOEWENTAL · F
(Illustration in Steguweit 1998, 120.)
[A] A two-sided bronze model
    (1) Der Königlichen Museen zu Berlin, Germany
[B] Cast bronze medal   93mm diameter   General issue
    (1) The Imperial War Museum, London  MED551
    (2) The Kadman Numismatic Pavilion, Tel-Aviv, Israel  K66796
    (3) Der Königlichen Museen zu Berlin, Germany.  MKB327/1916
       92mm diameter

### LOE098  1917  COUNTESS VON MALTZAN
No other details
[A] Bronze
    Exhibited at the Usher Art Gallery, Lincoln, in 1941/2.  **NOT LOCATED**

### LOE099  1917  'VICTOR OF KOWNO', KARL LITZMANN (1850–1936)
German general, the Victor of Kowno, 1917.
**Obv:** The profile head and shoulders portrait of a man in uniform, facing left.
Legend in relief along right hand rim: LITZMANN
Incised in two lines in field to right of portrait: ALOEWENTAL / 1917
**Rev:** Siegfried walking through flames.
Legend in relief around the rim: DURCH · LOHENDE · FLAMMEN · SCHRITT · KÜHN · SIEGFRID · DER · HELD
In relief in two lines at base: KOWNO / 1915
(Illustration in Steguweit 1998, 118)
[A] Cast bronze medal   68mm diameter   General issue
    An example exhibited at the Beaux Art Gallery, London, in 1935.
    An example exhibited at the Usher Art gallery, Lincoln, in 1941/2.
    An example of the obverse exhibited at the Usher art Gallery, Lincoln, in 1941/2.
    **NOT LOCATED**
    An example of the reverse exhibited at the Usher Art Gallery, Lincoln, in 1941/2.
    **NOT LOCATED**
    (1) The British Museum, London BM1937-1-2-1
    (2) The Ashmolean Museum, Oxford
    Presented by Loewental 15 December 1960
    (3) Der Königlichen Museen zu Berlin, Germany  MKB270/1927
       69mm diameter

**LOE106**

**LOE107**

### LOE100  1917  BARON HANS EBERHARD VON BODENHAUSEN-DEGENER (1868–1918)
German chemical industrialist. Served on the board of Krupps. Went into politics.
An important figure in German and European cultural movement at turn of the century.
No other details
[A] Bronze
    Exhibited at the Usher Art Gallery, Lincoln, in 1941/2.  **NOT LOCATED**

### LOE101  n.d.  DR JOHANNES HASS  Leader of the Centrum Party, Bavarian Catholics.
No other details
[A] Bronze
    Exhibited at the Usher Art Gallery, Lincoln, in 1941/2.  **NOT LOCATED**

### LOE102  1918  HARALD, portrait of a child
No other details
[A] Bronze
    Exhibited at the Usher Art Gallery, Lincoln, in 1941/2.  **NOT LOCATED**

**LOE103 1919 OTTO WOLFF** Steel industrialist of Cologne.
**No other details**
[A] **Bronze**
> Exhibited at the Beaux Art Gallery, London, in 1935.
> Exhibited at the Usher art Gallery, Lincoln, in 1941/2. **NOT LOCATED**

**LOE104 1920 PRINCESS FULVIA ORSINI of Italy**
No other details
[A] **Bronze**
> Exhibited at the Beaux Art Gallery, London, in 1935.
> Exhibited at the Usher Art Gallery, Lincoln, in 1941/2. **NOT LOCATED**

**LOE105 1920 HERR STERNE**
No other details
[A] **Bronze**
> Exhibited at the Usher Art Gallery, Lincoln, in 1941/2. **NOT LOCATED**

**LOE106 n.d. (1924) ANTONIA LOEWENTAL** (1850–1942) The sculptor Artur Loewental's mother.
**Obv:** The profile head and shoulders portrait of a lady, facing left.
Legend in relief in two lines in field to right of portrait: **ANTONIA / LOEWENTAL**
Incised on rim to right of portrait: **ALOEWENTAL**
**Rev:** Uniface
[A] **Cast bronze medal 130mm diameter**
> (1) The McNichol private collection, England
> Housed in original blue-lined case, with gold lettering: Sy & Wagner, Berlin.

**LOE107 1924 ANTONIA LOEWENTAL** (1850–1942)
**Obv:** The profile head and shoulders portrait of a lady, facing left. No legend.
Incised at lower right hand corner: **ALÖWENTAL · 1924**
**Rev:** Uniface
[A] **Cast bronze plaque 130 x 170mm**
> (1) The Jackson private collection, England
> Purchased at the 1980 Bauer sale.

**LOE108 n.d. PAULA AUGUSTE LOEWENTAL** (born 1882) The sculptor Artur Loewental's sister.
**Descr:** Model portrait bust of a lady's head, with short hair and wearing earrings.
No artist's monogram. The casting seam and pencil measuring points are clearly visible.
[A] **Plaster of Paris cast 375mm high**
> (1) The Collection, Lincoln **LCNUG:1927/2062**
> Presented by Loewental.

**LOE109 n.d. CLARA OTTILIE LOEWENTAL** (1875–1944) The sculptor Artur Loewental's sister.
**Descr:** Model portrait bust of a lady's head, with short hair and a side parting on her right.
No artist's monogram.
[A] **Plaster of Paris cast 390mm high**
> (1) The Collection, Lincoln **LCNUG:1927/2050**
> Presented by Loewental.

LOE108

LOE109

LOE110

LOE112

LOE113

LOE114

LOE115

LOE116

**LOE110 n.d. ARTUR IMMANUEL LOEWENTAL** (1879–1964) Self portrait of the sculptor.
**Obv:** The profile portrait of a man, facing left. No date or artist's signature.
In relief in two lines in field to right of portrait: **ARTUR / LÖWENTAL**
**Rev:** Uniface
**[A] Cast bronze medal   142mm diameter**
   (1) **The Collection, Lincoln  LCNUG:1927/1872**
   Purchased from Loewental in 1948.

**LOE111  1925  PAUL LUDWIG HANS ANTON VON BENECKENDORFF UND VON HINDENBURG** (1847–1934) President of the Wiemar Republic.
No other details
**[C] Silver**
   Exhibited at the Beaux Art Gallery, London, in 1935.
   Exhibited at the Usher Art Gallery, Lincoln, in 1941/2.  **NOT LOCATED**

**LOE112 n.d. 'ROSA LAVOROSA'** (1881-1958). The sculptor Artur Loewental's wife, Rosa Katharina Josepha.
**Obv:** The profile portrait of a lady wearing a headscarf, facing left.
Legend incised in three lines in field to right of portrait: **ROSA / LAVOROSA / A over L**
**Rev:** Uniface
**[A] Plaster of Paris cast   130mm diameter**
   Exhibited at the Usher Art Gallery, Lincoln, in 1944.
   Exhibited at the Usher Art Gallery, Lincoln, in 1946.
   (1) **The Bauer private collection, England**

**LOE113 n.d. 'ROSA LAVOROSA'**
**Obv:** The profile portrait of a lady wearing a headscarf, facing left.
Legend incised in three lines in field to right of portrait: **ROSA / LAVOROSA / A over L**
**Rev:** Uniface
**[A] Cast bronze medal   130mm diameter**
   (1) **The Collection, Lincoln  LCNUG:1927/1870**
   Purchased from Loewental in 1948.
   (2) **The Fennell private collection, England**
   Same legend but register of lettering differs.
   (3) **The American Numismatic Society, New York, USA  1999.39.30**
   **125mm diameter**
   Same legend but register of lettering differs.

**LOE114 n.d. [1926]  PROFESSOR FRITZ KREISLER** (1875–1962) Austrian-born violinist and composer. One of the most accomplished violinists of his time.
**Obv:** The profile portrait of a man, facing left.
Legend in relief around the rim: **PROFESSOR FRITZ KREISLER**
Incised on truncation: **ALÖWENTAL**
**Rev:** A classical nude male figure playing a lyre.
In relief at top rim: **ΟΡΦΕΥΣ**
Legend in relief in two lines in fields to either side of figure: **DEM · GROSSEN KÜNSTER · UND / EDLEN MENSCHEN**
**[A] Bronze medal   140mm diameter**
   Exhibited at the Beaux Art Gallery, London, in 1935.
   Exhibited at the Usher Art Gallery, London, in 1939.
   An example of the obverse exhibited at the Usher Art Gallery, Lincoln, in 1941/2.
   **NOT LOCATED**
   An example of the reverse exhibited at the Usher Art Gallery, Lincoln, in 1941/2.
   **NOT LOCATED**
   (1) **The Collection, Lincoln  LCNUG:1927/1878**

**LOE115 n.d. (1926) ADOLPH DONATH** (1876–1937) Czechoslovakian poet and connoisseur. To celebrate his 50th birthday.

**Obv:** The profile portrait of a man, facing left.
Legend in relief in two lines in field to right of portrait: ADOLPH / DONATH
In relief in two lines in field under chin: AETAT · S · AO / L ·
Incised on truncation: ALÖWENTAL · FEC ·
**Rev:** Uniface
[A] Cast bronze medal   188mm diameter
    (1) The Bauer private collection, England
[B] Cast brass medal   177mm diameter
    (1) Zezula Auction (Illustrated on website)

LOE118

**LOE116 1926 ADOLPH DONATH**

**Obv:** The profile portrait of a man, facing left.
Legend in relief in two lines in field to right of portrait: ADOLPH / DONATH
In relief in two lines in field under chin: AETAT · S · AO / L ·
Incised on truncation: ALÖWENTAL · FEC ·
**Rev:** A nude male figure, holding a small angel in his right hand and a book in the other.
Legend in relief around rim: ARTIBUS STUDIISQVE
In relief in three lines on the book: DER / KUNST / WAND
In relief in exergue: 1926 ·
[A] Bronze medal   80mm diameter
    (1) The Collection, Lincoln  LCNUG:1927/1874
    Purchased from Loewental in 1948.
    (2) The Ashmolean Museum, Oxford
    Presented by Loewental 15 December 1960.

LOE120

**LOE117 n.d. (1926) DR WILHELM VON BODE** (1845–1929). German art historian. General Director of German museums.

**Obv:** The profile portrait of a man, facing left.
Legend in relief in field to right of portrait: BODE
Incised along lower right rim: ALÖWENTAL · FECIT
**Rev:** Unknown
**(Illustration in *Der Kunstwanderer*, 1926/7)**
[A] Bronze medal   Size unknown
    An example exhibited at the Beaux Art Gallery, London, in 1935.
    Three examples exhibited at the Usher Art Gallery, Lincoln, in 1941/2.
    **NOT LOCATED**

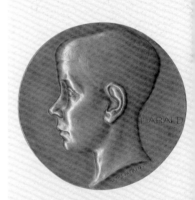

LOE121

**LOE118 1927 THEODOR DÄUBLER** (1876–1934) German poet, born in Italy.
**Obv:** The profile portrait of a bearded man, facing left.
Legend in relief down right hand rim: THEODOR · DÄVBLER
In relief in two lines in field to right of portrait: A over L / 1927
**Rev:** Uniface
[A] Cast bronze medal  78mm diameter
    (1) The British Museum, London  BM1981-9-16-1

**LOE119 1927 DR FRIEDRICH WILHELM KARL THIMME** (1868–1938)
Historian and political publicist
No other details
[A] Bronze plaque
    Reference: Lepsius, 1927, *Berliner Tageblatt*, morning edition, 1-3-1927.

LOE122

**LOE120  1927  DR ALFRED KERR** (1867–1948) Poet, journalist and dramatic critic.
**Obv:** The profile head and shoulders portrait of a man, facing left.
Legend in relief in three lines in field below chin: **DR · ALFRED / KERR / 1927**
In relief in two lines in field to right of portrait: **A · LOEWENTAL / FECIT**
**Rev:** Uniface
**[A] Cast bronze plaque  175mm x 210mm**
> Exhibited at the Usher Art Gallery, Lincoln, in 1941/2.
> **(1) The Bauer private collection, England**

**LOE121  n.d. (1927)  'HARALD', portrait of a child**
**Obv:** The profile portrait of a young boy, facing left.
Legend incised in field to right of portrait: **HARALD**
Incised below truncation: **ALÖWENTAL · F ·**
**Rev:** Uniface
**[A] Cast bronze medal  167mm diameter**
> An example exhibited at the Usher Art Gallery, Lincoln, in 1941/2.
> **(1) The Rezak private collection, USA**

**LOE122  n.d. (1927)  'HERBERT', portrait of a child**
**Obv:** The profile portrait of a young boy, facing left.
Legend in relief in field below chin: **HERBERT**
Incised below truncation: **ALÖWENTAL · F ·**
**Rev:** Uniface
**[A] Cast bronze plaque  155mm x 191mm**
> An example exhibited at the Usher Art Gallery, Lincoln, in 1941/2.
> **(1) The Collection, Lincoln  LCNUG:1927/1869**
> Purchased from Loewental in 1948.

**LOE123  1927  DR OTTO MERCKENS**
Managing Director and Chairman of the NSU-Werke, Neckarsulm.
**Obv:** The profile head and shoulders portrait of a man, facing left.
Legend in relief in three lines below truncation: **DR· OTTO / MERCKENS / 1927 ·**
Incised at lower right hand border: **A.LOEWENTAL**
**Rev:** Uniface
**[A] Cast bronze plaque  161 x 202.5mm**
> **(1) Example offered on German eBay auction, 2007**

**LOE124**

**LOE124  1927  DR OTTO MERCKENS**
**Obv:** The profile head and shoulders portrait of a man, facing left. No artist's signature.
Legend in relief in three lines below truncation: **DR· OTTO / MERCKENS / 1927 ·**
**Rev:** Uniface
**[A] Cast bronze plaque  165 x 197mm**
> **(1) The Ashmolean Museum, Oxford**
> Presented by Loewental 15 December 1960.

**LOE125**

**LOE125  1927  GUSTAV BÖSS** Progressive Mayor of Berlin.
**Obv:** The profile portrait of a bespectacled man, facing left. No artist's signature.
Legend in relief in four lines in field below truncation: **OBERBÜRGER / MEISTER / GUSTAV · BÖSS / · MCMXXVII ·**
Facsimile of Böss's signature incised in field below chin.
**Rev:** Uniface
**[A] Cast bronze plaque   Size unknown**
> Known from photograph only. **The Turner private collection, England**
> Two examples exhibited at the Usher Art Gallery, Lincoln in, 1941/2. Described in catalogue as 1928.  **NOT LOCATED**

**LOE126  1928  CHARLES AHL** Finnish goldsmith.
**Obv:** The profile portrait of a bespectacled man, facing left.
Legend in relief in three lines in field to right of portrait: **CHARLES / AHL / AURIFEX**
Incised in two lines below truncation: **ALOEWENTAL · FEC · / 1928**
**Rev:** Uniface
**[A] Cast bronze medal   143mm diameter**
> Exhibited at the Beaux Art Gallery, London, in 1935.
> Exhibited at the Usher Art Gallery, Lincoln, in 1941/2.
> **(1) The Ashmolean Museum, Oxford**
> Presented by Loewental 15 December 1960.

LOE126

**LOE127  1928  ROBERT WEISMANN** The last democratic Secretary of State of Prussia.
No other details
**[A] Bronze**
> Exhibited at the Usher Art Gallery, Lincoln, in 1941/2.  **NOT LOCATED**


**LOE128  1928  HERR MATTER** Clerk to the Mayor of Berlin.
No other details
**[A] Bronze**
> Exhibited at the Usher Art Gallery, Lincoln, in 1941/2.  **NOT LOCATED**


**LOE129  1928  DR JOHANNES HASS** Leader of the Centrum Party, Bavarian Catholics.
No other details
**[A] Bronze**
> Exhibited at the Beaux Art Gallery, London, in 1935.
> Exhibited at the Usher Art Gallery, Lincoln, in 1941/2.  **NOT LOCATED**


**LOE130  1928  PAUL LOEBE** President of the Reichstag.
No other details
**[A] Bronze**
> Two examples exhibited at the Usher Art Gallery, Lincoln, in 1941/2.
> **NOT LOCATED**


**LOE131  1928  ALFRED FLECHTHEIM** (1878–1937)
German art dealer of international fame.
No other details
**[A] Bronze**
> Exhibited at the Usher Art Gallery, Lincoln, in 1941/2.  **NOT LOCATED**


**LOE132  1928  UNIDENTIFIED SITTER**
**Obv:** The profile head and shoulders portrait of a bearded man, unidentified, facing left.
No legend.
In relief in three lines in field to right of portrait: **1928 / ALÖWENTAL / FEC ·**
**Rev:** Uniface
**[A] Cast bronze medal   142mm diameter**
> **(1) The Bauer private collection, England**

LOE132

**LOE133**

**LOE133  1928  PROFESSOR EMMO FRIEDRICH RICHARD ULRICH VON WILAMOWITZ-MOELLENDORFF** (1848–1931). Greek historian and rector of the University of Berlin.

Obv: The profile head and shoulders portrait of a man, facing left.
Legend in relief around the rim: **ULRICH VON WILAMOWITZ-MOELLENDORFF**
In relief in two lines in field to right of portrait: **ALÖWENTAL / 1928**
Rev: Uniface
[A] **Cast bronze medal   156mm diameter**
      Exhibited at the Beaux Art Gallery, London, in 1935.
      Exhibited at the Usher Art Gallery, Lincoln, in 1941/2.
      (1) The British Museum, London  BM1984-11-1-2

**LOE135**

**LOE134  1928  CAPTAIN GEYGER** A noted connoisseur.
No other details
[A] **Bronze**
      Exhibited at the Usher art gallery, Lincoln, in 1941/2   **NOT LOCATED**

**LOE135  1928  MAX JACOB FRIEDLAENDER** (1867–1958) German art historian and Director General of German museums, successor to Bode.

Obv: The profile portrait of a man, facing left.
Legend incised in field below portrait: **MAX · FRIEDLAENDER**
Incised along lower border: **ALÖWENTAL  F · MCMXXIIX** [sic]
Rev: Uniface
[A] **Cast bronze plaque   172mm x 210mm**
      (1) The Bauer private collection, England

**LOE136**

**LOE136  1929  BARON EHRENFRIED GÜNTHER VON HÜNEFELD** (1892–1929) German aviation pioneer and initiator of the first transatlantic flight in east-west direction.

Obv: The profile portrait of a man, facing left.
Legend in relief around the rim: **GÜNTHER · EHRENFRIED · FREIHERE VON · HÜNEFELD ·· I · 1929**
In relief below truncation: **ALOEWENTAL ·**
Rev: Uniface
[A] **Cast bronze medal   124mm diameter**
      An example exhibited at the Beaux Art Gallery, London, in 1935.
      Two examples exhibited at the Usher Art Gallery, Lincoln, in 1941/2.
      (1) The Rezak private collection, USA

**LOE137  1929  PROFESSOR JACOB GOULD SCHURMAN** (1854–1942) American ambassador to Germany between 1925 and 1929.
No other details
[A] **Bronze**
      Exhibited at the Beaux Art Gallery, London, in 1935.
      Exhibited at the Usher Art Gallery, Lincoln, in 1941/2.  **NOT LOCATED**

**LOE138**

**LOE138  1929  UNIDENTIFIED SITTER**

Obv: The profile portrait of a man, facing left.
In relief on right hand lower border: **MCMXXIX**
Incised on left hand lower border: **ALOEWENTAL · FEC ·**
Obv: Uniface
[A] **Cast bronze plaque   180mm x 210mm**
      (1) The Bauer private collection, England

**LOE139  n.d. (1929)  MAX JACOB FRIEDLAENDER** (1867–1958) German art historian and Director General of German museums, successor to Bode.

**Obv:** The profile portrait of a man, facing left.
Legend in relief around right hand side rim: MAX · FRIEDLAENDER
No artist's monogram.

**Rev:** Uniface

**[A] Plaster of Paris cast   178mm diameter**
> An example exhibited at the Beaux Art Gallery, London, in 1935.
> Two examples exhibited at the Usher Art Gallery, Lincoln, in 1941/2.
> **(1) The Collection, Lincoln  LCNUG:1927/2054**
> Presented by Loewental.

LOE139

**LOE140  1929  THEODOR DÄUBLER** (1876–1934) German poet, born in Italy

**Obv:** The profile portrait of a bearded man, facing left.
Legend in relief in two lines in field below truncation: THEODOR / DÄUBLER
In relief in field to right of portrait: MCMXXIX
Incised on truncation: ALÖWENTAL

**Rev:** Uniface

**[A] Cast bronze medal   132mm diameter**
> Exhibited at the Usher Art Gallery, Lincoln, in 1941/2.
> Exhibited at the Usher Art Gallery, Lincoln, in 1955.
> **(1) The Collection, Lincoln  LCNUG:1983/38**
> Purchased in 1982.

LOE140

**LOE141  1929  DR HERMANN HÖPKER-ASCHOFF** (1883–1954)
The last democratic Minister of Finance of Prussia 1925 to 1931.

**Obv:** The profile portrait of a man, facing right.
Legend in relief in four lines in field to left of portrait: DR· / HÖPKER / -ASCHOFF / 1929 ·
Incised on truncation: ALÖWENTAL · F ·

**Rev:** Uniface

**[A] Cast bronze medal   174mm diameter**
> Exhibited at the Beaux Art Gallery, London, in 1935.
> Exhibited at the Fine Art Society, London, in 1939.
> Two examples exhibited at the Usher Art Gallery, Lincoln, in 1941/2.
> **(1) The Bauer private collection, England**

LOE141

**LOE142  1929  DR HERMANN HÖPKER-ASCHOFF**

**Obv:** The profile portrait of a man, facing right.
Legend in relief around the rim: DR· HÖPKER-ASCHOFF · PREUSSISCHER · FINANZ MINISTER
Date in relief in field to left of portrait: 1929
Incised below truncation: ALÖWENTAL

**Rev:** Eagle with outstretched wings.
Legend in relief around the rim: DURCH · ARBEIT · UND · SPARSAMKEIT · ZU · NEUEM · GLANZ (small oak leaf)

**[A] Bronze medal   91mm diameter**
> **(1) The Ashmolean Museum, Oxford**
> Presented by Loewental 15 December 1960.

LOE142

**LOE143**

**LOE145**

**LOE146**

**LOE147**

**LOE148**

**LOE143  1930 DR FRIEDRICH EICHBERG** Famous as an inventor of electrical machinery.

**Obv:** The profile head and shoulders portrait of a man, facing left.

Legend in relief in three lines in field below truncation: **DR· FRIEDRICH / EICHBERG / 1930**

In relief to right on lower border: **ALOEWENTAL · FECIT ·**

**Rev:** Uniface

[A] **Cast bronze plaque   182mm x 240mm**

      An example exhibited at the Usher Art Gallery, Lincoln, in 1941/2.

      (1) **The Rezak private collection, USA**


**LOE144  1930  PAUL LUDWIG HANS ANTON VON BENECKENDORFF UND VON HINDENBURG** (1847–1934) As president of the Weimar Republic 1925 to 1934.

**Obv:** The head and shoulders portrait of a man, facing left.

Legend in relief in four lines at base. No details.

**Rev:** Uniface

[A] **Cast bronze plaque   102mm x 137mm**

      (1) **Example sold on German eBay 17 May 2009**


**LOE145  1930  PROFESSOR ALBERT EINSTEIN** (1879–1955)

German-born theoretical physicist

**Descr:** The life-size portrait bust of a man, truncated at neck.

Incised at rear at the base of the neck: **ALOEWENTAL 1930**

[A] **Cast bronze bust   345mm high**

      Exhibited at the Beaux Art Gallery, London, in 1935.

      Exhibited at the Usher Art Gallery, Lincoln, in 1941/2.

      (1) **The Collection, Lincoln  LCNUG:1927/1846**

      Black patina and mounted on a polished stone base.

      Purchased from Loewental in 1945.


**LOE146  1930  PROFESSOR ALBERT EINSTEIN**

**Obv:** The profile portrait of a man, facing left.

Legend in relief in two lines along the top border: **ALBERT EINSTEIN / 1930**

Facsimile of Einstein's signature incised in field below truncation.

Incised along left bottom border: **ALOEWENTAL · FECIT ·**

**Rev:** Uniface

[A] **Cast bronze plaque   186mm x 216mm**

      (1) **The Jewish Museum, New York, USA  FB1062**

      Said to be 177mm x 209mm and undated.

      (2) **Unknown private collection, USA 178mm x 216mm   NOT LOCATED**

      Sold by auction by Alexander Autographs Inc., USA, in 2005.


**LOE147  n.d.  DR WILFRID GREIF** Director of I. G. Farben, New York, USA. To celebrate his 50th birthday.

**Obv:** The profile portrait of a man, facing left.

Legend in relief along lower rim: **DR· WILFRID · GREIF ·**

In relief in two lines in field to right of portrait: **AO · AETAT · S · / L ·**

Incised on truncation: **ALOEWENTAL · F ·**

**Rev:** Uniface

[A] **Cast bronze medal   178mm diameter**

      An example exhibited at the Beaux Art Gallery, London, in 1935.

      An example exhibited at the Usher Art Gallery, Lincoln, in 1941/2.

      (1) **The Rezak private collection, USA**

**LOE148  1930  PAUL LOEBE** President of the Reichstag.
**Obv:** The profile portrait of a bespectacled man, facing left.
Legend in relief around the rim: **PAUL · LOEBE · PRAESIDENT · DES · REICHSTAGES**
Incised in two lines in field to right of portrait: **ALOEWENTAL · / 1930**
**Rev:** Uniface
**[A] Cast bronze medal   175mm diameter**
     (1) **The Bauer private collection, England**

LOE149

**LOE149  n.d. (1930)  DR OTTO BRAUN** (1872–1955)
The last democratic Prime Minister of Prussia.
**Obv:** The profile portrait of a bespectacled man, facing left. No legend.
Facsimile of Braun's signature incised in field below truncation.
In relief on truncation: **ALOEWENTAL · F ·**
**Rev:** Uniface
**[A] Cast bronze medal   189mm diameter**
     An example exhibited at the Beaux Art Gallery, London, in 1935.
     An example exhibited at the Usher Art Gallery, Lincoln, in 1941/2.
     (1) **The Rezak private collection, USA**

LOE150

**LOE150  n.d. (1930)  DR OTTO BRAUN**
**Obv:** The profile portrait of a man, facing left.
Legend in relief in two lines in field to right of portrait: **OTTO / BRAUN**
Incised on truncation: **ALOEWENTAL . FECIT**
Facsimile of Braun's signature incised in field below neck.
**Rev:** Uniface
**[A] Cast bronze medal   187mm diameter**
     Two examples exhibited at the Usher Art Gallery, Lincoln, in 1941/2.
     (1) **The Bauer private collection, England**

LOE151

**LOE151  n.d. (1930)  DR OTTO BRAUN**
**Obv:** The profile portrait of a man, facing left. No legend.
Incised in field below truncation: **ALÖWENTAL · F ·**
**Rev:** Uniface
**[A] Cast bronze medal   94mm diameter**
     (1) **The Ashmolean Museum, Oxford**
     Presented by Loewental 15 December 1960.

**LOE152  1930  DR OTTO BRAUN**
**Obv:** The profile portrait of a man, facing left. No legend.
Incised below truncation: **ALOEWENTAL · FEC ·**
**Rev:** German eagle at the top and three oak leaves at base.
Legend in relief in seven lines in centre field: **OTTO / BRAUN / MINISTER /
PRAESIDENT / VON / PREUSSEN / 1930**
**[A] Bronze medal   97mm diameter**
     An example exhibited at the Beaux Art Gallery, London, in 1935.
     (1) **The Bauer private collection, England**
     (2) **The Ashmolean Museum, Oxford**
     Presented by Loewental in December 1960.

**LOE153  n.d.  'ALLEGORY OF WORLD TRADE'**
No other details
**[A] Bronze**
     Exhibited at the Usher Art Gallery, Lincoln, in 1941/2.  **NOT LOCATED**

LOE152

LOE154

**LOE154 n.d. 'ALLEGORY OF WORLD TRADE'**
**Obv:** Nude male figure striding over the globe towards the left. His right arm outstretched and holding a purse. His left arm holding a staff. A ship to the left and a lighthouse to the right. No legend or artist's monogram.
**Rev:** Uniface
[A] Plaster of Paris cast   95mm diameter
     (1) The Bauer private collection, England

LOE155

**LOE155 n.d. 'ALLEGORY OF WAR'?**
**As below but in reverse**
**Obv:** Nude male figure walking to left but looking to the right, with a flaming torch in his left hand and his right held aloft. Supplicating figures to both sides. Mountains with lightning flashes in background. No legend or artist's monogram.
**Rev:** Uniface
[A] Plaster of Paris cast of mould   103mm diameter
     (1) The Bauer private collection, England

LOE156

**LOE156 n.d. 'ALLEGORY OF WAR'?**
**As below but in reverse**
**Obv:** Nude male figure walking to left but looking to the right, with a flaming torch in his left hand and his right held aloft. Supplicating figures to both sides. Mountains with lightning flashes in background. No legend or artist's monogram.
**Rev:** Uniface
[A] Plaster of Paris cast of mould   103mm diameter
     (1) The Bauer private collection, England

LOE157

**LOE157 n.d. UNIDENTIFIED SITTER**
**As below but in reverse**
**Obv:** The profile portrait of a lady, facing left. No legend or artist's monogram.
**Rev:** Uniface
[A] Plaster of Paris cast of mould   112mm diameter
     (1) The Bauer private collection, England

**LOE158 n.d. (1931) THEODOR DÄUBLER** (1876–1934) German poet, born in Italy.
**Obv:** The profile portrait of a bearded man, facing left. No legend or artist's signature.
[A] Wax model on slate   63mm diameter
     (1) The Ashmolean Museum, Oxford
     Presented by Loewental in June 1961.

LOE158

**LOE159 1931 THEODOR DÄUBLER**
**Obv:** The profile portrait of a bearded man, facing left.
Legend in relief along the right hand rim: THEODOR · DÄVBLER
Incised in field to right of portrait: A over L
Date in relief below truncation: **1931**
**Rev:** Uniface
[A] Bronze medal   78mm diameter
     Exhibited at the Beaux Art Gallery, London, in 1935.
     Exhibited at the Usher Art Gallery, Lincoln, in 1941/2.
     (1) The Ashmolean Museum, Oxford
     Presented by Loewental 15 December 1960.

**LOE160 n.d. (1931) PROFESSOR MAX KARL ERNST LUDWIG VON PLANCK**
(1858–1947) German physicist and President of the Academy of Science. The expounder of
the Quantum Theory.

Obv: The profile portrait of a man, facing left.
Legend in relief along right hand side rim: **MAX VON PLANCK**
Facsimile of Planck's signature incised below truncation.
Incised on truncation: **ALOEWENTAL · F**
Rev: Uniface
[A] **Cast bronze medal   176mm diameter**
   Exhibited at the Beaux Art Gallery, London, in 1935.
   Exhibited at the Usher Art Gallery, Lincoln, in 1941/2.
   Exhibited at the Usher Art Gallery, Lincoln, in 1955.
   **(1) The British Museum, London  BM1984-11-1-3**

LOE159

**LOE161 1931 PROFESSOR MAX KARL ERNST LUDWIG VON PLANCK**
Obv: The profile portrait of a man, facing left.
Legend in relief in two lines in field below chin: **DR· MAX / PLANCK**
Incised in field to right of portrait: **MCMXXXI**
Incised on truncation: **ALOEWENTAL · F**
Rev: Uniface
[A] **Cast bronze medal   172mm diameter**
   **(1) Münzkabinett, Staatliche Museen zu Berlin, Germany  18217811**
   **(Illustration on website)**

LOE160

**LOE162 1932 JOHANN WOLFGANG VON GOETHE** (1749–1832) German poet,
dramatist, novelist and scientist (To commemorate the centenary of his death).
No other details
[A] **Bronze medal**
   An example of the obverse exhibited at the Beaux Art Gallery, London, in 1935.
   An example of the reverse exhibited at the Beaux Art Gallery, London, in 1935.
   An example exhibited at the Usher Art Gallery, Lincoln, in 1941/2.
   An example of the reverse exhibited at the Usher Art Gallery, Lincoln, in 1941/2.
   **NOT LOCATED**

**LOE163 1932 PROFESSOR ROBERT SCHMIDT** Director of the Schloss Museum, Berlin.
Obv: The profile portrait of a man, facing left.
Legend in relief in three lines in field to right of portrait: **ROBERT / SCHMIDT / 1932**
Rev: Uniface
[A] **Cast bronze medal   169mm diameter**
   Exhibited at the Usher Art Gallery, Lincoln, in 1941/2.
   **(1) The Ashmolean Museum, Oxford**
   Presented by Loewental 15 December 1960.

LOE163

**LOE164 1932 ALEX VEECK**
Obv: The profile head and shoulders portrait of a man, facing left.
Legend in relief in three lines in field to right of portrait: **ALEX · / VEECK / 1932**
Incised along right hand side rim: **A · LOEWENTAL · FECIT**
Obv: Uniface
[A] **Plaster of Paris cast   148mm diameter**
   Exhibited at the Usher Art Gallery, Lincoln, in 1941/2.
   **(1) The Collection, Lincoln  LCNUG:1927/2055**
   Presented by Loewental.

LOE164

**LOE165**

**LOE165 n.d. (1933) 'CORNELIA'**
**Obv:** The profile portrait of a lady, facing left.
Legend incised in field to left of portrait: **CORNELIA**
Incised in field to right of portrait: **A** over **L**
**Rev:** Uniface
[A] **Wax model on slate   75 x 80mm**
   (1) The Ashmolean Museum, Oxford
   Presented by Loewental in June 1961.

**LOE166**

**LOE166 n.d. (1933) 'CORNELIA'**
**Obv:** The profile portrait of a lady, facing left. No artist's signature.
Legend in relief in field to left of portrait: **CORNELIA**
**Rev:** Uniface
[A] **Plaster of Paris cast   74 x 86mm**
   (1) The Ashmolean Museum, Oxford

**LOE167 n.d. (1933) 'CORNELIA'**
**Obv:** The profile portrait of a lady, facing left.
Legend in relief in field to left of portrait: **CORNELIA**
In relief in field to right of portrait: **A** over **L**
**Rev:** Uniface
[A] **Cast bronze medal   77 x 91mm**
   (1) The Ashmolean Museum, Oxford
   Presented by Loewental in June 1961.

**LOE167**

**LOE168 1933 JEAN BABELON** (1889–1978). Conservateur du Cabinet des Médailles at the Bibliothéque Nationale de France, Paris.
No other details
[A] **Bronze**
   An example exhibited at the Beaux Art Gallery, London, in 1935.
   An example exhibited at the Usher Art Gallery, Lincoln, in 1941/2.
   **NOT LOCATED**

**LOE169**

**LOE169 n.d. 'A LADY SPINNING'** Is this a reverse?
**Obv:** A seated classical lady spinning, sitting facing forward and looking slightly to the left. No legend.
Incised at base: **ALÖWENTAL · F**
**Rev:** Uniface
[A] **Cast bronze medal   180mm diameter**
   (1) The Bauer private collection, England

**LOE170 n.d. 'LA SEMEUSE'**
No other details
[A] **Silver**
   An example exhibited at the Beaux Art Gallery, London, in 1935.  **NOT LOCATED**

**LOE171**

**LOE171 n.d. MRS ANNA WINKLER of Vienna**
**Obv:** The profile portrait of a lady wearing earrings, facing left. No legend.
Incised at lower right hand border: **ALÖWENTAL · FECIT ·**
**Rev:** Uniface
[A] **Cast bronze plaque   150mm x 177mm**
   (1) The Bauer private collection, England

**LOE172 n.d. (1934) SIR ROBERT HENRY EDWARD ABDY, 5<sup>TH</sup> BT (1896–1976)**
Connoisseur, collector and antiques dealer. Served in the 15<sup>th</sup> Hussars. He was one of the sponsors of Loewental's application for British nationality in 1940.
**Obv:** The profile head and shoulders portrait of a man, facing left.
Legend in relief in three lines in field to right of portrait: **SIR / ROBERT / ABDY**
Incised on right hand side rim: **ALOEWENTAL · F ·**
**Rev:** Uniface
**[A] Cast bronze medal  152mm diameter**
> An example exhibited at the Beaux Art Gallery, London, in 1935.
> Two examples exhibited at the Usher Art Gallery, Lincoln, in 1941/2.
> **(1) The Bauer private collection, England**

LOE172

**LOE173 n.d. (1934)  SIR ROBERT HENRY EDWARD ABDY, 5<sup>TH</sup> BT**
**Obv:** The profile head and shoulders portrait of a man, facing left.
No legend or artist's monogram visible on photograph.
**Rev:** Uniface
**[A] Cast bronze medal  *c.*73mm diameter**
> Exhibited at the Usher Art Gallery, Lincoln, in 1955.
> **(Illustration in photograph of display)  NOT LOCATED**

**LOE174 n.d. (1935)  BARON GEORG VON UND ZU FRANCKENSTEIN** (1878-1953)
Austrian Minister to the court of St James in London 1920-38. Knighted in 1938 to become Sir George Franckenstein.
**[A] Wax model**  No other details known
> Two examples exhibited at the Beaux Art Gallery, London, in 1935. It is likely that this is the wax model modified for the 1946 medal q.v.

**LOE175 n.d. (1935)  BARON GEORG VON UND ZU FRANCKENSTEIN**
**[A] Plaster of Paris cast**  No other details known
> Two examples exhibited at the Beaux Art Gallery, London, in 1935.
> **NOT LOCATED**

**LOE176 1935  BARON GEORG VON UND ZU FRANCKENSTEIN**
**Obv:** The profile portrait of a man, facing left.
Legend in relief around the rim: **GEORG · FREIHERR VON ZU FRANCKENSTEIN · OESTERREICHISCHER · GESANDTER · LOND ·**
In relief in two lines in field to right of portrait: **ALÖWENTAL / 1935**
**Rev:** Uniface
**[A] Cast bronze medal  115mm diameter**
> Exhibited at the Fine Art Gallery, London, in 1939.
> Exhibited at the Usher Art Gallery, Lincoln, in 1941/2.
> **(1) The Collection, Lincoln  LCNUG:1927/1875**
> Purchased from Loewental in 1948.

LOE176

**LOE177 n.d. (1934)  LADY ELIZABETH HAMBRO (1920–1995)**
**Obv:** The profile head and shoulders portrait of a lady, facing left. No legend.
Incised on right hand side rim: **ALÖWENTAL · F ·**
**Rev:** Uniface
**[A] Cast bronze medal  150mm diameter**
> **(1) The Jackson private collection, England**
> Purchased at the 1980 Bauer sale.

LOE177

LOE178

LOE178 1934 LADY ELIZABETH HAMBRO
Obv: The profile head and shoulders portrait of a lady, facing left. No legend.
Incised on right hand side rim: · ALOEWENTAL · 1934 ·
Rev: Uniface
[A] **Cast bronze medal   405mm diameter**
　　　Exhibited at the Beaux Art Gallery, London, in 1935.
　　　(1) **The Bauer private collection, England**
　　　'Hambro' written in chalk on the reverse.

LOE180

LOE179 n.d. (1934) COLIN CHRISTOPHER PAGET TENNANT (Born 1926).
The first son of Lord Christopher Glenconnor.
[A] **Plaster of Paris cast   No other details known**
　　　Exhibited at the Usher Art Gallery, Lincoln, in 1941/2.   **NOT LOCATED**

LOE180 1934 COLIN CHRISTOPHER PAGET TENNANT
Obv: The profile head and shoulders portrait of a young boy, facing left. No legend.
Incised along right hand side rim: · **A LOEWENTAL · 1934**
Rev: Uniface
[A] **Cast bronze medal   320mm diameter**
　　　Exhibited at the Beaux Art Gallery, London, in 1935.
　　　Exhibited at the Usher Art Gallery, Lincoln, in 1941/2.
　　　(1) **The Fennell private collection, England**

LOE182

LOE181 n.d. (1935) JAMES GREY HERBERT TENNANT (1929–1992).
The son of Lord Christopher Glenconnor.
[A] **Plaster of Paris cast   No other details known**
　　　Exhibited at the Usher Art Gallery, Lincoln, in 1941/2.   **NOT LOCATED**

LOE182 1935 JAMES GREY HERBERT TENNANT
Obv: The profile head and shoulders portrait of a young boy, facing left. No legend.
Incised below truncation: ALÖWENTAL · FECIT · 1935
Rev: Uniface
[A] **Cast bronze medal   159mm diameter**
　　　An example exhibited in Antwerp in 1959.
　　　(1) **The Ashmolean Museum, Oxford**
　　　Presented by Loewental in 1960.

LOE183

LOE183 n.d. (1935)  JAMES GREY HERBERT TENNANT
Obv: The profile head and shoulders portrait of a young boy, facing left. No legend or
artist's monogram.
Rev: Uniface
[A] **Cast bronze medal   154mm diameter**
　　　(1) **The Lee private collection, England**

LOE184

LOE184 n.d.  LORD CHRISTOPHER GLENCONNOR (CHRISTOPHER GREY
TENNANT 2ND BARON GLENCONNOR) (1899–1983). He was one of the sponsors of
Loewental's application for British Nationality in 1940.
Obv: The profile head and shoulders portrait of a man, facing left. No legend.
Incised along right hand side rim: ALOEWENTAL · F ·
Rev: Uniface
[A] **Plaster of Paris cast   162mm diameter**
　　　Exhibited at the Usher Art Gallery, Lincoln, in 1941/2.
　　　(1) **The Collection, Lincoln   LCNUG:1927/2061**
　　　Has the pencilled outline for a smaller medal.
　　　Presented by Loewental.

**LOE185** n.d. **LORD CHRISTOPHER GLENCONNOR (CHRISTOPHER GREY TENNANT 2ᴺᴰ BARON GLENCONNOR)**
[A] Cast bronze medal   No other details known
> Exhibited at the Beaux Art Gallery, London, in 1935.   **NOT LOCATED**

**LOE186** n.d. **UNIDENTIFIED SITTER**
**Obv:** The profile head and shoulders portrait of a bearded man, facing left. No legend.
In relief in field to right of portrait: **A over L**
**Rev:** Uniface
[A] Cast bronze plaque   147 x 194mm
> (1) Example offered for sale in Germany, 2007

**LOE187** 1935 **SIR GEORGE FRANCIS HILL** (1867–1948). Keeper of the Department of Coins and Medals at the British Museum 1912-30. Director and Principal Librarian at the British Museum 1931-36. Knighted 1933. He was one of the sponsors of Loewental's application for British Nationality in 1940.
**Obv:** The profile head and shoulders portrait of a man, facing left.
Legend in relief around the rim: **SIR · GEORGE · F · HILL · K·C·B · DIRECTOR · OF · THE · BRITISH · MUSEUM ·**
In relief in three lines in field to right of portrait: **ALÖWENTAL · / LONDON / 1935**
**Rev:** A griffin, seated with right forepaw raised.
Legend in relief around the rim: **THESAVROPHYLAX**
[A] Bronze medal   140mm diameter
> An example exhibited in Antwerp in 1959, 145mm diameter.
> (1) The Collection, Lincoln  LCNUG:1927/1873
> Purchased from Loewental in 1948.
> (2) The Victoria and Albert Museum, London  A51-1940
> Presented by Sir George Hill.
> (3) The Ashmolean Museum, Oxford
> Presented by Sir George Hill 1 August 1940.

**LOE187**

**LOE188** 1935 **JOSEPH RUDYARD KIPLING** (1865–1936).
English short story writer, poet and novelist. To celebrate his 70ᵗʰ birthday.
**Obv:** The profile head and shoulders portrait of a bespectacled man, facing left.
Legend in relief along right hand side rim: **RUDYARD · KIPLING**
Incised in three lines in field to right of portrait: **A over L / MCM / XXXV**
**Rev:** Uniface
[A] Plaster of Paris cast   140mm diameter
> (1) The Bauer private collection, England

**LOE188**

**LOE189** 1935 **JOSEPH RUDYARD KIPLING**
**Obv:** The profile head and shoulders portrait of a bespectacled man, facing left.
Legend in relief along right hand side rim: **RUDYARD · KIPLING**
In relief in three lines in field to right of portrait: **A over L / MCM / XXXV**
**Rev:** Uniface
[A] Plaster of Paris cast   140mm diameter
> (1) The Bauer private collection, England

**LOE189**

**LOE190** 1935 **JOSEPH RUDYARD KIPLING**
**Obv:** The profile head and shoulders portrait of a bespectacled man, facing left.
Legend in relief along right hand side rim: **RUDYARD · KIPLING**
In relief in three lines in field to right of portrait: **A over L / MCM / XXXV**
**Rev:** Uniface
[A] Plaster of Paris cast   140mm diameter
> (1) The Bauer private collection, England

**LOE190**

**LOE191**

**LOE192**

**LOE193**

**LOE194**

**LOE191 1935 JOSEPH RUDYARD KIPLING**
**Obv:** The profile head and shoulders portrait of a bespectacled man, facing left.
Legend in relief along right hand side rim: **RUDYARD · KIPLING**
In relief in three lines in field to right of portrait: **A over L / MCM / XXXV**
**Rev:** Uniface
**[A] Cast bronze medal   140mm diameter**
> An example exhibited at the Usher Art Gallery, Lincoln, in 1941/2.
> **(1) The American Numismatic Society, USA  1951.58.1**
> **(2) The Fennell private collection, England**
> **(3) The Bauer private collection, England**

**LOE192 1935 RUFUS DANIEL ISAACS, 1ST MARQUESS OF READING** (1860–1935).
Politician , Lord Chief Justice, Ambassador and Viceroy of India.
**Obv:** The profile head and shoulders portrait of a man, facing left.
Legend in relief around the rim: **RUFUS · D · ISAACS · MARQVIS · OF · READING -**
**G·C·B - G·C·S·I - G·C·I·E - G·C·V·O**
In relief in two lines in field to right of portrait: **1860- / -1935**
Incised in two lines below dates: **LÖWENTAL / FECIT ·**
**Rev:** Uniface
**[A] Cast bronze medal   223mm diameter**
> An example exhibited at the Fine Art Society, London, in 1939.
> **(1) The Collection, Lincoln  LCNUG:1927/1877**
> Purchased from Loewental in 1948.
> **(2) The British Museum, London  M0674**

**LOE193 1936 RUFUS DANIEL ISAACS, 1ST MARQUESS OF READING**
**Obv:** The profile head and shoulders portrait of a man, facing left.
Legend in relief around the rim: **RVFVS · D · ISAACS · MARQVIS · OF · READING -**
**G·C·B - G·C·S·I - G·C·I·E - G·C·V·O · 1860-1935**
Incised in four lines in field to right of portrait: **A · LÖWENTAL · / FECIT / LONDON /**
**1936**
**Rev:** Uniface
**[A] Cast bronze medal   232mm diameter**
> Two examples exhibited at the Usher Art Gallery, Lincoln, in 1941/2.
> An example exhibited in Antwerp in 1959, 230mm diameter.
> **(1) The Collection, Lincoln  LCNUG:1927/2056**
> Presented by Loewental.
> **(2) The Jewish Museum, Camden Town, England**
> Presented by Antony de Rothschild.
> **(3) The Middle Temple Library, London**
> **(4) The Ashmolean Museum, Oxford**
> Presented by Loewental in December 1960.
> **(5) The Fennell private collection, England**
> **(6) The National Portrait Gallery, London  NPG.D7203**
> Presented by R. Charleston, 1967.
> **(7) The Rezak private collection, USA**
> **(8) Upton House, Oxford  UPT0452**
> **(9) The British Museum, London  M0674**
> **(10) The Jewish Museum, New York, USA  FB154**

**LOE194 1936 SIR GEORGE FRANCIS HILL** (1867–1948). Keeper of the Department
of Coins and Medals at the British Museum 1912-30. Director and Principal Librarian at
the British Museum 1931-36. Knighted 1933. He was one of the sponsors for Loewental's
application for British Nationality in 1940.
**Obv:** The profile head and shoulders portrait of a man, facing left.

Legend in relief around the rim: SIR · GEORGE · F · HILL · K·C·B · DIRECTOR · OF · THE · BRITISH · MVSEVM · 1936 ·
In relief in field to right of portrait: 19 A over L 36
Incised on truncation: ALÖWENTAL ·
**Rev:** Uniface
[A] **Cast bronze medal   140mm diameter**
   An example exhibited in Antwerp in 1959. 145mm diameter.
   (1) The Ashmolean Museum, Oxford
   Presented by Sir George Hill in 1946.
   (2) The Bauer private collection, England

**LOE195**

**LOE195  1936  SIR GEORGE FRANCIS HILL**
**Obv:** The profile head and shoulders portrait of a man, facing left.
Legend in relief in four lines in field to right of portrait: SIR / GEORGE · F · / HILL · / 1936
Incised in two lines on truncation: ALOEWENTAL · FECIT / LONDON
**Rev:** Uniface
[A] **Bronze medal   190mm diameter**
   (1) The Ashmolean Museum, Oxford
   Presented by Sir George Hill 1 August 1940.

**LOE196  1936  LADY BEARSTED**  Wife of Lord Bearsted.
**Obv:** The profile portrait of a lady with drop earrings, facing left. No legend.
Incised in field to right of portrait: 19 A over L 36
**Rev:** Uniface
[A] **Cast bronze medal   230mm diameter**
   (1) Upton House, Bamford  UPT0306
   Mounted on wooden square.
   (2) Upton House, Bamford  UPT0307
   Mounted on wooden square.
   (3) Upton House, Bamford  UPT0308
   Mounted on wooden square.

**LOE196**

**LOE197  1936  MARY GASCOIGNE-CECIL, MARCHIONESS OF HARTINGTON**
(1895-1988). Married Edward Cavendish, Lord Hartington in 1917, who succeeded his father as 10th Duke of Devonshire in 1938, whereupon Mary became the Duchess of Devonshire.
**Obv:** The profile portrait of a lady, facing left. No legend.
Incised in field to right of portrait: 19 A over L 36
Incised on truncation: LONDON
**Rev:** Uniface
[A] **Cast bronze medal   237mm diameter**
   Exhibited at The Fine Art Society, London, in 1939.
   Exhibited at the Usher Art Gallery, Lincoln, in 1941/2.
   (1) The Fennell private collection, England

**LOE197**

**LOE198  1936  JOSEPH RUDYARD KIPLING** (1865–1936).
English short story writer, poet and novelist
**Obv:** The profile head and shoulders portrait of a bespectacled man, facing left.
Legend in relief around the rim: RUDYARD · KIPLING 1865-1936
Incised in four lines in field to right of portrait: A / LÖWENTAL / FECIT / 1936
**Rev:** Uniface
[A] **Cast bronze medal   239mm diameter**
   (1) The Kipling Society Museum, Bateman's, Burwash
   (2) The wreck of HMS Kipling
   (3) The British Museum, London  M6985
   Presented by Captain John Ball, 1936.

**LOE198**

**LOE199**

**LOE199  1937  HENRY PAUL GUINNESS CHANNON** (1935–2007). The only child of Sir Henry Channon and Lady Honor Guinness Channon. Conservative MP and Minister.
**Obv:** The profile head and shoulders portrait of a young boy, facing left. No legend.
Incised on right hand side rim: A · LOEWENTAL · F · 1937 ·
**Rev:** Uniface
**[A] Plaster of Paris cast  172mm diameter**
 Exhibited at the Usher Art Gallery, Lincoln, in 1941/2.
 **(1) The Collection, Lincoln  LCNUG:1927/1934**
 Presented by Loewental.

**LOE200  1937  HENRY PAUL GUINNESS CHANNON**
**Obv:** The profile head and shoulders portrait of a young boy, facing left. No legend.
Incised on right hand side rim: A · LOEWENTAL · F · 1937
**Rev:** Uniface
**[A] Steel die produced from above**
 Exhibited at the Usher Art Gallery, Lincoln, in 1941/2.  **NOT LOCATED**

**LOE201  1937  HENRY PAUL GUINNESS CHANNON**
**Obv:** The profile head and shoulders portrait of a young boy, facing left. No legend.
Incised on right hand side rim: A · LOEWENTAL · F · 1937
**Rev:** Uniface
**[A] Struck medal from above die**
 Exhibited at the Usher Art Gallery, Lincoln, in 1941/2.  **NOT LOCATED**

**LOE202  1937  JEAN BABELON** (1889–1978). Conservateur du Cabinet des Mèdailles at the Bibliothèque Nationale de France, Paris.
**[A] Bronze medal**  No other details known
 An example exhibited at the Usher Art Gallery, Lincoln, in 1955.
 An example exhibited in Antwerp in 1959. 157mm diameter.  **NOT LOCATED**

**LOE203  1938  LADY BEARSTED** The wife of Lord Bearsted.
**Obv:** The profile head and shoulders portrait of a lady, facing left. No legend.
Incised along the right hand rim: ALOEWENTAL · F · 1938
**Rev:** Uniface
**[A] Cast bronze medal  230mm diameter**
 **(1) Upton House, Banbury  UPT0996**
 Mounted on wooden square.

**LOE203**

**LOE204  1938  ANTON MARIC of Dalmatia**
**[A] Bronze medal**  No other details known
 Exhibited at the Usher Art Gallery, Lincoln, in 1941/2.  **NOT LOCATED**

**LOE205  1938  SIR GEORGE FRANCIS HILL** (1867–1948). Keeper of the Department of Coins and Medals at the British Museum 1912-30. Director and Principal Librarian at the British Museum 1931-36. Knighted 1933. He was one of the sponsors of Loewental's application for British Nationality in 1940.
**Obv:** The profile head and shoulders portrait of a man, facing left.
Legend in relief around the rim: SIR · GEORGE · FRANCIS · HILL · K·C·B · DIRECTOR · OF · THE · BRITISH · MUSEUM
In relief in two lines in field to right of portrait: 19 A over L 38 / LONDON
**Rev:** Uniface
**[A] Plaster of Paris cast  134mm diameter**
 Exhibited at the Usher Art Gallery, Lincoln, in 1941/2.
 **(1) The Collection, Lincoln  LCNUG:1927/2060**
 Presented by Loewental.

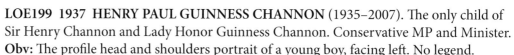

**LOE205**

**LOE206 n.d. (1939) WALTER SAMUEL BEARSTED, 2ᴺᴰ VISCOUNT** (1882–1948). Prominent art collector. Chairman of Shell between 1927-1948, and British Peer. He was one of the sponsors of Loewental's application for British Nationality in 1940.
[B] **Plaster of Paris cast bust**   No other details known
           Exhibited at the Usher Art Gallery, Lincoln, in 1941/2.   **NOT LOCATED**

LOE207

**LOE207  1939  WALTER SAMUEL BEARSTED, 2ᴺᴰ VISCOUNT**
**Obv:** The profile head and shoulders portrait of a man, facing right. No legend.
Incised in two lines in field to left of portrait: **ALOEWENTAL · / 1939**
**Rev:** Uniface
[A] **Cast bronze medal   230mm diameter**
           (1) Upton House, Banbury  UPT0453

**LOE208  1941  SIR GEORGE FRANCKENSTEIN** (1878–1953). Formerly Baron Georg von und zu Franckenstein. Knighted in 1938.
**Obv:** The profile portrait of a man, facing left.
Legend in relief around the rim: **SIR · GEORGE FRANCKENSTEIN**
Incised in field to right of portrait: **19 A over L 41**
**Rev:** Uniface
[A] **Plaster of Paris cast   94mm diameter**
           Exhibited at the Usher Art Gallery, Lincoln, in 1941/2.
           (1) The Collection, Lincoln  LCNUG:1927/2057
           Presented by Loewental.

LOE208

**LOE209  1944  SIR GEORGE FRANCKENSTEIN**
**Obv:** The profile portrait of a man, facing left.
Legend in relief around the rim: **SIR GEORGE FRANCKENSTEIN**
In relief in field to right of portrait: **19 A over L 44**
**Rev:** Uniface
[A] **Plaster of Paris cast   93mm diameter**
           Exhibited at the Usher Art Gallery, Lincoln, in 1944.
           Exhibited at the Usher Art Gallery, Lincoln, in 1946.
           (1) The Collection, Lincoln  LCNUG:1927/2058
           Presented by Loewental.

LOE209

**LOE210  1944  LADY ANN BONTIAL**
**Obv:** The profile head and shoulders portrait of a young girl, facing left. No legend.
Incised in field to right of portrait: **19 A over L 44**
**Rev:** Uniface
[A] **Plaster of Paris cast   162mm diameter**
           Exhibited at the Usher Art Gallery, Lincoln, in 1944.
           (1) The Collection, Lincoln  LCNUG:1927/1936
           Presented by Loewental.

LOE210

**LOE211  1944  FRANCIS JOHN COOPER** Director of the City of Lincoln Libraries, Museum and Art Gallery 1936–1961. A friend and supporter of Loewental during his time in Lincoln; he arranged exhibitions of Loewental's work at the Usher Art Gallery as well as minor displays at the Lincolnshire Artists Society annual exhibitions.
**Obv:** The profile head and shoulders portrait of a bespectacled man, facing left.
Legend in relief along the right hand rim: **F · J · COOPER**
Incised in field to right of portrait: **19 A over L 44**
**Rev:** Uniface
[A] **Cast bronze medal   113mm diameter**
           (1) Sold on eBay September 2007, USA   **NOT LOCATED**

LOE211

**LOE212** 1944 WINSTON SPENCER CHURCHILL (1874–1965). Politician, author and Prime Minister of Great Britain during WW2. (Preliminary portrait for the commissioned 'Victory' medal).

**Obv:** The profile head and shoulders portrait of a man, facing left.

Legend in relief along right hand side rim: **CHURCHILL**

In relief in field to right of portrait: **1944**

Incised in two lines on truncation: **ALOEWENTAL / FECIT**

**Rev:** Uniface

**[A] Plaster of Paris cast   175mm diameter**

       Exhibited at the Usher Art Gallery, Lincoln, in 1944.

       **(1)** The Collection, Lincoln  **LCNUG:1927/2051**

       Presented by Loewental.

**LOE212**

**LOE213** 1944 WINSTON SPENCER CHURCHILL (Preliminary portrait for the commissioned 'Victory' medal).

**Obv:** The profile head and shoulders portrait of a man, facing left.

Legend in relief along right hand side rim: **CHURCHILL**

In relief in field to right of portrait: **1944**

Incised in two lines on truncation: **A · J · LOEWENTAL · F · / 1944**

**Rev:** Uniface

**[A] Cast bronze medal   172mm diameter**

       **(1)** The Collection, Lincoln  **LCNUG:1927/2263**

       Purchased from Loewental in 1955.

**LOE213**

**LOE214** n.d. (1944)  WINSTON SPENCER CHURCHILL (Preliminary reverse for the commissioned 'Victory' medal).

**Obv:** A right hand rising out of a cloud and holding a flaming torch.

Legend in relief around the rim: · **UNFLINCHING · INDOMITABLE · HIS · SPIRIT · SAVED · BRITAIN · AND · SO · THE · WORLD· ·**

Legend in relief in five lines to either side of torch: **WE · WILL FIGHT · ON / LAND ON · SEA / AND · IN THE · AIR / UNTIL VICTORY / IS WON**

No artist's monogram.

**Rev:** Uniface

**[A] Plaster of Paris cast   174mm diameter**

       Exhibited at the Usher Art Gallery, Lincoln, in 1944.

       **(1)** The Collection, Lincoln  **LCNUG:1927/2052**

       Presented by Loewental.

**LOE214**

**LOE215** n.d. (1944)  WINSTON SPENCER CHURCHILL (Preliminary reverse for the commissioned 'Victory' medal).

**Obv:** A right hand rising out of a cloud and holding a flaming torch.

Legend in relief around the rim: · **UNFLINCHING · INDOMITABLE · HIS · SPIRIT · SAVED · BRITAIN · AND · SO · THE · WORLD ··**

Legend in relief in five lines to either side of torch: **WE · WILL FIGHT · ON / LAND ON · SEA / AND · IN THE · AIR / UNTIL VICTORY / IS WON**

Incised in field below torch: **A over L**

**Rev:** Uniface

**[A] Cast bronze medal   172mm diameter**

       **(1)** The Bauer private collection, England

**LOE215**

**LOE216  1945  'TO THOSE WHO FOUGHT'**
**Obv:** A semi-nude winged Victory stands to the right with outstretched right arm holding an olive branch. To the left is an altar on a double plinth with flames issuing from the top. At the base of the altar a discarded helmet, shield and sword. The Sun rises in the background behind the altar.
Legend in relief around top rim: **TO · THOSE · WHO · FOUGHT**
Incised in two lines on altar: **FOR / LIBERTY**
Incised in exergue: **1939-1945**
Incised at right hand side lower rim: **A · LOEWENTAL · F**
**Rev:** Uniface
[A] **Cast bronze medal   202mm diameter**
      (1) The Fennell private collection, England

LOE216

**LOE217  1945  WINSTON SPENCER CHURCHILL** (Revised portrait for the commissioned 'Victory' medal).
**Obv:** The profile head and shoulders portrait of a man, facing left.
Legend in relief along right hand side rim: **CHURCHILL**
In field to right of portrait: **1945** in relief over an incised **V**
Incised in two lines on truncation: **A · LOEWENTAL / LINCOLN**
**Rev:** Uniface
[A] **Cast bronze medal   172mm diameter**
      Exhibited at the Usher Art Gallery, Lincoln, in 1955.
      **(Illustration in photograph of display, p.43)   NOT LOCATED**

**LOE218  1945 WINSTON SPENCER CHURCHILL** (Die for the obverse for the commissioned 'Victory' medal).
**As below but in reverse**
**Obv:** The profile head and shoulders portrait of a man, facing left.
Legend in relief along right hand side rim: **CHURCHILL**
In field to right of portrait: **1945** in relief over an incised **V**
Incised in two lines on truncation: **A · LOEWENTAL · / LINCOLN**
[A] **Steel working die**
      (1) The Collection, Lincoln  LCNUG:1977/2786a
      Purchased at auction in 1977.

LOE218

**LOE219  n.d. (1945)  WINSTON SPENCER CHURCHILL** (Die for the reverse for the commissioned 'Victory' medal).
**As below but in reverse**
**Obv:** A right hand rising out of a cloud and holding a flaming torch.
Legend in relief around the rim: · **UNFLINCHING · INDOMITABLE · HIS · SPIRIT ·
SAVED · BRITAIN · AND · SO · THE · WORLD ···**
Legend in relief in five lines to either side of torch: **WE · WILL FIGHT · ON / LAND ON ·
SEA / AND · IN THE · AIR / UNTIL VICTORY / IS WON**
In relief in field below torch: **A over L**
[A] **Steel working die**
      (1) The Collection, Lincoln  LCNUG:1977/2786b
      Purchased at auction in 1977.

LOE219

**LOE220**

**LOE221**

**LOE223**

**LOE220  1945  WINSTON SPENCER CHURCHILL** (The commissioned 'Victory' medal).
**Obv:** The profile head and shoulders portrait of a man, facing left.
Legend in relief along right hand side rim: CHURCHILL
In field to right of portrait: **1945** in relief over an incised **V**
Incised in two lines on truncation: A · LOEWENTAL · / LINCOLN
**Rev:** A right hand rising out of a cloud and holding a flaming torch.
Legend in relief around the rim: · UNFLINCHING · INDOMITABLE · HIS · SPIRIT ·
SAVED · BRITAIN · AND · SO · THE · WORLD ···
Legend in relief in five lines to either side of torch: WE · WILL FIGHT · ON / LAND ON ·
SEA / AND · IN THE · AIR / UNTIL VICTORY / IS WON
In relief in field below torch: A over L
**[A] Struck bronze medal   63mm diameter   General issue**
      Promoted by Harry Burrows, Jeweller, Manchester.
      Struck by John Pinches (Medallists) Ltd., London.
      General issue, 1,000 struck in bronze. Some  appear to have been silver plated.
      **(1) The Collection, Lincoln  LCNUG:1927/1598**
      **(2) The V&A Museum, London  A215-1946**
      **(3) The Spalding Gentlemen's Society Museum, Spalding**
      **(4) The Ashmolean Museum, Oxford**
      Presented by Sir George Hill, 8 October 1946.

**LOE221  1946  SIR GEORGE FRANCKENSTEIN** (1878–1953).
Formerly Baron Georg von und zu Franckenstein. Knighted in 1938.
**Obv:** The profile portrait of a man, facing left.
Legend incised around the rim: SIR · GEORGE · FRANCKENSTEIN
Incised in field to right of portrait: **19 A over L 46**
**Rev:** Uniface
**[A] Wax  model on slate   94mm diameter**
      Exhibited at the Usher Art Gallery, Lincoln, in 1941/2.
      **(1) The Ashmolean Museum, Oxford**
      Presented by Loewental in 1961.
      The ticket with this wax states 1936, so likely to be the original 1936 wax model,
      modified to suit his changed status.

**LOE222  1946  SIR GEORGE FRANCKENSTEIN**
**Obv:** The profile portrait of a man, facing left.
Legend in relief around the rim: SIR GEORGE FRANCKENSTEIN
In relief in field to right of portrait: **19 A over L 46**
**Rev:** Uniface
**[A] Cast bronze medal   91mm diameter**
      Exhibited at the Usher Art Gallery, Lincoln, in 1947.
      Exhibited at the Usher Art Gallery, Lincoln, in 1955.
      **(Illustration in photograph of display)   NOT LOCATED**
      Exhibited in Antwerp in 1959.

**LOE223  1946  NEAL CORNELIUS FRIEND GREEN.** (1885–1974). Trawler owner,
gentleman farmer, inventor and JP, although as a painter his first love was the arts. He
befriended Loewental during his time in Lincoln and would invite him to lunch at Holbeck
Manor about once a fortnight, although Rosa usually declined.
**Obv:** The profile head and shoulders portrait of a bespectacled man, facing left.
Legend in relief in four lines in field to right of portrait: NEAL / GREEN / 1946 / A over L
**Rev:** Uniface
**[A] Plaster of Paris cast   176mm diameter**
      Exhibited at the Usher Art Gallery, Lincoln, in 1946.
      **(1) The Bauer private collection, England**

**LOE224  1946  NEAL CORNELIUS FRIEND GREEN**

**Obv:** The profile head and shoulders portrait of a bespectacled man, facing left.

Legend in relief in four lines in field to right of portrait: **NEAL / GREEN / 1946 / A over L**

Incised in two lines below truncation: **ALOEWENTAL · / FECIT**

**Rev:** Uniface

**[A] Cast bronze medal   176mm diameter**

> An example exhibited at the Usher Art Gallery, Lincoln, in 1947.
>
> **(1) The Lee private collection, England**

LOE224

**LOE225  n.d. (c.1948)   THE LINCOLNSHIRE RED SHORTHORN ASSOCIATION**

Award medal awarded at agricultural shows for the best animal in show.

**Obv:** A Lincoln Red Shorthorn bull, facing left. View of south face of Lincoln cathedral in background at top.

Legend in relief in three lines in exergue: **THE · LINCOLNSHIRE / RED SHORTHORN / ASSOCIATION**

Incised along lower right hand side rim: **ALOEWENTAL · F ·**

**Rev:** Reverse ground flat in order to accommodate engraved winner's name and details.

**[A] Struck bronze medal   63mm diameter   General issue**

> General issue award medal struck by John Pinches (Medallists) Ltd., London.
>
> **(1) The Gilbert private collection, England**
>
> Example awarded in 1948.

LOE225

**LOE226  n.d.  'HADASSA'**

No other details

**[B] Plaster of Paris cast**

> Exhibited at the Usher Art Gallery, Lincoln, in 1946.
>
> Exhibited at the Usher Art Gallery, Lincoln, in 1949.   **NOT LOCATED**

**LOE227  n.d.  'VJERA', a Swedish girl**

**Obv:** The profile head and shoulders portrait of a young girl, facing left.

Legend in relief in field to right of portrait: **VJERA**

No artist's monogram.

**[A] Plaster of Paris cast   153mm diameter**

> Exhibited at the Usher Art Gallery, Lincoln, in 1947.
>
> **(1) The Collection, Lincoln  LCNUG:1927/1935**
>
> Presented by Loewental.

LOE227

**LOE228  1948  JAMES WILLIAM FRANCIS HILL** (1899–1980). Alderman and sometime Mayor of Lincoln, solicitor and senior partner at Andrew & Company, solicitors of Lincoln. He befriended Loewental during his time in Lincoln.

**Obv:** The profile portrait of a man, facing left.

Legend in relief in two lines in field to right of portrait: **J · W · F · HILL · / 1948**

Incised on truncation: **ALOEWENTAL · F ·**

**Rev:** Uniface

**[A] Plaster of Paris cast   175mm diameter**

> **(1) The Bauer private collection, England**

LOE228

LOE229

LOE229 1948 JAMES WILLIAM FRANCIS HILL

**Obv:** The profile portrait of a man, facing left.

Legend in relief in two lines in field to right of portrait: J · W · F · HILL · / 1948

Incised on truncation: A LOEWENTAL · F ·

**Rev:** Uniface

**[A] Cast bronze medal   175mm diameter**

> Exhibited at the Usher Art Gallery, Lincoln, in 1949.
> Exhibited at the Fine Art Society, London, in 1949.
> Exhibited at the Royal Academy, London, in 1955.
> **(1) The Collection, Lincoln   LCNUG:1975/130**
> Presented by Hill in 1975.

LOE230

LOE230 1949 ARTUR IMMANUEL LOEWENTAL (1879–1964).

Self portrait of the sculptor to mark his 70th birthday.

**Obv:** The profile self portrait of the artist, facing left.

Legend in relief along right hand side rim: ARTUR · I · LOEWENTAL

In relief in two lines in field to right of portrait: MCM / XLVIIII [sic]

In relief in two lines in field below chin: AO · AET · S · / LXX

Incised on truncation: LINCOLN

**Rev:** Uniface

**[A] Cast bronze medal   140mm diameter**

> An example exhibited at the Usher Art Gallery, Lincoln, in 1954.
> An example exhibited at the Usher Art Gallery, Lincoln, in 1955.
> An example exhibited in Antwerp in 1959.
> **(1) The Collection, Lincoln   LCNUG:1927/2262**
> This example has a green patina.
> Purchased from Loewental in 1955.
> **(2) The Fennell private collection, England**
> No patina
> **(3) The Gretton private collection, England**
> This example has a green patina.

LOE231

LOE231 n.d. (1948) PROFESSOR ALBERT EINSTEIN (1879–1955). German-born theoretical physicist. To mark his 70th birthday.

**Obv:** The profile portrait of a man, facing left.

Legend incised in field to right of portrait: EINSTEIN

Incised on truncation: A · LOEWENTAL · F ·

**Rev:** Uniface

**[C] Cast bronze medal   165mm diameter**

> **(1) The Spalding Gentlemen's Society Museum, Spalding**
> Presented by Ashley K. Maples.

LOE232

LOE232 1948 PROFESSOR ALBERT EINSTEIN To mark his 70th birthday.

**Obv:** The profile portrait of a man, facing left.

Legend incised in field to right of portrait: EINSTEIN

Facsimile of Einstein's signature incised in field under chin.

Incised in two lines on truncation: A · LOEWENTAL · F · / 1948

**Rev:** Uniface

**[A] Cast bronze medal   165mm diameter**

> **(1) The Ashmolean Museum, Oxford**
> Presented by Loewental 15 December 1960.
> **(2) The Bauer private collection, England**

**LOE233 1948 ASHLEY K. MAPLES** (1868–1950). President of the Spalding Gentlemen's Society. He arranged for the Society to purchase Loewental's valuable collection of Chinese glass and ceramics etc in 1948. The medal was commissioned by the members of the Spalding Gentlemen's Society.

Obv: The profile head and shoulders portrait of a man, facing left.
Legend in relief along right hand side rim: **ASHLEY · K · MAPLES**
Incised in two lines in field to right of portrait: **SPALDING / 1948**
Incised in two lines on truncation: **A LOEWENTAL · / FECIT**
Rev: Uniface

[A] **Cast bronze medal   195mm diameter**
       Exhibited at the Usher Art Gallery, Lincoln, in 1949.
       **(1) The Spalding Gentlemen's Society Museum, Spalding**
       This example is mounted upon a rectangular wooden board. Mounted below is a small cast bronze plaque with the legend, in two lines in relief:
       **HON · SECRETARY · 24 · APRIL · 1899 / PRESIDENT · 25 · SEPT · 1930**

LOE233

**LOE234 1948 UNIDENTIFIED SITTER** (Thought to be DWIGHT D. EISENHOWER (1890–1969), Supreme Commander of the troops invading France on D-Day, 1944.)
Obv: The profile portrait of a man, facing left. No legend.
Incised in four lines in field to right of portrait: **A over L / MCM / XXXX / VIII**
Rev: Uniface

[A] **Plaster of Paris cast   140mm diameter**
       **(1) The Bauer private collection, England**

LOE234

**LOE235 1948 UNIDENTIFIED SITTER** (Thought to be DWIGHT D. EISENHOWER).
Obv: The profile portrait of a man, facing left. No legend.
In relief in four lines in field to right of portrait: **A over L / MCM / XXXX / VIII**
Rev: Uniface

[A] **Cast bronze medal   142mm diameter**
       **(1) The Rezak private collection, USA**
       Green patina.

LOE235

**LOE236 n.d. UNIDENTIFIED AIRMAN**
**As below but in reverse**
Obv: The head and shoulders portrait of an airman in uniform and wearing a beret, facing slightly to the left. A small flash on his left shoulder with the letters AG. No legend.
In relief in field to left of portrait: **A over L**
Rev: Uniface

[A] **Plaster of Paris cast of mould   160mm diameter**
       **(1) The Bauer private collection, England**

LOE236

**LOE237 n.d. UNIDENTIFIED AIRMAN**
Obv: The head and shoulders portrait of an airman in uniform and wearing a beret, facing slightly to the left. A small flash on his left shoulder with the letters AG. No legend.
In relief in field to left of portrait: **A over L**
Rev: Uniface

[A] **Plaster of Paris cast   160mm diameter**
       **(1) The Bauer private collection, England**

LOE237

LOE238

**LOE238 1948 FRANCIS JOHN COOPER** Director of the City of Lincoln Libraries, Museum and Art Gallery 1936-1961. A friend and supporter of Loewental while in Lincoln; he arranged exhibitions of Loewental's work at the Usher Art Gallery as well as minor displays at the Lincolnshire Artists Society annual exhibitions.
**As below but in reverse**
Obv: The profile head and shoulders portrait of a bespectacled man, facing left.
In relief along right hand border: **F · J · COOPER**
In relief in two lines in field to right of portrait: **MCM / XLVIII**
No artist's monogram.
**Ref:** Uniface
**[A] Plaster of Paris cast of mould   133mm diameter**
      (1) The Bauer private collection, England

LOE239

**LOE239 1948 FRANCIS JOHN COOPER**
Obv: The profile head and shoulders portrait of a bespectacled man, facing left.
In relief along right hand border: **F · J · COOPER**
In relief in two lines in field to right of portrait: **MCM / XLVIII**
No artist's monogram.
**Ref:** Uniface
**[A] Plaster of Paris cast   133mm diameter**
      Exhibited at the Usher Art Gallery, Lincoln, in 1949.
      (1) The Bauer private collection, England

LOE240

**LOE240 1948 'A DEER'**
Obv: The profile image of a deer, facing left.
Incised at bottom right hand corner: **19 A over L 48**
**Rev:** Uniface
**[A] Cast bronze plaque   96mm x 155mm**
      Exhibited at the Usher Art Gallery, Lincoln, in 1949.
      (1) The Collection, Lincoln  LCNUG:1927/2261
      Purchased from Loewental in 1955.

LOE241

**LOE241 1948 'A LIONESS'**
**As below but in reverse**
Obv: The profile image of a lioness, facing left.
Incised at bottom right hand corner: **19 A over L 48**
**Rev:** Uniface
**[A] Plaster of Paris cast of mould   100mm x 210mm**
      (1) The Bauer private collection, England

LOE242

**LOE242 1949 'A LIONESS'**
Obv: The profile image of a lioness, facing left.
Incised at bottom right hand corner: **19 A over L 49**
**Rev:** Uniface
**[A] Cast bronze plaque   100mm x 210mm**
      Exhibited at the Usher Art Gallery, Lincoln, in 1949.
      Exhibited at the Usher Art Gallery, Lincoln, in 1955.
      (1) The Collection, Lincoln  LCNUG:1927/2260

**LOE243 1949 'TYRTAIOS'**
No further details
[A] **Cast bronze medal   87mm diameter**
>   Exhibited at the Usher Art Gallery, Lincoln, in 1955.
>   Exhibited in Antwerp in 1959.   **NOT LOCATED**

**LOE244 n.d. (c.1951) THE LINCOLN RED SHORTHORN SOCIETY**
Award medal awarded at agricultural shows for the best animal in show.
**Obv:** A Lincoln Red Shorthorn bull, facing left. View of south face of Lincoln cathedral in background at top.
Legend in relief in three lines in exergue: **LINCOLN / RED SHORTHORN / SOCIETY**
Incised along lower right hand side rim: **ALOEWENTAL · F ·**
**Rev:** Reverse ground flat in order to accommodate engraved winner's name and details.
[A] **Struck bronze medal   63mm diameter**
>   General issue award medal struck by John Pinches (Medallists) Ltd., London.
>   (1) The Gilbert private collection, England
>   Four examples awarded in 1951.

**LOE244**

**LOE245 1950 UNIDENTIFIED SITTER**
**Obv:** The profile head and shoulders portrait of a man, facing right.
In relief in three lines in field to left of portrait: **A over L / MCM / L**
**Rev:** Uniface
[A] **Plaster of Paris cast   150mm diameter**
>   (1) The Bauer private collection, England

**LOE245**

**LOE246 1950 FRANCIS JOHN COOPER** Director of the City of Lincoln Libraries, Museum and Art Gallery 1936-1961. A friend and supporter of Loewental during his time in Lincoln; he arranged exhibitions of Loewental's work at the Usher Art Gallery as well as minor displays at the Lincolnshire Artists Society annual exhibitions.
**Obv:** The profile head and shoulders portrait of a bespectacled man, facing left.
Legend in relief along the right hand rim: **F · J · COOPER**
Incised in four lines in field to right of portrait: **A over L / MCM /L / LINCOLN**
**Rev:** Uniface
[A] **Cast bronze medal   133mm diameter**
>   Exhibited at the Usher Art Gallery, Lincoln, in 1954.
>   Exhibited at the Usher Art Gallery, Lincoln, in 1955.
>   (1) The Lucas private collection, Canada

**LOE246**

**LOE247 1950 JAMES M. EFROSS**
**Obv:** The profile portrait of a man, facing right.
Legend in relief along right hand rim: **JAMES · M · EFROSS**
In relief in three lines in field to left of portrait: **A over L / MCM / L ·**
**Rev:** Uniface
[A] **Cast bronze medal   145mm diameter**
>   (1) The Bauer private collection, England

**LOE247**

**LOE248**

**LOE248 1950 PROFESSOR ALBERT EINSTEIN** (1879–1955).
German-born theoretical physicist.
Obv: The profile portrait of a man, facing left.
Legend incised in four lines in field to right of portrait: **A / EINSTEIN / 1950 / A over L**
Incised in two lines below truncation: **COPYRIGHT / RESERVED**
Rev: Uniface
[A] Wax model on slate   165mm diameter
  (1) The Ashmolean Museum, Oxford
  Cased as a medal.
  Presented by Loewental 1961.


**LOE249 1950 PROFESSOR ALBERT EINSTEIN**
Obv: The profile portrait of a man, facing left.
Legend incised in four lines in field to right of portrait: **A / EINSTEIN / 1950 / A over L**
Incised in two lines below truncation: **COPYRIGHT / RESERVED**
Rev: Uniface
[A] Cast bronze medal   165mm diameter
  Exhibited at the Usher Art Gallery, Lincoln, in 1954.
  Exhibited at the Usher Art Gallery, Lincoln, in 1955.
  **(Illustration in photograph of display)   NOT LOCATED**

**LOE250**

**LOE250 1954 DR AUGUSTINE JOSEPH FENNELL** (1900–1980).
Loewental's friend and GP during his time in Lincoln. Born in Cork, Eire, in 1900 he
purchased a practice on Yarborough Road, Lincoln.
Obv: The profile head and shoulders portrait of a bespectacled man, facing right.
Legend in relief along the right hand rim: **DR · AUGUSTINE · J · FENNELL**
Incised in three lines in field to left of portrait: **A · LOEWENTAL / FECIT / 1954**
Incised on truncation: **LINCOLN**
Rev: Uniface
[A] Cast bronze medal   182mm diameter
  (1) The Fennell private collection, England

**LOE251**

**LOE251 1954 DR AUGUSTINE JOSEPH FENNELL, revised portrait**
Obv: The profile head and shoulders portrait of a bespectacled man, facing right.
Legend in relief along the right hand rim: **DR · AUGUSTINE · J · FENNELL**
Incised in three lines in field to left of portrait: **A · LOEWENTAL · / FECIT / 1954**
Incised on truncation: **LINCOLN**
Rev: Uniface
[A] Cast bronze medal   182mm diameter
  Exhibited at the Usher Art Gallery, Lincoln, in 1955.
  (1) The Fennell private collection, England


**LOE252**

**LOE252 n.d. (1955) JOHN DESMOND FENNELL** (1933–2011).
The son of Dr Augustine Joseph Fennell, he knew Loewental during his time in Lincoln.
Obv: The profile head and shoulders portrait of a young man, facing right.
Legend in relief in field to left of portrait: **DESMOND**
No artist's monogram.
Rev: Uniface
[A] Plaster of Paris cast   165mm diameter
  (1) The Bauer private collection, England

**LOE253** n.d. (1955) JOHN DESMOND FENNELL
**Obv:** The profile head and shoulders portrait of a young man, facing right.
Legend in relief in field to left of portrait: **DESMOND**
No artist's monogram.
**Rev:** Uniface
**[A] Plaster of Paris cast** 165mm diameter
    (1) The Bauer private collection, England

LOE253

**LOE254** 1955 JOHN DESMOND FENNELL
**Obv:** The profile head and shoulders portrait of a young man, facing right.
Legend in relief in field to left of portrait: **DESMOND**
Incised in two lines below truncation: **ALOEWENTAL · F · / 1955**
**Rev:** Uniface
**[A] Plaster of Paris cast** 165mm diameter
    (1) The Fennell private collection, England

LOE254

**LOE255** 1955 JOHN DESMOND FENNELL
**Obv:** The profile head and shoulders portrait of a young man, facing right.
Legend in relief in field to left of portrait: **DESMOND**
Incised in two lines below truncation: **ALOEWENTAL · F · / 1955**
**Rev:** Uniface
**[A] Cast bronze medal** 165mm diameter
    (1) The Fennell private collection, England
      This example is mounted on a wooden board.

LOE255

**LOE256** n.d. (c.1958) SIR JAMES WILLIAM FRANCIS HILL (1899–1980). Alderman and sometime Mayor of Lincoln, solicitor and senior partner at Andrew & Company, solicitors of Lincoln. He was knighted in 1958. He befriended Loewental during his time in Lincoln.
**Obv:** The profile head of a man, facing left.
Legend incised in three lines in field to right of portrait: **SIR / FRANCIS / HILL**
Incised on truncation: **ALOEWENTAL · F ·**
**Rev:** Uniface
**[A] Cast bronze medal** 175mm diameter
    (1) Andrew & Company LLP, Lincoln
      This example has a black patina and mounted on a square wooden board.

LOE256

**LOE257** **?** DR JAKOB BAUER A doctor who studied medicine in Poland at Warsaw University, and received his MD from there in 1926. He arranged for Loewental to lodge in his house at Wellingore when Rosa died.
No details known **NOT LOCATED**

**LOE258** **?** GIZELLA (GITTA) BAUER The second wife of Dr Jakob Bauer. Looked after Loewental at Wellingore for the last five years of his life.
No details known **NOT LOCATED**

**LOE259**

**LOE260**

**LOE261**

**LOE259 n.d. RALPH BAUER** The son of Dr Jakob Bauer by his first wife.
**Obv:** The profile head and shoulders portrait of a young man, facing left.
Legend in relief along right hand rim: **RALPH**
No artist's monogram.
**Rev:** Uniface
[A] **Plaster of Paris cast   140mm diameter**
    (1) The Bauer private collection, England

**LOE260 1962 GERARD MIET BAUER** (Born 1956). The younger son of Dr Jakob Bauer
by his second wife, Gizella. Has memories of Loewental during his time at Wellingore.
**Obv:** The profile head and shoulders portrait of a young boy, facing left.
Legend incised in three lines in field to right of portrait: **GERARD / MIET / BAUER**
Incised in two lines on truncation: **A · LOEWENTAL / 1962**
**Rev:** Uniface
[A] **Cast bronze medal   140mm diameter**
    (1) The Bauer private collection, England

**LOE261 1963 ERAN NICODEMUS BAUER** (Born 1954). The elder son of Dr Jakob
Bauer by his second wife, Gizella. Has memories of Loewental during his time at
Wellingore.
**Obv:** The profile head and shoulders portrait of a young boy, facing right.
Legend incised in three lines in field to left of portrait: **ERAN / BAUER / 1963**
Incised on truncation: **A · LOEWENTAL**
**Rev:** Uniface
[A] **Cast bronze medal   140mm diameter**
    (1) The Bauer private collection, England

**LOE262 1965 SIR WINSTON CHURCHILL**
**Descr.** A die for the Churchill 'Death' medal obverse, manufactured by John Pinches
(Medallists) Ltd., London.
[A] **Steel die**
    (1) The British Museum, London  BM465

**LOE263 1965 SIR WINSTON CHURCHILL**
**Descr.** A puncheon for the Churchill 'Death' medal obverse, manufactured by John
Pinches (Medallists) Ltd., London.
[A] **Steel puncheon**
    (1) The British Museum, London  BM466

**LOE264 1965 SIR WINSTON CHURCHILL**
**Descr.** A die for the Churchill 'Death' medal reverse, manufactured by John Pinches
(Medallists) Ltd., London.
[A] **Steel die**
    (1) The British Museum, London  BM467

**LOE265 1965 SIR WINSTON CHURCHILL**
**Descr.** A die for the Churchill 'Death' medal reverse, manufactured by John Pinches
(Medallists) Ltd., London.
[A] **Steel die**
    (1) The British Museum, London  BM468

**LOE266 1965 SIR WINSTON CHURCHILL**
**Descr.** A puncheon for the Churchill 'Death' medal reverse, manufactured by John Pinches (Medallists) Ltd., London.
[A] Steel puncheon
  (1) The British Museum, London BM469

**LOE267 1965 SIR WINSTON CHURCHILL, 'Death' medal, promoted by B. A. Seaby, Ltd, London.** Politician and prime minister of Great Britain during WW2.
**Obv:** The profile head and shoulders portrait of a man, facing left.
Legend in relief along right hand side rim: **CHURCHILL**
In field to right of portrait: **1945** in relief over an incised **V**
Incised in two lines on truncation: **A · LOEWENTAL / LINCOLN**
In relief on rim below truncation: **OB · 24 · JAN · 1965**
**Rev:** A right hand rising out of a cloud and holding a flaming torch.
Legend in relief around the rim: **· UNFLINCHING · INDOMITABLE · HIS · SPIRIT · SAVED · BRITAIN · AND · SO · THE · WORLD ··**
Legend in relief in five lines to either side of torch: **WE · WILL FIGHT · ON / LAND ON · SEA / AND · IN THE · AIR / UNTIL VICTORY / IS WON**
In relief in field below torch: **A over L**
[A] Struck bronze medal   50mm diameter
  General issue, 1,421 struck by John Pinches (Medallists) Ltd, London
    (1) The Collection, Lincoln  LCNUG:1977/2851
    (2) The British Museum, London  BM1966-7-4-3
[B] Struck sterling silver medal   50mm diameter
  General issue, 736 struck by John Pinches (Medallists) Ltd, London
    (1) The British Museum, London  BM1966-7-4-2
[C] Struck .375 gold medal   50mm diameter
  General issue, 200 struck by John Pinches (Medallists) Ltd, London
    (1) The British Museum, London  BM1966-7-4-1
[D] Struck .916 gold medal   50mm diameter
  General issue, 500 struck by John Pinches (Medallists) Ltd, London

LOE267

# INDEX OF PEOPLE PORTRAYED BY ARTUR LOEWENTAL

ABDY, Sir Robert Henry Edward, 5th Bt (1896-1976). Connoisseur, collector and antiques dealer; served in the 15th Hussars. He was one of the sponsors of Loewental's application for British nationality in 1940. Sculpted: 1934. **LOE172, 173**

ADELGUNDE, Princess, of Bavaria (1823-1914). Née Adelgunde Auguste Charlotte Caroline Elisabeth Amalie Marie Sophie Luise von Bayern. Consort Duchess of Modena, Italy, by her marriage to Francis V, Duke of Modena. Sculpted: 1905 (Christmas 1905). **LOE021**

AHL, Charles. Finnish goldsmith. Sculpted: 1928. **LOE126**

BABELON, Jean (1889-1978). Conservateur du Cabinet des Mèdailles at The Bibliothéque Nationale de France, Paris. Sculpted: 1933, 1937. **LOE168, LOE202**

BARING, Evelyn, 1st Earl of Cromer (1841-1917). British diplomat and administrator. Consul general and virtual ruler of Egypt between 1883 and 1907. Sculpted: 1906 (65th birthday). **LOE023**

BAUER, Eran Nicodemus (born 1954). The elder son of Dr Jakob Bauer by his second wife, Gizella. Has memories of Loewental lodging at Wellingore. Sculpted: 1963. **LOE261**

BAUER, Gerard Miet (born 1956). The younger son of Dr Jakob Bauer by his second wife, Gizella. Has memories of Loewental lodging at Wellingore. Sculpted: 1962. **LOE260**

BAUER, Gizella (Gitta). The second wife of Dr Jakob Bauer. Looked after Loewental for the final five years of his life at Wellingore. Sculpted: c.1959. **LOE258**

BAUER, Dr Jakob (Jacob) (died 1961). A doctor who had studied medicine in Poland and received his MD at Warsaw University in 1926. He arranged for Loewental to lodge in his house at Wellingore when Rosa Loewental died. Sculpted: c.1959 **LOE257**

BAUER, Ralph. The son of Dr Jakob Bauer by his first wife. Sculpted: c.1961. **LOE259**

BEARSTED, Lady. The wife of Lord Bearsted. Sculpted: 1936, 1938. **LOE196, LOE203**

BEARSTED, Walter Samuel 2nd Viscount (1882-1948). Prominent art collector; Chairman of Shell between 1927 and 1948, and British Peer. He was one of the sponsors of Loewental's application for British nationality in 1940. Sculpted: 1939. **LOE206, 207**

BEETHOVEN, Ludwig van (1770-1827). German composer, considered one of the greatest musicians of all time. Sculpted: 1912. **LOE032, 033, 034, 035**

BISSING, Baron Moritz Ferdinand von (1844-1917). Former Prussian General der Kavallie; Governor General of occupied Belgium from 1914 until his death. Sculpted: 1916. **LOE083**

BISSING, Baroness Alice von, née Countess Königsmarck. The wife of Baron Moritz Ferdinand von Bissing. Sculpted: 1916 **LOE084**

BODE, Dr Wilhelm von (1845-1929). German art historian. He was the creator and first curator of the Kaiser Friedrich Museum in 1904. Became General Director of German Museums in 1905. Sculpted: 1914 (70th birthday) 1926 (80th birthday). **LOE050, LOE117**

BODENHAUSEN-DEGENER, Baron Hans Eberhard von (1868-1918). German chemical industrialist. In 1910 he was the leader in the formation of the Iron and Steel Association. Served on the board of Krupps. Went into politics. Was one of the most important figures in the German and European cultural movement at the turn of the century. Sculpted: 1917 (50th birthday). **LOE100**

BONTIAL, Lady Ann. Sculpted: 1944. **LOE210**

BÖSS, Gustav. Progressive Mayor of Berlin. Sculpted: 1927. **LOE125**

BRAUN, Dr Otto (1872-1955). German Social Democratic politician who intermittently served as Prime Minister of Prussia from 1920 to 1932. Sculpted: 1930. **LOE149, 150, 151, 152**

BÜLOW, Karl von (1846-1921). German Field Marshal who commanded the German 2nd Army during World War 1 from 1914 to 1916. Sculpted: 1916, to commemorate the battle at St Quentin. **LOE090**

CANDIDA, Maria. Possibly Maria Candida of the Eucharist (1884-1949). Sculpted: c.1913. **LOE036**

CHANNON, Henry Paul Guinness (1935-2007). The only child of Sir Henry Channon and Lady Honor Guinness Channon. Conservative MP and Minister. He was created a life peer as Baron Kelvedon of Ongar in 1997. Sculpted: 1937, as a child. **LOE199, 200, 201**

CHURCHILL, Winston Spencer, later Sir (1874-1965). Politician and Prime Minister of Great Britain during World War 2, he was knighted in 1953. Sculpted: 1944 (Victory medal) **LOE212, 213, 214, 215**; 1945 (Victory medal) **LOE217, 218, 219, 220**; 1965 (posthumous death commemorative) **LOE262, 263, 264, 265, 266, 267**

COHEN, Salo (c.1842-1917). Director of the Jewish community in Vienna, died 1917 aged 75. Sculpted: 1901 (60th birthday). **LOE009**

COOPER, Francis John (?) Director of the City of Lincoln Libraries, Museum and Art Gallery, 1936-1961. Friend and supporter of Loewental during his time in Lincoln. He arranged exhibitions of Loewental's work at the Usher Art Gallery in 1941/2 and 1955, as well as minor displays at the Lincolnshire Artists Society's annual exhibitions. Sculpted: 1944, 1948, 1950. **LOE211, LOE238, 239, LOE246**

DÄUBLER, Theodor (1876-1934). German poet, born in Trieste, Austria-Hungary (now in Italy), whose extraordinary vitality and optimism sharply contrasted with the despair expressed by many writers of his time. Sculpted: 1927 (50th birthday), 1929, 1931 (55th birthday). **LOE118, LOE140, LOE158, 159**

**DOHNA-SCHLODIEN, Count Nikolaus Paul Richard zu** (1879-1956). German naval officer and author. Commandant of the minelayer and armed merchantman *Möwe* (*Seagull*). Sculpted: 1916. **LOE091**

**DOMANIG, Dr Karl** (1850-1913). Director of the Vienna Münzkabinetts. Sculpted: 1914. **LOE040**

**DONATH, Adolph** (1876-1937). Czechoslovakian poet and connoisseur. Sculpted: 1926 (50th birthday). **LOE115, 116**

**DONNERSMARCK, Prince Guido Henckel von** (1830-1916). Major Silesian industrialist and landowner. Member of the Prussian Upper Chamber. Sculpted: 1915 (85th birthday) and 1916 to commemorate his death. **LOE068, 069** and **LOE087, 088**

**DUCHESS OF DEVONSHIRE, see GASCOYNE-CECIL, Mary Alice, Marchioness of Hartington.**

**EFROSS, James M.** Possibly the American of the same name. Sculpted: 1950. **LOE247**

**EICHBERG, Dr Friedrich.** Famous as an inventor of electrical machinery. Sculpted: 1930. **LOE143**

**EINSTEIN, Professor Albert** (1879-1955). German-born theoretical physicist, widely regarded as the most important scientist of the 20th century. He developed the special and general theories of relativity and made significant contributions to quantum mechanics. Sculpted: 1930 **LOE145, 146**; 1948 **LOE231, 232**; 1950 (70th birthday) **LOE248, 249**.

**FENNELL, Dr Augustine Joseph** (1900-1980). Born in Cork, Eire, he purchased a practice on Yarborough Road, Lincoln. He was Loewental's friend and GP during his time in Lincoln. Sculpted: 1954. **LOE250, 251**

**FENNELL, John Desmond, later Sir** (1933-2011). The son of Dr Augustine Joseph Fennell. He knew Loewental during his time in Lincoln. Sculpted: 1955. **LOE252, 253, 254, 255**

**FERDINAND I, Tzar of Bulgaria** (1861-1948). Born Prince Ferdinand Maximilian Karl Leopold Maria of Saxe-Coburg and Gotha-Koháry. Author, botanist, entomologist and philatelist Sculpted: 1916. **LOE097**

**FLECHTHEIM, Alfred** (1878-1937). German art dealer of international fame. Sculpted: 1928 (50th birthday). **LOE131**

**FRANCKENSTEIN, Baron Georg von und zu** (1878-1953). Austrian Minister to the Court of St James in London from 1920-1938. Knighted in 1938 to become **Sir George Franckenstein**. Sculpted: 1935; 1941; 1944; 1946. **LOE174, 175, 176; LOE 208; LOE209; LOE221, 222.**

**FRIEDENSBERG, Walter.** German naval lieutenant. Sculpted: 1915. **LOE065**

**FRIEDLAENDER, Max Jacob** (1867-1958). German art historian and Director General of German museums. Sculpted: 1928 (60th birthday) and 1929. **LOE135** and **LOE139**

**GÄRTNER.** Musician. Possibly Eduard Gärtner (1862-1918) Austrian composer. Sculpted: 1901. **LOE008**

**GAERTNER, Eduard.** Austrian singer of light opera. Sculpted: 1900. **LOE006**

**GASCOIGNE-CECIL, Mary Alice, Marchioness of Hartington** (1895-1988). Married, in 1917, Edward Cavendish,

Lord Hartington, who succeeded his father as 10th Duke of Devonshire in 1938, whereupon Mary became **Duchess of Devonshire**. Sculpted: 1936 (40th birthday). **LOE197**

**GEYGER, Captain.** Noted connoisseur. Sculpted: 1928. **LOE134**

**GIRARDI, Alexander** (1850-1918). Austrian singer of light opera. Sculpted: 1905 (55th birthday) and 1915 (65th birthday). **LOE022** and **LOE062**

**GOETHE, Johann Wolfgang von** (1749-1832). German poet, dramatist, novelist and scientist. One of the key figures in German literature and the movement of Weimar Classicism in the late 18th and 19th centuries. Sculpted: 1932, to mark the centenary of his death. **LOE162**

**GREEN, Neal Cornelius Friend** (1885-1974). Trawler owner, gentleman farmer, although as a painter his first love was the arts. He befriended Loewental and invited him for lunch at Holbeck Manor about once a fortnight, though Rosa usually declined. Sculpted: 1946 (60th birthday?). **LOE223, 224**

**GREIF, Dr Wilfrid.** A director of I. G. Farben, New York. Sculpted: c.1930? (50th birthday). **LOE147**

**HAESELER, Count Ferdinand Albert Alexis von** (1836-1919). German general field marshal. Sculpted: 1915 (80th birthday). **LOE070, 071**

**HAMBRO, Lady Elizabeth** (1920-1995). Sculpted: 1934. **LOE177, 178**

**HARTMANN, Dr Franz** (1838-1912). German theosopher and author. In 1896 he founded a German theosophical society. Sculpted: 1904. **LOE018**

**HASS, Dr Johannes.** Leader of the Centrum Party, Bavarian Catholics. Sculpted: c.1918, 1928. **LOE101, LOE129**

**HERZOG, Rudolf** (1869-1943). German writer, journalist, poet and story teller. Sculpted: 1914 (45th birthday). **LOE049**

**HILL, James William Francis, later Sir Francis** (1899-1980). Alderman and sometime Mayor of Lincoln; solicitor and senior partner of Andrew & Company, solicitors of Lincoln. His services to local government were recognised by a knighthood in 1958. He befriended Loewental during his life in Lincoln. Sculpted: 1948 and c.1958 to commemorate his knighthood. **LOE228, 229** and **LOE256**

**HILL, Sir George Francis** (1867-1948). Knighted 1933. Keeper of the Department of Coins and Medals at the British Museum 1912-30; Director and Principal Librarian at the British Museum 1931-36. He was one of the sponsors of Loewental's application for British nationality in 1940. Sculpted: 1935, 1936, 1938. **LOE187, LOE194, 195, LOE205**

**HINDENBURG, Paul Ludwig Hans Anton von Beneckendorff und von** (1847-1934). German general and field marshal who scored a notable victory at Tannenberg in August 1914. Later tried starving Britain into surrender by unrestricted submarine warfare. Became President of the Weimar Republic 1925-1934. Sculpted: 1914 (the victory at Tannenberg) **LOE043, 044, 045, 046. 047, 048**; 1916 **LOE075**; 1925, as President of the Weimar Republic **LOE111**; 1930 **LOE144**.

**HOFFMANN, Dr Adolph.** Possibly the same person as below?Sculpted: 1902. **LOE013**

**HOFFMANN, Dr Alfred.** Sculpted: 1906 (80th birthday). **LOE024**

**HÖPKER-ASCHOFF, Dr Hermann** (1883-1954). Last democratic Minister of Finance of Prussia 1925 to 1931. Sculpted: 1929. **LOE141, 142**

**HÜNEFELD, Baron Ehrenfried Günther von** (1892-1929). German aviation pioneer and initiator of the first transatlantic flight in east-west direction. Sculpted: 1929, to commemorate his death. **LOE136**

**ISAACS, Rufus Daniel, First Marquess of Reading** (1860-1935). Politician, Lord Chief Justice, and Ambassador and Viceroy of India. Sculpted: 1935 (75th birthday), 1936, to commemorate his death. **LOE192, LOE193**

**JOSEPH I, Franz, of Austria** (1830-1916). Emperor of Austria. Sculpted: 1914 (Austro-German Alliance). **LOE064**

**KANITZ, Moriz.** Sculpted: 1898. **LOE002**

**KERR, Dr Alfred** (1867-1948). Poet, journalist and dramatic critic. Sculpted: 1927 (60th birthday). **LOE120**

**KIPLING, Joseph Rudyard** (1865-1936). English short story writer, poet and novelist. Sculpted: 1935 (70th birthday) and 1936, to commemorate his death. **LOE188, 189, 190, 191** and **LOE198**

**KLUCK, Alexander Heinrich Rudolph von** (1846-1934). German field commander who led the First Army in the opening campaigns of the Western Front from August 1914. He was almost successful in defeating France, his forces being halted 13 miles from Paris in the battle of the Marne from 6-9 September 1914. Sculpted: 1915 (the drive on Paris). **LOE052, 053, 054, 055**

**KREISLER, Professor Fritz** (1875-1962). Austrian-born violinist and composer. His brilliant technique brought him recognition as one of the most accomplished violinists of his time. Sculpted: 1912. **LOE031**; 1926 (50th birthday). **LOE114**

**KREISLER, Harriet, previously Harriet Woerz, née Lies.** The wife of Fritz Kreisler. Sculpted: 1912. **LOE031**

**KRUPP VON BOHLEN UND HALBACH, Gustav** (1870-1950). Major German industrialist. Chosen by Wilhelm II to marry Bertha Krupp and add Krupp to his name. The Krupp field gun 'Big Bertha' played a vital role in the German advance in 1914 and at Verdun in 1916. In 1918 a new cannon, the 'Paris Gun', shelled Paris from a 75-mile distance. Sculpted: 1916. **LOE076**

**KRUPP VON BOHLEN UND HALBACH, Alfried** (1907-1967). German industrialist. The eldest son of Gustav Krupp von Bohlen und Halbach. He joined the family firm in 1936 and helped rearm Nazi Germany. May have been instrumental in aiding Loewental's flight from Germany in 1934. Sculpted: c.1916, as a child. **LOE079**

**(KRUPP) VON BOHLEN UND HALBACH, Claus Arthur Arnold** (1910-1940). The son of Gustav Krupp von Bohlen und Halbach. Sculpted: 1916, as a child. **LOE080**

**KRUPP, Margarethe** (1854-1931). The wife of Friedrich Alfred Krupp. Daughter of the Prussian Baron August von Ende. She was involved in the planning and building of the Margarethenhöhe housing estate, which like the other company benefit schemes, became a lifetime commitment. Sculpted: 1916 (60th birthday). **LOE077, 078**

**LEWIS, Mrs, of Vienna.** Sculpted: 1902. **LOE012**

**LICHTENSTERN, Wilhelm.** Advocate. Sculpted: 1904. **LOE017**

**LITZMANN, KARL** (1850-1936). German general, the victor of Kowno, 1917. Sculpted: 1917 (as the victor of Kowno). **LOE099**

**LOEBE, Paul.** President of the Reichstag. Sculpted: 1928, 1930. **LOE130, LOE148**

**LOEHR, August Ritter von.** Vice president of the first camera club in Austria. Sculpted: 1899. **LOE005**

**LOEWENTAL, Antonia** (1850-1942). The mother of the sculptor Artur Immanuel Loewental. Sculpted: 1924. **LOE106, 107**

**LOEWENTAL, Clara Ottilie** (1875-1944). Sister of the sculptor Artur Immanuel Loewental. Sculpted ? (n.d.) **LOE109**

**LOEWENTAL, Paula Auguste** (born 1882). Sister of the sculptor Artur Immanuel Loewental. Sculpted ? (n.d.) **LOE108**

**LOEWENTAL, Artur Immanuel** (1879-1964). Self-portrait. Sculpted: n.d. c.1929? (50th birthday), 1949 (70th birthday). **LOE110, LOE230**

**LOEWENTAL, Rosa Katharina Josepha** (1881-1958). The wife of the sculptor Artur Immanuel Loewental. Sculpted: 1910 (marriage to Artur); 1914; n.d. c1926? (45th birthday). **LOE028, 029; LOE042; LOE112, 113**

**LOOS, Adolf** (1870-1933). Austrian architect whose planning of private residences strongly influenced European Modernist architects after World War 1. Sculpted: 1910 (40th birthday). **LOE025, 026**

**MACKENSEN, August von** (1849-1945). Considered one of the best field commanders of the German army during World War One. Promoted to Field Marshal in 1915. Sculpted: 1915, to commemorate the Galician offensive, and c.1916. **LOE072, 073** and **LOE075**

**MALTZAN, Count Andreas.** Sculpted: 1916. **LOE089**

**MALTZAN, Countess von.** Sculpted: 1917. **LOE098**

**MAPLES, Ashley K** (1868-1950). President of the Spalding Gentlemen's Society. He arranged for the SGS to purchase Loewental's valuable collection of Chinese glass, ceramics, hardstone carvings, etc in 1948. Sculpted: 1948, medallion commissioned by members of the Spalding Gentlemen's Society. **LOE233**

**MARIC, Anton, of Dalmatia.** Sculpted: 1938. **LOE204**

**MATTER, Herr.** Clerk to the Mayor of Berlin. Sculpted: 1928. **LOE128**

**MENGERSON, Countess.** German head of the Red Cross in Belgium. Sculpted: 1916. **LOE092**

**MERCKENS, Dr Otto.** Managing director and chairman of the NSU-Werke in Neckarsulm. Sculpted: 1927, to celebrate his becoming chairman. **LOE123, 124**

**NEWLINSKI, Baroness.** Sculpted: 1903. **LOE015**

**ORSINI, Princess Fulvia, of Italy.** Sculpted: 1920. **LOE104**

**PLANCK, Professor Max Karl Ernst Ludwig von** (1858-1947). German physicist and Nobel laureate who was the originator of quantum theory. Sculpted: 1931. **LOE160, 161**

POSADOWSKY-WIEHNER, Count Arthur von (1845-1932). Minister of State. Sculpted: 1915 (70th birthday). **LOE061**

RAUSENBERGER, Professor Fritz (1868-1926). Professor at the Militärtechn. Akademie in Charlottenburg. Sculpted: n.d. (WW1, 1918? 50th birthday) **LOE093**

RUSS, Dr V. W. Member of the Austrian Parliament. Sculpted: 1902. **LOE014**

SCHLESWIG-HOLSTEIN-SONDERBURG-GLÜCKSBURG, Alexandra Victoria von (1887-1957). Princess August Wilhelm of Prussia. Sculpted: 1916 (30th birthday). **LOE086**

SCHMIDT, Professor Robert. Director of the Schloss Museum, Berlin. Sculpted: 1932. **LOE163**

SCHMOLLER, Professor von. Scientist and political economist Sculpted: 1914. **LOE041**

SCHURMAN, Professor Jacob Gould (1854-1942). American educationist who served as United States Ambassador to China between 1921 and 1925, and then Ambassador to Germany between 1925 and 1929. Sculpted: 1929 (75th birthday and retirement) **LOE137**

SPEE, Count Maximilian Johannes Maria Hubertus von (1861-1914). German Vice Admiral. At the Battle of the Falkland Islands, 8 December 1914, heavily outgunned, six German ships, including Spee's own flagship, were sunk, with some 2,200 sailors drowned, among them Spee himself. Sculpted: 1914, to commemorate the Falkland Islands battle. **LOE074**

STERNE, Herr. Sculpted: 1920. **LOE105**

STIASSING, Dr H. A lawyer from Prague. Sculpted: 1904. **LOE019**

TENNANT, Christopher Grey, in 1920 became 2nd **BARON GLENCONNOR** (1899-1983). He was a named sponsor of Loewental's application for British nationality in 1940, although he was unable to be contacted due to his war service. Sculpted: c1934 (35th birthday). **LOE184, 185**

TENNANT, Colin Christopher Paget, in 1983 became 3rd **BARON GLENCONNOR** (born 1926). First son of Christopher Grey Tennant. Sculpted: 1934, as a child. **LOE179, 180**

TENNANT, James Grey Herbert (1929-1992). Son of Christopher Grey Tennant. Sculpted: 1935, as a child. **LOE181, 182, 183**

THIMME, Dr Friedrich Wilhelm Karl (1868-1938). Historian and political publicist. Sculpted: 1927 (60th birthday). **LOE119**

TIRPITZ, Alfred von (1849-1930). German Grand Admiral and Secretary of State of the Imperial Naval Office. Was chiefly responsible for the build-up of the German navy, including its submarine fleet. He retired in 1916. Sculpted: 1915. **LOE058, 059, 060**

TRINKS, Wilhelm. Viennese numismatist. Sculpted: 1899. **LOE003, 004**

TWAIN, Mark (Pseudonym of **Samuel Langhorne Clemens**) (1835-1910). American humorist, writer, and lecturer, who won a worldwide audience for his stories of youthful adventures. Sculpted: 1898. **LOE001**

VEECK, Alex. Sculpted: 1932. **LOE164**

WAGNER, Professor Adolph (1835-1917). Economist and financier, professor of political science at Berlin University. Sculpted: 1915 (80th birthday). **LOE063**

WALDHOF, Rudolph Alter von. Chief of the Austrian judiciary. Sculpted: 1900. **LOE007**

WEDDIGEN, Otto (1882-1915). A daring German submarine commander. He was killed with all hands on 18 or 25 March 1915 when the new U-boat U-29 which he was commanding sank after being rammed by the British battleship HMS Dreadnought. Sculpted: 1915. **LOE066**

WEISMANN, Robert. Last democratic Secretary of State of Prussia. Sculpted: 1928. **LOE127**

WILAMOWITZ-MOELLENDORFF, Professor Emmo Friedrich Richard Ulrich von (1848-1931). Greek historian and rector of the University of Berlin. Sculpted: 1916 (70th birthday) and 1928 (80th birthday). **LOE094, 095 and LOE133**

WILHELM II (1859-1941). Last Kaiser of Germany and King of Prussia. Abdicated 9 November 1918. Sculpted: 1914, 1915, 1916. **LOE064, LOE056, 057, LOE096, 097**

WINKLER, Mrs Anna, of Vienna. Sculpted: n.d. **LOE171**

WOLFF, Otto. Steel industrialist of Cologne. Sculpted: 1916, 1919. **LOE085, LOE103**

**Sitters named by forename only**

CORNELIA Sculpted: 1933. **LOE165, 166, 167**

FELIX ?Silk merchant. Sculpted: c1901. **LOE011**

HARALD Sculpted: 1918, 1927. **LOE102, LOE121**

HERBERT Sculpted: 1927. **LOE122**

TITY Sculpted: 1903. **LOE016**

VJERA A Swedish child. Sculpted: n.d. **LOE227**

# SOURCES

## [A] ORIGINAL DOCUMENTS ETC (date order)

**Birth certificate:** Arthur Imanuel Löwenthal, 28 August 1879.

**Pencil sketch:** Samuel Löwenthal drawn by his son Artur, n.d. (The McNichol private collection, England).

**Marriage certificate:** Artur Immanuel Löwenthal and Rosa Sagorc, 4 January 1910.

**Photographic print:** Rosa Löwenthal, n.d. (The McNichol private collection, England).

**Photographic print:** Bronze plaque of Gustav Böss, n.d., ?1927. © *The New York Times Bild-Dienst Wide World Photos*, Berlin. (The Turner private collection, England).

**Photographic print:** Loewental sculpting Albert Einstein, Berlin, 1930. © *The New York Times GmbH,* Berlin. Taken by Wide World Photos, Berlin. (The Collection, Lincoln).

**Photograph:** Loewental sculpting Albert Einstein's bust, Berlin, 1930 (© collections CEGES/SOMA – Brussels. Image No.126746).

**Alien Registration Card:** Artur Loewental, 20 November 1934. (The National Archives, Kew).

**Alien Registration Card:** Rosa Loewental, 20 November 1934. (The National Archives, Kew).

**Glass plate negative:** 11 intaglios from 1939 exhibition of Loewental's work, n.d., *c.*1939. (The Lucas private collection, Canada).

**Glass plate negative:** 6 casts from intaglios by Loewental, n.d. ?1939. (The Lucas private collection, Canada).

**Home Office, Aliens Department file:** HO405/33202, 1940/1, formerly L3041/3; files L3041/1, /2, /4 and /5 have been consolidated. Loewental's application for British nationality. (The National Archives, Kew).

**Alien Registration Card Dead Section:** Artur Loewental, 25 January 1941. (The National Archives, Kew).

**Photographic prints:** Two views of Loewental's collection of Chinese glass, etc as displayed at the Usher Art Gallery, Lincoln, n.d., photographer unknown. (The Collection, Lincoln).

**Photographic print:** Artur and Rosa Loewental at home in West Parade, Lincoln, n.d. (The McNichol private collection, England).

**Appointment diaries:** Sir Francis Hill, 1948, 1957/8 and 1958/9. (Lincolnshire Archives Office, Lincoln).

**Photographic print:** Portrait of Artur Loewental dated August, 1955. Photographer unknown. (The Collection, Lincoln).

**Negative:** Loewental's display board at 1955 exhibition in Usher Art Gallery, Lincoln. Taken by Record & General Photographs Limited, Lincoln. (© Lincolnshire Illustrations Index, Lincoln, image number LC26052).

**Photographic print:** Loewental in front of display at exhibition in Usher Art Gallery, Lincoln, 1955. © *The Lincolnshire Echo.* (Spalding Gentlemen's Society, Spalding).

**Death Certificate:** Rosa Loewental, 13 January 1958.

**Last Will and Testament:** Artur Loewental, 3 June 1959.

**Photographic print:** An elderly Artur Loewental seated on a garden bench, n.d. (The McNichol private collection, England).

**Death Certificate:** Artur Loewental, 17 November 1964.

**Deposition by Anthony Lucas:** 25 November 1964. Memorandum re *vasa murrina.* (The McNichol private collection, England).

**Deposition by Anthony Lucas:** 30 December 1964. Digest of letters written by Loewental. (The McNichol private collection, England).

**Deposition by Anthony Lucas:** 23 January 1965. Memorandum of meeting with Coopers. (The McNichol private collection, England).

**Probate Certificate:** Granted to Gizella Bauer, 12 March 1965.

## [B] CORRESPONDENCE ETC

### (a) Extracts of letters written in German by Loewental, retained in Germany, published in Steguweit 1998

Essen, 22 February 1916

Berlin, 4 May 1916

Berlin, 5 May 1916

Brussels, 17 July 1916

Brussels, 1 August 1916

*c.*1916 n.d.

Schloß Militsch, Bezirk Breslau, 6 November 1916.

### (b) Letters retained in the Albert Einstein Archive, Jerusalem

**Albert Einstein** to the director of the Metropolitan Museum, NY, 24 March 1930. Einstein praises Loewental's artistic productions, saying that there is no future in Europe for an artist like him, trying to encourage the museum's directors to invite Loewental to the USA. (Poor carbon copy only).

**Albert Einstein** to Mr Boyce Thompson, a noted lapidary, NY, 16 October 1930. Einstein praises Loewental's skill in crafting gems and calls attention to his qualifications. (Poor carbon copy only).

**Albert Einstein** to Max Liebermann, 30 March 1930. AEA 34-124.00. Praising Loewental 's work.

**Loewental** to Albert Einstein, October/November, 1930, with handwritten reply. AEA 47-253.00. Pleading on behalf of his friend Carlo Klein. (Fragment only).

### (c) Copies of correspondence, etc, retained at The National Archives, Kew:

**Letter:** Sir George Hill to Oswald Peake MP, 12 July 1940, urging Loewental's naturalisation.

**Letter:** Sir George Hill to Oswald Peake MP, 12 July 1940. Follow-up note to above.

**Letter:** Ian Roy to Sir George Hill, July 1940. Acknowledgement of above.

**Memo:** Summary of Loewental's qualifications and background, 19 July 1940.

**Letter:** Sir George Hill to Ian Roy, 21 July 1940, urging Loewental's naturalisation.

**Letter:** Ian Roy to Sir George Hill, 23 July 1940. Not in a position to give a definite reply.

**Memo:** Re suspension of ordinary applications, August 1940.

**Letter:** A. Lenfestey to Sir George Hill, 20 August 1940. Application to be allowed.

Letter: Sir George Hill to A. Lenfestey, 24 August 1940. Acknowledgement of above.

Memo: Re letter from the Department of Scientific and Industrial Research (now destroyed) received as proof of Loewental's worth, 26 September 1940.

Reference form: By Lord Bearsted, 2 October 1940.

Reference form: By Sir George Hill, 3 October 1940.

Reference form: Returned as Lord Glenconnor not contactable, 4 October 1940.

Letter: Loewental to Under Secretary of State, 5 October 1940, re location of Lord Glenconnor.

Reference form: By Sir Robert Abdy, 6 October 1940.

Memo: Re letter from Ministry of Supply, Diamond Dies Control, to Loewental, (now destroyed) commissioning him to set up a laboratory, 10 October 1940.

Special report: By Metropolitan Police Special Branch, 18 October 1940. Report on Loewental and his family.

Memo: To proceed with only three referees, 5 November 1940.

Memo: Loewental meets all of the necessary requirements, 6 December 1940.

Form: Listing Loewental's details for inclusion on his certificate of naturalisation, 21 December 1940.

Letter: Loewental to Under Secretary of State, 21 December 1940. Fee for naturalisation certificate.

Letter: Rosa Loewental to Under Secretary of State, n.d., requesting British nationality.

Letter: Loewental to Under Secretary of State, 20 February 1941. Registering his certificate of naturalisation.

Letter: Lincoln's Chief Constable to Central Register of Aliens, 18 October 1941. Rosa Loewental granted certificate of naturalisation.

### (d) A selection of correspondence in German from Loewental to his nephew Tony Lucas. (The McNichol private collection, England)

1940 Letter: 24 August 1940, re Amethyst cup.

1941 Letter: 2 December 1941. (1/119) His collections to be left to Tony.

1948 Letter: May/June 1948, re *vasa murrina*, letter from Einstein, etc.

1955 Letter: 7 October 1955, re rock crystal engraving of Einstein.

1957 Letter: 1 December 1957 (78/119). Re visit to Berlin re reparations.

1958 Letter: February 1958 (80/119). First letter after his wife's death.

1958 Letter: 16 March 1958 (82/119). Re new will making Tony chief beneficiary.

1958 Letter: 23 March 1958 (83/119) to arrange meeting to discuss many things.

1958 Letter: 30 March 1958 (84/119) thanking Tony for restoring and rebinding copy of Dante.

1959 Letter: 30 January 1959 (92/119) thanking Tony for completing Appian, urging him once again to take up restoration and bookbinding as a career, fate of astrakhan fur coat.

1959 Letter: 24 February 1959 (93/119). Fine conditions at Wellingore, please return the astrakhan fur coat.

1959 Letter: 7 April 1959 (94/119). Thanking Tony for return of coat; has been away in hospital; cheque for Appian.

1959 Letter: 22 April 1959 (95/119) re discussion of private matters.

1959 Letter: 5 May 1959 (96/119) in answer to Tony's request for a loan for house purchase.

1959 Letter: September 1959 (98/119) re Tony's home move.

1960 Letter: May 1960 (99/119) re Tony's new occupation.

1960 Postcard: 1 July 1960 (100/119) complaining of Tony's long silence.

1960 Letter: 21 July 1960 (101/119). Loewental cannot get around as much as he would like; does not wish Tony to come to Wellingore.

1960 Letter: Woodhall Spa, 1 September 1960 (102/119). Staying at Woodhall Spa for three weeks as Bauers are away on holiday.

1960 Letter: 8 October 1960 (103/119). Not able to visit Tony in Leatherhead as Dr Bauer has had an accident and has new car.

1961 Letter: 17 May 1961 (104/119). Apologies for long silence; could he come to stay for two days.

1961 Letter: 21 July 1961 (105/119).

1961 Letter: 16 September 1961 (106/119). Loewental ill the whole of August.

1961 Letter: 1 November 1961. (107/119). Notice of Dr Bauer's death.

1962 Letter: 19 February 1962 (108/119) urging Tony to repay £50 loan.

1962 Letter: 21 February 1962 (109/119) urging Tony to repay £50 loan.

1962 Letter: 24 April 1962 (110/119). Receipt for £25 received; Loewental is under pressure.

1962 Letter: 25 May 1962 (111/119). Receipt for repayment.

1962 Letter: 14 June 1962 (112/119). Receipt for balance of loan.

1962 Letter: 1 November 1962 (113/119). 'There is no need for you to spend time and money to look after me'.

1962 Letter: 15 November 1962 (114/119). Does not wish to see Tony again.

1963 Letter: 5 September 1963 (115/119) thanking Tony for letter.

1964 Postcard: From nursing home, 9 April 1964 (116/119) asking Tony to obtain coffee percolator for him as he is returning to Wellingore.

1964 Letter: 16 April 1964 (117/119) thanking Tony for percolator.

1964 Letter: 13 May 1964 (118/119). Payment for coffee percolator and chocolates for Tony's children.

1964 Letter: Whitsun 1964 (119/119). A few personal lines; the last letter to Tony.

### (e) Correspondence etc, retained by The Collection, Lincoln:
1946 Letter: Sir George Hill to the Fitzwilliam Museum. 18 February 1946. Gift of Loewental's Churchill medal.

n.d. Receipt: Items returned to Loewental from the Usher Gallery: Bronze bust Otto Braun, ditto small head, plaster busts of Lord Bearsted (2), plus pieces of marble. n.d.

**1952 Receipt:** Items returned to Loewental from the Usher Gallery: Wax of Trinks, stone matrix 'Labour and Wealth', ditto 'Vial Glock', ditto 'Bode', plus pieces of gemstone. 18 June 1952.

**1954 Letter:** Paul Fierens, Musées Royaux des Beaux-Arts de Belgique, to Mr F. T. Baker, 19 March 1954, re Stoclet's libation cup.

**1954 Letter:** Mr F. T. Baker to Mr Jacques Stoclet, written on behalf of Loewental, 23 April 1954, re Stoclet's libation cup.

**1954 Receipt:** Item returned to Loewental from the Usher Gallery: plaster horse in case. 1 October 1954.

**1955 Receipt:** Items from Loewental to be delivered to the Royal Academy: display board of 13 bronze medals and bronze medal on mahogany mount. 17 February 1955.

**1956 Receipt:** Items returned to Loewental from the Usher Gallery: display board of 13 medals. 21 January 1956.

**1961 Typewritten list:** Loewental's plaster casts stored by the Usher Gallery, on loan since November 1947. 16 June 1961.

**1964 Letter:** Mr F. T. Baker to Dr Donald Harden, 19 November 1964 re Loewental's funeral and the fate of the *vasa murrina*.

**1964 Letter:** Mr F. T. Baker to Mr R. J. Charleston, V&A Museum, 19 November 1964, re Loewental's death.

**1964 Letter:** Dr Donald Harden to Mr F. T. Baker, 4 December 1964. Regret at Loewental's death and what has happened to the *vasa murrina*.

**1964 Letter:** Mr F. T. Baker to Dr Donald Harden, 11 December 1964. Location of the *vasa murrina* and its final fate.

**(f) Correspondence etc retained by the Spalding Gentlemen's Society, Spalding:**

**1948 Letter:** Loewental to Ashley Maples, 25 July 1948, re medal of Maples.

**1948 Letter:** Loewental to Mr Bailey, 25 September 1948, re medal of Maples.

**1948 Letter:** Loewental to Mr Bailey, 30 September 1948, re his collection.

**1948 Letter:** Loewental to Mr Bailey, 5 October 1948, re exhibition.

**1948 Letter:** Ashley Maples to Mr Turner, 31 October 1948, re purchase of Loewental's collection of Chinese glass, etc.

**1948 Letter:** Ashley Maples to Mr Turner, 22 November 1948, re purchase of Loewental's collection of Chinese glass, etc.

**1948 Letter:** Loewental to Mr Bailey, 22 November 1948, re proposed lecture by Loewental.

**1948 Handwritten draft for speech** by Ashley Maples, 24 November 1948, re support for the purchase of Loewental's collection of Chinese glass, etc.

**1949 Letter:** Ashley Maples to Mr Turner, 5 February 1949, re the purchase of Loewental's collection of Chinese glass, etc.

**1949 Letter:** Loewental to Mr Bailey, 1 April 1949, re newspaper articles and photographs.

**1949 Letter:** Loewental to Ashley Maples, 18 December 1949, re final disposal of his collections and works.

**1949 Letter:** Mr Turner to Loewental, 21 December 1949, re final disposal choices.

**1953 Letter:** Loewental to Mr Bailey, 20 Dec 1953, re his illness.

**(g) Other miscellaneous correspondence:**

**1948 Letter:** Albert Einstein to Loewental, 30 July 1948. Possibly in connection with selling his *vasa murrina* (sold in the USA in 2005 to an unknown buyer).

**[C] PUBLISHED REFERENCES**

**Attwood, Philip and Powell, Felicity,** *Medals of dishonour,* (London, The British Museum Press, 2009).

**Babelon, J.,** 'Graveurs en pierres fines contemporains', in *Demareteion Numismatique-Glyptique-Archaeologie, Haute Curiosite, I,* (Paris, 1935), pp.178, 180.

**Barnett, R. D. (editor),** *Catalogue of the permanent and loan collections of the Jewish Museum London,* (London, Harvey Miller, 1974).

**Bénézit, E.,** *Dictionnaire critique et documentaire des peintres sculpteurs dessinateurs et graveurs de tous les temps et de tous les pays par un groupe d'écrivains spécialistes français et étrangers. Tome 8 Köster-Magand,* (Paris, Éditions Gründ, nouvelle edition, 1999).

**Brown, Laurence,** *A catalogue of British historical medals 1760-1960, Volume III. The accession of Edward VII to 1960,* (London, Spink & Son Ltd, 1995).

**Carrington, Charles,** *Rudyard Kipling, his life and work,* (Macmillan London Limited, third edition, 1978).

**City of Lincoln Libraries, Museums and Art Gallery, 1963.** *City of Lincoln Libraries, Museums and Art Gallery review for the year 1962.*

**Cooper, Denis R.,** *The art and craft of coinmaking. A history of minting technology,* (London, Spink & Son, 1988).

**Cooper, Francis J.,** 'The mystery of *vasa murrina* solved', in *The Connoisseur,* Volume 127, January-June, 1951, (London), pp.16-17.

**Dougan, A.M., and Furlong, M,** *Art index: a cumulative author and subject index to a selected list of fine arts periodicals and museum bulletins, volume 1935/1938, K-Z,* (H. W. Wilson, 1938).

**Ebenezer Baylis & Son Ltd., 1935.** *Who's who in Lincolnshire,* (Worcester: Ebenezer Baylis & Son Ltd).

**Eimer, Christopher,** *British commemorative medals and their values,* (London, A. Seaby, 1987).

**Engstrom, J. Eric,** *The medallic portraits of Sir Winston Churchill,* (London: Spink & Son Ltd, 1972).

**Fearon, Daniel,** *Spink's catalogue of British commemorative medals 1558 to the present day with valuations,* (Exeter, Webb & Bower Publishers Ltd, 1984).

**Fine Art Society,** *Intaglio carvings in crystal, cornelian, agate and other semi-precious stones by A. I. Loewental (May 1939),* (London, The Fine Art Society Ltd, 1939).

**Ford, Trevor D.,** *Derbyshire Blue John,* (Ashbourne, Ashbourne Editions, second edition, 2005).

**Forrer, L.,** *Biographical dictionary of medallist coin, gem, and seal-engravers, mint-masters, &c. ancient and modern, with references to their works B.C.500-A.D.1900, volume VII supplement A-L,* (London, Spink & Son Ltd, 1923).

**Franckenstein, Sir George,** *Facts and features of my life,* (London, Cassell and Company Ltd, 1939).

**Frankenhuis, M.,** *Collection M. Frankenhuis. Catalogue of medals – medalets and plaques relative to the World War 1914-1919,* (Enschede, Holland, 1919).

Friedenberg, Daniel M. (ed), *Great Jewish portraits in metal: selected plaques and medals from the Samuel Friedenberg collection of the Jewish Museum*, (New York, Schocken Books Inc, 1963).

Friedenberg, Daniel M., *Jewish minters and medallists*, (Philadelphia, The Jewish Publication Society of America, 1976).

Friedenberg, Daniel M., 'Jews and the art of the medal', in *The Numismatist*, July 1969, pp.891-919.

Friedländer, Saul, *The years of persecution: Nazi Germany and the Jews 1933-1939*, (London, Phoenix, 2007).

Fry, Helen, *The King's most loyal enemy aliens, Germans who fought for Britain in the Second World War*, (Stroud: Sutton Publishing, 2007).

Giodsenhoven, J. P. van, *Adolphe Stoclet collection (part 1). Selection of the works belonging to Madame Feron-Stoclet*, (Brussels, J. P. van Giodsenhoven, 1956).

Grant, Colonel M. H., 'Catalogue of British medals since 1760, part IV (1910-1937)', in *The British Numismatic Journal*, (London, The British Numismatic Society, 1940/41), pp.455, 456, 470.

Grodzinski, Paul, *Diamond technology: production methods for diamond and gem stones*, (N. A. G. Press Ltd., second edition, 1953).

Gunstone, Antony, *Sylloge of coins of the British Isles, vol. 27, coins in the Lincolnshire collections*, (Oxford University Press, 1981).

Hill, Sir Francis, *Medieval Lincoln*, (Stamford, Paul Watkins, reprint of 1948 first edition with added biography of Hill, 1990).

Hill, George F., *The commemorative medal in the service of Germany*, (London, Longmans, Green and Co, 1917).

Hill, George F. and Brooke, G. C, *A guide to the exhibition of historical medals in the British Museum*, (London, British Museum, 1924).

Harden, D. B., '*Vasa Murrina* again', in the *Journal of Roman Studies*, 44, (The Society for the Promotion of Roman Studies, 1954), p.53.

Henry Spencer & Sons. *By order of Mrs G. Bauer and in the estate of the late Dr J. Bauer. The contents of The Old Rectory Wellingore Lincoln to be sold by auction on the premises Tuesday & Wednesday 28 & 29 October 1980*, (Retford: Henry Spencer & Sons, 1980).

'Het Sterckshof', *Internationale Tentoonstelling Hedendaagse Penningkunst 27 Juni – 27 September 1959 Catalogus*, ("Het Sterckshof", Provinciaal Museum vorr Kunstambachten, 1959).

Historisches Museum der Stadt Wien, *Traum und Wirklichkeit, Wien 1870-1930*, (Vienna, Historisches Museum der Stadt Wien, 1985).

Hutchinson & Co, *The year's art 1940*, (London, Hutchinson and Co Publishers Ltd, 1940).

*Illustrated London News*, 15 June 1935, (London), p.1062.

Isaacson, Walter, *Einstein his life and universe*, (London, Simon & Schuster UK Ltd, 2007).

*Jewish Chronicle*, 'The Jewish Museum', in *Jewish Chronicle*, 14 February 1936.

Judd, Denis, *Lord Reading. Rufus Isaacs, First Marquess of Reading, Lord Chief Justice and Viceroy of India, 1860-1935*, (London, Weidenfeld and Nicolson Ltd, 1982).

Kenna, V. E. G., *Cretan seals with a catalogue of the Minoan gems in the Ashmolean Museum*, (Oxford, The Clarendon Press, 1960).

Kraus, Karl (editor), 'In stillen Hören versenkt', in *Die Fackel*, Dreifache Nummer, Nr.360/361/362, November 1912, (Vienna: 'Die Fackel', 1912), pp.35-6.

Kunze, Irene, 'Neuerwerbungen der Gemäldegalerie des Kaiser=Friedrich=Museum zu Berlin', in *Der Kunstwanderer*, (1926/7), (Berlin: *Der Kunstwanderer* G.m.b.H, 1927), pp182-4. Lincoln City Council, *Lincoln register of electors*, (Lincoln City Council, 1939, 1945-1962).

Lincoln Public Libraries, *City of Lincoln Public Libraries Museum & Art Gallery. Readers' book list, February, 1942*, (Lincoln, 1942).

Lincolnshire Family History Society, *An index to Lincoln cemetery burial registers*, (Lincoln, Lincolnshire Family History Society Trustees, 2007).

Lincolnshire Museums, *The collection of the late Sir Francis Hill 1899-1980. An exhibition of paintings, watercolours, prints and coins bequeathed to the Usher Gallery, 7 November – 13 December, 1981*, (Lincoln, Lincolnshire Museums, 1981).

Loewental, Artur, 1926. 'Technik und Geschichte der Steinschneidekunst', in *Der Kunstwanderer* (1925-6), (Berlin, *Der Kunstwanderer*, GmbH), pp.452-7, 489-492.

Loewental, Artur, 1929. 'Wie ich Girardi porträtierte', in *Der Kunstwanderer*, (1928/9), (Berlin, *Der Kunstwanderer* GmbH), pp.458-9.

Loewental, Artur, 'Les grands vases de crystal de roche et leur origine', in *La Gazette des Beaux-Arts*, Janvier 1934, (Paris: Éditions de Gazette des Beaux-Arts, 1934), pp.43-8.

Loewental, Artur I., and Harden, D. B., '*Vasa Murrina*' in the *Journal of Roman Studies* 39, (The Society for the Promotion of Roman Studies, 1949), pp.31-37 and PL.V-VII.

London, Louise, *Whitehall and the Jews, 1933-1948. British immigration policy, Jewish refugees and the Holocaust*, (Cambridge University Press, 2000).

Mackay, James, *The dictionary of sculptors in bronze*, (Woodbridge, Antique Collectors' Club Ltd, reprint of 1977 edition, 1992).

Major, Edward R., *Lincolnshire artists. One hundred years 1906-2006*, (The Lincolnshire Artists' Society, 2006).

Muhlen, Norbert, *The incredible Krupps: the rise, fall, and comeback of Germany's industrial family*, (New York, Award Books, 1969).

*Numismatic Chronicle*, 'German war medals', in *The Numismatic Chronicle and Journal of the Royal Numismatic Society*, series 4, volume 16 (1916/17), pp.107-112.

*Numismatic Chronicle*, 'More German war medals', in *The Numismatic Chronicle and Journal of the Royal Numismatic Society*, series 4, volume 17 (1916/17), pp.402-406.

Ormond, Richard, and Rogers, Malcolm, *Dictionary of British portraiture, in four volumes, volume 4. The twentieth century – historical figures born before 1900*, compiled by Dr Adriana Davies, (London, The National Portrait Gallery, 1981).

Pinches, John Harvey, *Medals by John Pinches. A catalogue of works struck by the company from 1840 to 1969*, (London, Heraldry Today, 1987).

Pyke, E. J., *A biographical dictionary of wax modellers*, (Oxford, The Clarendon Press, 1973).

Royal Academy of Arts, *Royal Academy exhibitors 1905-1970: a complete dictionary of artists and their works shown at exhibitions of the Royal Academy of Arts: volume 5: Lawr-Sher.*, (EP Publishing Ltd, 1981).

Royal Society of Arts, *Exhibition of European medals 1930-1955 held by The Royal Society of Arts in association with The Royal Numismatic Society and La Fédération Internationale des Éditeurs de Médailles 8-29 June 1955*, (London, The Royal Society of Arts, 1955).

Schmidt, Robert, 'Der Dionyson-Kristall von Artur Loewental', in *Der Kunstwanderer* (1932), (Berlin, *Der Kunstwanderer GmbH*, 1932), pp.185-189.

Schulz, Karl, 'Die Wiener Secession und die Medaille', in *The Medal*, No.31, Autumn 1997, (London, The British Art Medal Society, 1997), pp.59-67.

Seaby Ltd., *Sir Winston Churchill 1874-1965* (flyer for Churchill death medal) (London, B. A. Seaby Ltd, 1965).

Sicree, Andrew A., 'Fluorite in the Ancient World', in *Popular Mineralogy*, No.8, Jan 2008, (Sandiego Lapidary Society, 2008).

Singer, Isidore and Adler, Cyrus (editors), 1901-06. *The Jewish Encyclopedia*, (New York, Funk and Wagnall).

Sotheby's, *Catalogue of English and foreign coins, in gold, silver and bronze together with historical and commemorative medals. The property of various owners*, (London, Sotheby's, 1977).

Spalding Gentlemen's Society, *Loewental collection*, (Spalding, Spalding Gentlemen's Society, c.1948).

Steguweit, Wolfgang, *Das münzkabinett der Königlichen Museen zu Berlin und die Förderung der Medaillenkunst, Künstlerbriefe und Medailleneditionen im Ersten Weltkrieg*, (Berlin, Staatliche Museen zu Berlin, 1998).

Suhle, Arthur, 'Der Medailleur Artur Loewental', in *Berliner Museen*, XLVIII, Jahrgang, Heft 6, 1927, (Berlin: G. Grotesche Verlagsbuch Handlung, 1927), pp.140-143.

Svarstad, Carsten, *Medals of actors, singers & dancers*, (London, Spink & Son Ltd, 1963).

Thos Mawer & Son Ltd, *Thos Mawer & Son Limited sale catalogue, 2 June 2007*, (Lincoln, Thos Mawer & Son Ltd, 2007).

Usher Art Gallery, *An exhibition of the works of Professor Artur Loewental including sculpture, medals and engravings in gems and hardstones*, (Lincoln, Usher Art Gallery, 1941).

Verdi, Richard, *Saved! 100 years of the National Art Collections Fund*, (London, Hayward Gallery Publishing, 2003).

Vollmer, Hans, *Allgemeines Lexikon der Bildenden Künstler von der Antike bis zur Gegenwart, Dreiundzwanzigster Band*, (Leipzig, E. A. Seemann Verlag, c.1930).

Weber, Frederick Parkes, *Aspects of death and correlated aspects of life in art, epigram, and poetry. Contributions towards an anthology and an iconography of the subject. Illustrated especially by medals, engraved gems, jewels, ivories, antique pottery, &c.*, (London, T. Fisher Unwin, Ltd, fourth edition, 1922).

Whittick, G. Clement, '*Vasa Murrina* and the Lexica', in the *Journal of Roman Studies*, vol. 42, parts 1 and 2, (1952)pp.66-67.

Zetzmann, G., *Deutsche Silbermedaillen des I Weltkriegs auf die militärischen Handlungen und denkwürdigen Ereignisse von 1914 bis 1919*, (Regenstauf: H. Gietl Verlag & Publikationsservice GmbH, 2002).

**SHORT NOTICES IN PERIODICALS, in date order.**

*The Magpie Annual*, 1937, (Lincoln, Elpeeko Limited), p68. (Francis Cooper appointed to Lincoln Library).

*The Kipling Journal*, No.48, Dec 1938. (Notice of Kipling medal).

*The Kipling Journal*, No.49, April 1939. (Kipling medal ordered).

*The Kipling Journal*, No.54, July 1940, pp.2-3, 19-22. (Presentation of Kipling medal).

*Lincolnshire Artists' Society annual exhibition catalogue*, 1944, p.9. (Loewental's exhibits).

*Seaby's Coin and Medal Bulletin*, No.343, September 1946, p.60. (Advertisement for Loewental's Churchill victory medal).

*Seaby's Coin and Medal Bulletin* No.344, November/December 1946, rear cover. (Illustrated advertisement for Loewental's Churchill victory medal).

*Lincolnshire Artists' Society annual exhibition catalogue*, 1946, p.9. (Loewental's exhibits).

*Lincolnshire Artists' Society annual exhibition catalogue*, 1947, p.9. (Loewental's exhibits).

*Spalding Gentlemen's Society annual report*, 1948. (Loewental meets members).

*Spalding Gentlemen's Society annual report*, 1949. (Report on Loewental's medal).

*Lincolnshire Artists' Society annual exhibition catalogue*, 1949, p.10. (Loewental's exhibits).

*Lincolnshire Artists' Society annual exhibition catalogue*, 1950. (Loewental listed as member).

*Lincolnshire Artists' Society annual exhibition catalogue*, 1951. (Loewental listed as member).

*Lincolnshire Artists' Society annual exhibition catalogue*, 1952. (Loewental listed as member).

*Lincolnshire Artists' Society annual exhibition catalogue*, 1953. (Loewental listed as member).

*Lincolnshire Artists' Society annual exhibition catalogue*, 1954, p.9. (Loewental's exhibits).

*Lincolnshire Artists' Society annual exhibition catalogue*, 1955. (Loewental listed as member).

*Lincolnshire Artists' Society annual exhibition catalogue*, 1956. (Loewental listed as member).

*Lincolnshire Artists' Society annual exhibition catalogue*, 1957. (Loewental listed as member).

*Lincolnshire Artists' Society annual exhibition catalogue*, 1958. (Loewental no longer listed as member).

*Spalding Gentlemen's Society annual report*, 1959. (Loan of *vasa murrina*).

*The Ashmolean Museum report*, 1960, p.33. (Loewental's gift to the museum).

*The Ashmolean Museum report*, 1961, p.36. (Loewental's gift to the museum).

*The British Medical Journal*, 7 October 1961, p.970. (Death of Dr Jacob Bauer).

*Seaby's Coin and Medal Bulletin*, No.561, March, 1965, cover and frontis. (Notice of Loewental's Churchill death medal).

*Seaby's Coin and Medal Bulletin*, No.563, May 1965, p.159. (Revised prices for Churchill death medal).

*Seaby's Coin and Medal Bulletin,* No.567, Sept/Oct. 1965, p.297. (Delivery delays of Churchill death medal).

*Seaby's Coin and Medal Bulletin,* No.576, July 1966, p.244. (Sales of Churchill death medal).

*Seaby (Rare Books) Ltd. Antiquarian and secondhand books.* List No.21, January, 1981. (Books formerly in Loewental's collection).

*Seaby (Rare Books) Ltd. Antiquarian and secondhand books.* List No.27, July, 1981. (Book formerly in Loewental's collection).

*Seaby's Coin and Medal Bulletin,* No.757, September 1981, pp.252-3. (Loewental's Hill medal).

*Spinks Numismatic Circular,* XCII, 5, June 1984, p.152. (Obituary Mr A. J. H. Gunstone).

*The Kipling Journal,* No.284, December 1997. (Reproductions of Kipling medal).

*The Kipling Journal,* No.286, June 1998. (Reproductions of Kipling medal).

*The Kipling Journal,* No.288, Dec 1998. (Kipling medal cleaned).

*Spalding Gentlemen's Society annual report,* 2002. (Lists their Loewental collection).

## SHORT NOTICES IN NEWSPAPERS, in date order.

*The New York Times,* 13 November 1898, p.19. (Loewental sculpts Mark Twain).

*Watertown Daily Times,* 18 December 1926. (Kreisler medal by Loewental).

*Berliner Tageblatt,* morning edition, 1-3-1927, pp.1, 3. (Loewental's portrait of Dr Thimme).

*The New York Times,* 13 April 1930, p.63. (Photograph of Loewental sculpting Einstein).

*The Times,* 31 May 1935, p.22. (Beaux Arts Gallery exhibition *review).*

*The Times,* 8 June 1935, p.17. (Visit by royalty to exhibition).

*The Times,* 10 February 1936, p.9. (Donation of two of Loewental's medals).

*The Times,* 13 May 1937, p.6. (Royal Society's annual exhibition review).

*The Times,* 20 May 1939, p.10. (Fine Art Society exhibition review).

*The Daily Telegraph,* 29 June 1940. (Notice of application by Loewental for British citizenship).

*The Hampstead News,* 4 July 1940. (Notice of application by Loewental for British citizenship).

*The London Gazette,* 18 March 1941, p.1597. (Notice of Loewental's naturalisation).

*Lincolnshire Echo,* 6 May 1949. (Royal Academy exhibition review).

*Lincolnshire Echo,* 9 January 1950. (Loewental's memories of Einstein).

*Lincolnshire Echo,* 26 April 1955. (Einstein's death).

*The Times,* 24 June 1955, p.5. (Royal Society of Arts exhibition review).

*Lincolnshire Echo,* 20 December 1955. (Exhibition review).

*Lincolnshire Echo,* 12 June 1958. (Francis Hill knighted).

*Lincolnshire Echo,* 21 September 1959. (Antwerp exhibition review).

*The Times,* 7 February 1961, p.12. (Loewental gifts 20 medals).

*Lincolnshire Echo,* 18 November 1964. (Notice of Loewental's death).

*The Times,* 19 November 1964, p.14. (Loewental's obituary).

*Lincolnshire Echo,* 20 November 1964. (Notice of Loewental's funeral).

*Lincolnshire Echo,* 20 October 1977. (Purchase by Lincoln museum of the dies used for the Churchill victory medal).

*Lincolnshire Echo,* 4 December 1981. (Exhibition review).

*Lincolnshire Echo,* 19 July 1984. (Bequest to Ashmolean Museum by the late Antony Gunstone)

*New York Times,* 12 May 2002. (Article on Einstein includes 1930 photograph of Loewental sculpting Einstein)

*Financial Times,* 27 May 2005. (*Vasa Murrina*)

## [D] ARCHIVE SOURCES.

*The Sir Francis Hill deposit.* (Lincolnshire Archives, Lincoln). The letters and papers belonging to Sir Francis Hill.

*The Lincoln Red Cattle Society Archives.* (Lincolnshire Showground, Grange-de-Lings.)
Items checked:
    Lincolnshire Red Shorthorn Association minute books for 1943 – 1947.
    Volumes of news-cuttings from 1945 – 1950.
    Scrap book compiled by Mona Skehel.

*Lincolnshire Artists' Society annual exhibition catalogues.* (The Collection, Lincoln.)
Issues checked:
    1944, 1945, 1946, 1947, 1948, 1949, 1950, 1951, 1952, 1953, 1954, 1955, 1956, 1957, 1958.

*Lincolnshire Illustrations Index.* (Lincolnshire Archives, Lincoln). An archive of negatives etc relating to Lincolnshire. Index checked by staff for Loewental – only one photo found.

*Loewental file* (The Collection, Lincoln). Compiled by Anthony Gunstone during the 1980s consolidating The Collection's records of Loewental and the results of his own outline research.

*Spalding Gentlemen's Society annual reports.* (Lincoln Central Library, Lincoln).
Issues checked:
    1930, 1935, 1938, 1945, 1946, 1947, 1948, 1949, 1950, 1951, 1952, 1953, 1958/9, 1959/60, 1960/61, 1961/62, 1962/63, 1963/64, 1964/65, 1965/66, 1966/67, 1967/68, 1969/70, 1970/71, 1971/72, 1972/73, 1973/74, 1974/75, 1976/77, 1977/78.

*Usher Art Gallery exhibition catalogues,* bound in volumes. (The Collection, Lincoln.)
Years checked:
    1938/40, 1940/42, 1942/44, 1944/46, 1946/47, 1947/48, 1948/49, 1949/50, 1950/51, 1952/53, 1953/54, 1954/55, 1955/56, 1956/57, 1957/58, 1958/59, 1959/60.

# INDEX

Page numbers in **bold** refer to illustrations in Chapters 1 to 6